Models of Curriculum-Based Assessment

A Blueprint for Learning

ॐ *Third Edition* ॐ

Lorna Idol
Ann Nevin
Phyllis Paolucci-Whitcomb

pro·ed
An International Publisher
8700 Shoal Creek Boulevard
Austin, Texas 78757-6897

© 1999, 1996, 1986 by PRO-ED, Inc.
8700 Shoal Creek Boulevard
Austin, Texas 78757-6897

Library of Congress Cataloging-in-Publication Data

Idol, Lorna.
    Models of curriculum-based assessment : a blueprint for learning /
Lorna Idol, Ann Nevin, Phyllis Paolucci-Whitcomb. — 3rd ed.
        p.   cm.
    Includes bibliographical references (p.   ) and index.
    ISBN 0-89079-787-0 (alk. paper)
    1. Curriculum-based assessment—United States—Handbooks, manuals,
etc.   2. Educational tests and measurements—United States—
Handbooks, manuals, etc.   3. Handicapped children—Education—
United States—Handbooks, manuals, etc.   I. Nevin, Ann.
    II. Paolucci-Whitcomb, Phyllis.   III. Title.
LB3060.32.C74I36   1999
371.26'4—dc21   98-28690
                                                          CIP

This book is designed in Goudy, Frutiger, and Palatino.

Production Manager: Alan Grimes
Production Coordinator: Dolly Fisk Jackson
Managing Editor: Chris Olson
Art Director: Thomas Barkley
Designer: Jason Crosier
Reprints Buyer: Alicia Woods
Preproduction Coordinator: Chris Anne Worsham
Project Editor: Suzi Hunn
Staff Copyeditor: Martin Wilson
Publishing Assistant: John Means Cooper

Printed in the United States of America

  2   3   4   5   6   7   8   9   10   02   01   00

Models of Curriculum-Based Assessment

Contents

5
CBAs for Science ৯৩ *125*

6
CBAs for Dictionary Skills ৯৩ *157*

7
CBAs for Following Directions and Using Study Skills ৯৩ *197*

Preface

We are pleased to bring you the third edition of this book on curriculum-based assessments. Curriculum-based assessments (CBAs) are teacher-constructed tests designed to measure directly students' skill achievements at specified grades. The results of a CBA provide a blueprint for learning, a blueprint tht delineates specific skills that are then targeted for additional remedial instruction. The assessments are criterion-referenced, and their content reflects the curricula used in general education classrooms.

Generating and revising CBA systems require continuous communication between special education and classroom teachers. We hope the detailed "how-to" focus of this book will be helpful to all educators responsible for ensuring the best practices in the education of exceptional learners. Curriculum-based assessment is a dramatic demonstration of the power of collaborative consultation, in that it represents current practice in general and special education that must rely on the expertise of both the general educator and the special educator. The how-to focus is crucial. It is in fact considered to be the *sine qua non* of successful collaborative consultation.

Models of Curriculum-Based Assessment is intended to supplement our book *Collaborative Consultation* (Idol, Nevin, & Paolucci-Whitcomb, in press). The contents of both books are a direct result of the collaboration we practice as consultants with general and special educators. In our respective collaborative efforts, we are committed to generating better educational programs for students with mild to moderate learning difficulties. Such learners are identified by the teacher or special educator as being in need of consultation services. The identified students include both those who are sent to a special education resource room but who spend most of their day with the classroom teacher and those who spend most of their day in a special class and are sent to selected general education classes. Other low-achieving students who are not receiving special education services are also recipients of consultation services.

The Collaborative Consultation Model has been successfully implemented at all educational levels (preschool through high school) in rural as well as urban areas. A key ingredient in this success is the ability of the model to permit people with diverse expertise to generate creative solutions to mutually defined problems. The outcome is thus enhanced and altered and made quite different from the solution that a single individual might have produced independently (Idol et al., in press). This same ingredient is inherent in CBA practices.

The book is organized simply. The Introduction provides a rationale and discussion of the factors that make the CBA an important alternative to traditional testing practices. It notes that the use of CBAs facilitates two important outcomes in the education of students: skill acquisition by the learner, and cooperation between special educators and classroom teachers working in collaboration.

In the Introduction, we present a case for CBAs as a viable alternative assessment practice, a review of recent CBA literature, the general attributes of the CBA, and a discussion of CBAs in inclusive classrooms. Chapters 1 through 7 include examples of CBAs that have actually been constructed and used by teachers for a wide range of subjects (literary reading, writing, spelling, math, science, dictionary use, and study skills). Each CBA is accompanied by a description of its construction and procedures for administering it. These examples are intended to serve as models rather than as definitive statements; we will consider this book a success only when better models are generated by our readers.

We extend our sincere appreciation to our collaborators, whose dedication and perseverance resulted in the direct translation of theory into practice. Most importantly, we appreciate the steadfast and loving support of our friends and loved ones.

In the development of the third edition of this book, we feel honored to have had yet another opportunity to work together collaboratively. We continue to learn the most when we give each other feedback, when we coax and cajole each other to go beyond our self-imposed limits, and when we work together on revisions and new directions. Clearly, we are practicing to learn the major principles of collaborative consultation.

Introduction: The Case for Curriculum-Based Assessment

A curriculum-based assessment (CBA) is a criterion-referenced test that is teacher constructed and designed to reflect curriculum content. Curriculum-based assessments are intended for teachers to use in determining students' skills in various curricula taught in the classroom. The primary strength of a CBA is that, as teachers develop it, they also formulate the important goals and objectives of the school program. Goal-setting is a natural artifact of this process; as teachers organize the assessment tool, they are also organizing and prioritizing the scope and sequence of the curriculum. Thus, the teachers not only develop an assessment instrument that reflects what is being taught, but they also glean a clearer and better organized perspective of what will be achieved in the program. The science CBA presented in Chapter 5 is a clear example of how goals and objectives can emerge as a result of CBA development.

Curriculum-based assessments can be developed for various types of curricula: developmental, spiraling, or unestablished. Developmental curricula are those that are organized in a hierarchical fashion, in which content at any level reflects acquisition of prerequisite skills taught at earlier levels. Each level contains prerequisite information necessary for mastery of subsequent levels. Examples of developmental curricula are those for basal reading, language arts, writing, and spelling programs. Examples can be found in Chapters 1 and 2, as well as those for content area reading in Chapters 3 and 5.

Spiraling curricula are also organized by level, but their concepts are repeated at subsequent levels. The concepts are not necessarily expected to be completely mastered at a given level of the curriculum, because more difficult applications will appear at subsequent levels. Math, science, and, in some cases, social studies are examples of subjects that can be taught via spiraling curriculum. Specific examples can be found in Chapters 5 and 6.

Unestablished curricula are those that have been developed by teachers, often in response to students' needs. A formal, published curriculum is usually not used; instead, the teachers develop the curricula themselves. Examples of unestablished curricula that have been developed by teachers are those for written language, handwriting, study skills, thinking skills, and, in some cases, formal content areas such as social studies and science. Examples appear in Chapter 7.

Regardless of the type of curricula, CBAs can, and have been, developed and used in many classrooms, as documented in the following chapters.

The CBA as an Alternative

Curriculum-based assessments have been developed in various parts of the United States over the past several years. Various methods for implementing CBAs were first developed by individual researchers and practitioners in the 1980s (Blankenship, 1985; Blankenship & Lilly, 1981; Deno, 1985; Germann & Tindal, 1985; Gickling & Havertape, 1981; Gickling & Thompson, 1985; Idol, 1993). Others implemented CBAs in specific school programs (Marston & Magnusson, 1985; Peterson, Heistad, Peterson, & Reynolds, 1985; Van Zant & Brown, 1997).

The concept of curriculum-based assessment seems to have developed as a solution to certain problems in our educational society, most of which have to do with educating low-achieving and special needs learners in mainstreamed classrooms.

As special education monies and those earmarked for the education of students who experience cultural disadvantage have been made available to schools the need to assess problem learners' skills has grown. As a consequence, a vast industry has developed that is devoted to the construction and selling of a huge array of testing instruments. Some of these instruments have been used as a means of assigning categorical labels to children in order to qualify them to receive supplementary educational assistance. Since the 1970s a growing general discontent with such labeling practices (Foster & Salvia, 1977; Foster, Schmidt, & Sabatino, 1976; Gillung & Rucker, 1977; Gordon, 1995) gave way to a continuing line of research to verify the utility and efficacy of CBA (Elliott & Fuchs, 1977; Howell & Evans, 1995; Morison, White, & Feuer, 1996). It became clear that categorical labeling created certain problems.

Some of those concerned about influencing policy changes in special education asserted that a solution to the labeling problem is to establish noncategorical programs for students with mild handicaps (Idol-Maestas, 1981; Lilly, 1979; Wiederholt, 1974). In these proposals, the category of mild handicap included students who had previously been labeled as having learning disabilities, mild mental retardation, or mild behavior disorders. Curriculum-based assessment is a testing methodology that fits nicely with noncategorical special education because the emphasis is on testing curricular-based skills, as opposed to attempting to define a special education exceptionality, such as mental retardation, an attentional deficit, or a behavior problem.

A major cause of continuing social and educational unrest is the fact that there is often little correspondence between a test's content and the curricular and teacher demands that are placed on a student in the classroom. Teams of educational researchers have demonstrated that teachers can expect discrepant achievement scores from school children who take several different, well-known reading tests. Different achievement scores were also found between test and performance in several widely used basal reading programs (Armbruster, Stevens, & Rosenshine, 1977; Espin & Foegen, 1996; Jenkins & Pany, 1976a; Jenkins & Pany, 1976b; Roberts & Shapiro, 1996). Because standardized reading tests do not always test the same skills or reflect curriculum content, they sometimes serve as weak predictors of how well a student might perform in the classroom. The use of CBA is a solution to this problem, because teachers construct CBAs to test mastery of the very skills that are taught and required in the classroom.

Curriculum-based assessment is a natural, reality-based form of classroom assessment. Many people view it as a reasonable solution to the social ills that can occur with the use of standardized tests, categorical labeling, and inadequate matches between tests and curricula. Curriculum-based assessment has been recommended by many people involved in the reform of assessment practices in general (Bernauer & Cress, 1997; Brandt, 1996; Lewis, 1997; Nitko, 1995; Smith & Levin, 1996; Thompson, Beckmann, & Senk, 1997; Van Zant & Brown, 1997) as well as reform of assessment practices in mathematics (Clark, 1995; Graue & Smith, 1996; Wilcox & Ziellinski, 1997), language arts (Wixson, Peters, & Potter, 1996) and science (Pallrand, 1996). For additional information in this CBA context, the reader can consult the following excellent topical issues: Tucker's (1985) special issue on CBA in *Exceptional Children*; Rosenfield and Shinn's (1989) topical issue on CBA in *School Psychology Review;* and the topical issue on assessment in Brandt's (1996) issue of *Educational Leadership*.

Review of Recent CBA Literature

A search of the Education Resources Information Clearinghouse (ERIC, a nationwide education information network sponsored by the U.S. Department of Education) system for citations that included CBA yielded 131 separate citations between 1981 and 1994. There were 12 citations between 1981 and 1985, 66 between 1986 (the year the first edition of *Models of Curriculum-Based Assessment* was published) and 1994, and 53 between 1995 (when the second edition of *Models of Curriculum-Based Assessment* was published) and 1997. There were 3 CBA citations in 1981, 0 in 1982, 0 in 1983, 1 in 1984, 8 in 1985, 7 in 1986, 4 in 1987, 8 in 1988, 6 in 1989, 13 in 1990, 6 in 1991, 10 in 1992, 2 in 1993, 10 in 1994, 21 in 1995, 19 in 1996, and 13 in 1997.

It is clear from this rapidly growing literature that CBAs have become viable alternatives to other assessment practices. For example, CBAs have been applied to better assess various populations such as students with mental retardation (e.g., Smith & Dowdy, 1992; Umbreit, 1995, 1996); students with learning disabilities (e.g., Bursuck & Lessen, 1987; Fuchs, 1994; Fuchs, Fuchs, & Hamlett, 1994; Fuchs, Fuchs, & Karns, 1995; Fuchs, Fuchs, & Phillips, 1995; Fuchs, Roberts, & Barnes, 1996; Rogan, LaJeunesse, & Miller, 1995); students with attention deficit disorder (Stoner, Carey, & Ikeda, 1994; Umbreit, 1995, 1996); students with severe disabilities and medical challenges (e.g., Skakun, 1988; Thousand & Villa, 1990); students with emotional or behavioral problems (e.g., Algozzine, Ruhl, & Ramsey, 1991; Delfino, 1994; Epstein, Kinder, & Bursuck, 1989; Umbreit, 1995, 1996); students with speech impairments (Nelson, 1989); students at risk for school failure (Rydell, 1990); students in bilingual special education settings (Baker & Good, 1994; Coballes-Vega & Salend, 1988; Ortiz & Wilkinson, 1991); reading in English proficiency for bilingual students (Baker & Good, 1995; Cline & Frederickson, 1996); and students with gifts and talents (Joyce & Wolking, 1988).

Curriculum-based assessments have been validated for assessing children and youth of various ages. At the preschool level, several researchers are studying the application of CBAs (Bagnato, Neisworth, & Capone, 1986;

Bondurant-Utz & Luciano, 1994; Joyce & Wolking, 1988; Notari & Drinkwater, 1991). At the elementary level, in addition to the earlier work of Marston and Magnusson (1985) and Peterson, Heistad, Peterson, and Reynolds (1985), several researchers and practitioners have contributed important additional data showing the efficacy for this population (e.g., Guernsey, 1990; Hintze, Shapiro, & Lutz, 1994; Norris, Fuchs, & Fuchs, 1994; Tucker, 1985). Efficacy of CBAs for students at the secondary level has been investigated by Bol and Strage (1996), Espin and Deno (1995), Espin and Foegen (1996), Delfino (1994), Glickling, Shane, and Croskery (1989), Pallrand (1996), Russell (1995), Seidenberg (1986; 1987), Tindal and Nolet (1995), and Tindal and Parker (1989).

In addition to comprehensive literature reviews by Algozzine et al. (1991), Bagnato et al. (1986), and Mehrens and Clarizio (1993), researchers have reported the use of CBAs with various academic content areas. Several researchers (e.g., Bullard & McGee, 1984; Casteel, Roop, & Schiller, 1996, Elliott & Fuchs, 1997; Erpelding, 1990; Fuchs & Fuchs, 1995; Gable, Arllen, and Evans, 1997; Gersten, Vaughn, & Brengelman, 1996; Hintze et al., 1994; King-Sears, 1997; Lewis, 1997; Nelson, 1989; Roberts & Shapiro, 1996; and Wixson et al., 1996) reported the applications of CBAs for reading and language arts acquisition in elementary school children. Cawley, Miller, and Carr (1990) examined the reading performance of students with mild educational handicaps or learning disabilities through a combination of norm-referenced and curriculum-based assessment. Baker and Good (1995) used CBAs for reading in English in order to validate CBA sensitivity and reliability for bilingual (Spanish/English) readers. Mathes, Fuchs, and Fuchs (1995) used CBAs in reading to validate improved reading performance of students with disabilities. Shinn, Powell-Smith, and Good (1997) used CBAs in reading to verify the positive effects of reintegrating students who had been previously removed from the general education classroom.

Many researchers have expanded CBA research to include the area of mathematics (Fuchs, Fuchs, & Karns, 1995; Fuchs, Fuchs, & Phillips, 1995; Parke & Lane, 1996; Parker & Picard, 1996). Gable, Enright, and Hendrickson (1991) reported the applications of arithmetic CBAs for elementary school children, whereas Gickling et al. (1989) investigated the effects of CBA interventions on the performance of high school students who were achieving at a low level in general mathematics classes. Espin and Foegen (1996) established the validity of three CBA measures (oral reading, maze, and vocabulary) on comprehension, acquisition, and retention of content-area material for 184 urban middle school students including 13 with mild disabilities. The vocabulary CBA was found to be the most effective and efficient measure for predicting student achievement of content-area tasks. Pallrand (1996) recommended the use of sequential CBA activities for high school science to emphasize how secondary students can use knowledge to explain phenomena that builds upon what they previously learned. Rogan et al. (1995) reported an example at the junior high school level that was stimulated by Pennsylvania's instructional support initiative for including students with special needs in general education settings. Success for seventh and eighth grade students in one school was demonstrated for those with disabilities in regular English classes. Curriculum-based assessments, along with collaboration between general and special educators and the use of adaptations such as learning strategies, resulted in positive outcomes. Tindal and Parker (1989) found that using curriculum-based measurements in secondary settings was feasible, particularly for sampling written comprehension across content-area classes. Seidenberg (1986; 1987) reported the use of CBAs to assist youth with learning disabilities as they transition from high school to college, whereas Delfino (1994) suggested CBAs for assessing and remediating the academic progress of youth who had been adjudicated in the California prison systems.

Curriculum-based assessments have been extended to other areas of the curriculum. Parke and Lane (1996) described a CBA system for mathematical problem solving, reasoning, and communication skills that was implemented successfully by teachers in six schools. Tindal and Nolet (1995) presented examples of CBA for critical thinking skills for middle and high school students. Frey (1995) recommended using CBA as part of portfolio assessment procedures for adult education and job training curriculum.

In addition, CBA implementation guides have been developed by practitioners and state department of education personnel. Bondurant-Utz and Luciano (1994) developed one for infant and preschool assessment in special education; Coulter (1985) for the New Orleans public schools; Gilbert and Burger (1990) for the Colorado State Department of Education; Gong and Reidy (1996) described the use of CBA in Kentucky's school reform efforts, Rogan et al. (1995) described Pennsylvania's use of CBA in assessment reform; Shanks (1986) for the Nebraska Department of Education; and personnel from the Division for Handicapped Children and Pupil Services for the Wisconsin Department of Education (1985). Wixson, Peters, and Potter (1996) and Casteel, Roop, and Schiller (1996) described Michigan's collaboration between university, state department of education, and language arts professionals who generated language arts CBAs in listening, speaking, reading, writing, and literature.

Broader applications of CBAs have been recommended as well. For example, the use of CBAs has been suggested as a way of making decisions in special education (Cundari & Suppa, 1988), as an alternative for school psychologists (Coulter, 1985; Rosenfield & Shinn, 1989; Thomas & Grimes, 1990), and as a method for vocational assessment and decision making (Brolin, 1992; Frey, 1995; Stodden & Ianacone, 1986).

Other applications of CBAs have been reported, particularly as a means for program evaluation. For example, Tindal (1992) suggested that instructional programs in general can be better evaluated through curriculum-based measurement systems. Jonietz (1990) recommended CBAs as a method for evaluating and remediating the needs of students with problems at an international school. Swisher and Clark (1991) reported the curriculum-based vocational assessment of students with special needs at middle school or junior high school levels. Foster (1990) reported that school psychology services could be broadened through program evaluation and modifications that emphasize CBA.

There were 36 citations that focused on reporting CBA research. Two surveys (Shapiro & Eckert, 1993, 1994) and one comparative study (Roberts & Rust, 1994) of psychologists' use of CBA took place. Other studies included 11 comparisons of CBA performance with other measures (Cawley et al., 1990; Elliott & Fuchs, 1997; Fuchs, 1994; Fuchs & Deno, 1981; Fuchs & Fuchs, 1986a, 1986b; Fuchs, Fuchs, & Hamlett, 1989, 1990; Fuchs, Fuchs, & Maxwell, 1988; Fuchs, Fuchs, Tindal, & Deno, 1981; Notari & Drinkwater, 1991). Tindal and Nolet (1995) provided quantitative and qualitative examples of the impact of CBAs for critical thinking skills for eighth grade science students. In addition, there were two analyses of the impact of CBA (Germann & Tindal, 1985; Joyce & Wolking, 1988) and 13 evaluations of curriculum or other treatments using CBAs as the dependent variable (Allinder, 1995; Allinder & BeckBest, 1995; Espin & Deno, 1995; Fuchs, Fuchs, Hamlett, & Ferguson, 1992; Fuchs, Fuchs, & Karns, 1995; Fuchs, Fuchs, & Phillips, 1995; Fuchs, Roberts, & Barnes, 1996; Mathes, Fuchs, & Fuchs, 1995; Notari & Drinkwater, 1991; Shinn et al., 1997; Stoner et al., 1994; Umbreit, 1995, 1996).

Shapiro and Eckert (1993) conducted a national survey of school psychologists regarding their knowledge, use, and attitudes about CBA. With a 45% return rate of 500 randomly selected members of the National Association of School Psychology, the results showed that about 45% of the respondents indicated they used some form of CBA. About 18% reported they used CBAs on a consistent basis. However, although psychologists viewed CBAs as very important in conducting psychoeducational assessment, their actual use of CBAs was limited. These respondents viewed CBAs as being less biased than published standardized tests for assessment of children from culturally diverse groups and more acceptable for students and teachers. In a subsequent report (Shapiro & Eckert, 1994), acceptability ratings showed that psychologists viewed CBAs as being more acceptable than standardized tests. Of course, the usual limitations regarding survey research (as distinguished from direct observations) must be considered. The results may not reflect psychologists' actual use of CBAs. Several researchers have studied the validity and reliability of CBAs when they were compared to other, more traditional psychoeducational assessment systems. A classic example comes from Fuchs and Deno (1981), who found a high correlation between comparisons of CBAs, teacher judgment, and standardized test scores for the reading placements of 91 elementary students, although there was not a high congruence among the measures themselves (ranging from 48% to 69% agreement). Subsequent validation studies have expanded these findings (Elliott & Fuchs, 1997; Fuchs & Fuchs, 1986a, 1986b; Fuchs, Fuchs, & Maxwell, 1988). Joyce and Wolking (1988) evaluated the criterion validity of CBAs in identifying children with gifts and talents by comparing the performance of 286 kindergartners and first graders on CBAs and standardized measures. Their study found that the predictive validities of the measures were equivalent and noted that the CBA measure may be more practical because of its direct application to classroom instruction.

More recently, Baker and Good (1995) showed that the sensitivity of CBAs allowed them to track the reading progress of bilingual (Spanish–English) students more reliably and validly than language proficiency measures. Cawley et al. (1990) studied 28 adolescents with mild educational handicaps and 38 with learning disabilities, comparing their performance on CBAs and norm-referenced assessments in comprehension and word recognition. The CBA measures showed significant differences in comprehension that favored students with learning disabilities. Espin and Deno (1995) used correlational and multiple regression techniques to verify the validity of CBAs for reading from text and vocabulary when predicting performance on content-area study tasks for 121 10th graders. Tindal (1992) studied the reading ability of four elementary students with learning disabilities. He found that individual referenced tests (like CBAs) were best suited for understanding the impact of instruction, although the norm-referenced tests determined allocation of resources.

Since 1995, several researchers have systematically explored the impact of various conditions on teacher implementation and acceptance of CBA systems (Allinder, 1995, 1996; Allinder & BeckBest, 1995; Allinder & Oats, 1997; Eckert, Shapiro, & Lutz, 1995). For example, Allinder and Oats (1997) studied 21 teachers who used CBAs over a 4-month period. Children whose teachers had high ratings of CBA acceptability showed more progress on the CBA math measures when compared to children whose teachers had low ratings of CBA acceptability. These findings were corroborated by Allinder's (1996) study of 29 elementary special education teachers who each used CBAs to monitor two students with mild disabilities over a 16-week period. Children whose teachers implemented CBAs more accurately made significantly greater progress. Eckert et al. (1995) evaluated general and special educators' acceptability ratings of two assessment techniques (CBA and norm-referenced tests). For this evaluation, teachers rated a case study that presented data using either CBA or norm-referenced information. Both general and special education teachers consistently rated the CBA data presentation as the more acceptable method. Allinder and BeckBest (1995) studied 18 teachers who used

either self-monitoring (N = 10) or university-based consultation (N = 8) as they implemented CBAs in math computation. Results showed that children in both groups made comparable significant achievement gains in math computation and that the degree of CBA implementation was similar for both groups of teachers. In general, these studies provide an important database for teachers to receive careful instruction and coaching when they develop, implement, and use CBAs to make instructional decisions.

Studying the achievement of students who transfer from special education settings to general education classrooms is another recent area of research that uses CBAs as the dependent variable. Fuchs et al. (1996) studied 27 special education teachers in elementary and middle schools over a 2-year period. The use of CBA and transenvironmental programming prepared 47 students with learning disabilities to move from the resource room to the general education classroom for math instruction. Davis, Fuchs, and Fuchs (1995) studied the student perspective of CBAs. Thirty-three special education teachers selected two students with mild-to-moderate special needs in grades 2 through 8. Students were randomly assigned to the CBA group (N = 41) or control group (N = 22). After 17 weeks, students individually completed a questionnaire. Inferential statistics were applied to compare and contrast their responses. Results show that students enjoyed CBA participation and that CBA growth and feedback may have increased student involvement in the learning process. CBAs may have empowered the students to "feel more responsibility for their own learning" (p. 32).

In summary, reformers, researchers, and practitioners are in agreement that CBAs are a viable alternative to more traditional psychoeducational assessment techniques. There is strong encouragement by educators and researchers to continue the development, implementation, evaluation, and refinement of CBAs in more areas of the curriculum.

General Attributes of the CBA

All CBAs, regardless of curricula type, are constructed in the same general way. First, sample items either are selected from the curriculum or constructed to match the curriculum. These items are then ordered by difficulty and combined within a single test, which is given on the first day of assessment (Day 1). Then, two more forms of the same test, containing similar items and identical orders of difficulty, are constructed; these are administered on the second and third days of testing (Days 2 and 3). It is highly recommended that the assessment be conducted in this way—on three different forms on three separate occasions—to control for sporadic student response, a characteristic that is typical of learners with special needs.

In administering the CBA, the teacher tests the students across several levels of the curriculum. Ordinarily, student responses are measured for speed or proficiency, as well as for accuracy. A CBA assessment form is developed to record student responses. Performance criteria are then established to determine acceptable levels of student performance or mastery. These criteria should be established collaboratively, with the classroom teacher and the consulting teacher (learning specialist) functioning as an assessment team. For several of the CBAs presented in subsequent chapters, mastery criteria have been defined based on actual practice. However, the reader is cautioned not to rely necessarily upon these criteria but rather to develop other reasonable criteria that reflect typical classroom performance in the class in which the CBA is being used, established, and modified by the collaborating team.

Normative sampling is a useful procedure for establishing mastery criteria (Idol, 1993). This procedure involves taking samples of average and acceptable student performance in the inclusive class as a basis for deciding what the absolute mastery criteria ought to be. Some-

times, a student in question may be so far below the levels of acceptable performance that a type of changing criterion design might have to be implemented. Such a design allows the mastery criteria to reflect the classroom average, permits a lowering of the criteria for subsequent instruction, and then allows the criteria to be made more stringent until he or she reaches the changed classroom average.

Once this type of social validation has occurred and the mastery criteria have been established, the CBA is administered, either to individual students or to groups of students. For guidance in working together as a team to conduct this assessment, readers can consult Chapter 5 of *Collaborative Consultation* (Idol et al., in press).

CBAs in Inclusive Classrooms

Curriculum-based assessments can be used very effectively in inclusive classrooms in which heterogeneous groups of students are educated together.

During the decade of the '90s, the inclusion movement has become influential throughout the United States. Webb (1994) reported that, since 1993, every U.S. state has implemented inclusion at some level. Recently, educators have been using CBAs in classrooms in combination with portfolio assessments (Idol et al., 1994; Russell, 1995; Thompson, Beckman, & Senk, 1997) as a means of providing both classroom assessments and ongoing monitoring of student progress.

In these applications, every student in the classroom has a portfolio for a particular subject area (see Idol and West, 1993, for guidance in constructing and using portfolio assessments). In addition, students with special learning needs (i.e., those who are at risk for school failure or in special education or remedial classes) have CBA performance data in their portfolios. This allows the teacher and classroom assistants to readily see the relationship between diagnosed skill levels of the student (the CBA data) and actual classroom performance (the student portfolio). This method also enables the adults involved to monitor more easily the progress of such students and give repeated CBAs at later dates.

Karns et al. (1995) discussed using CBA as a measurement system to facilitate individualized instruction. Based on a review of the research and a CBA analysis of the impact of peer-mediated instruction, these authors concluded that CBAs are a viable means for accommodating diversity in the general education classroom.

The CBA can be used in its entirety, or sections of it may be given over time. Even if the entire CBA is given initially, teachers may wish to use it again later as a means of assessing student gains. If this option is chosen, it is recommended that a second form of the CBA be developed as a means of controlling for memory of test items. Teachers using CBAs often find that the same curriculum is being used by other teachers in their buildings or local school districts. In any event, teachers should work together with the guided facilitation of the collaborative team members to develop a CBA that can be used by all teachers using the same curriculum. This collaborative process makes it much easier to develop various forms of the same CBA.

Additional researchers and practitioners have found that CBAs in inclusive classrooms are often superior to other assessment systems for their sensitivity to analyzing the impact of classroom adaptations. Day and Skidmore (1996) showed the link between CBAs, student self-assessment, and achievement of improved learning of the curriculum goals. Parke and Lane (1996) described a situation in which teachers in six schools used a CBA system to assess students' mathematical problem solving, reasoning, and communication skills. Paulsen (1997) described a school-wide implementation of CBA systems in reading fluency, reading comprehension, word recognition, and computation. In this study, all 300 children were assessed once a week (with the exception of students with special education needs, who were assessed twice a week). Results indicated that all students progressed and that fewer students were referred for testing to psychologists and special educators. Van Zant and Brown (1997) reported a school-wide implementation of CBAs that occurred twice a month for all students. Teachers were given early release time twice a month to analyze the results and to plan data-based decisions about modifications to improve student achievement.

In summary, teachers who use CBAs to evaluate students' skill areas often find that instruction becomes more streamlined; students can be offered instruction for unmastered areas without receiving repetitive instruction in previously mastered areas. Curriculum-based assessments can be developed collaboratively with other teachers who use the same curriculum. They can be used at the beginning of the school year or in segments throughout the year. They can be used with groups of students or with individuals. If multiple forms are developed, they can be used to monitor progress over time. The results of this assessment technique are specific to the curriculum they represent and can be easily communicated to parents, other teachers, and program administrators. Teachers, parents, advocates, support personnel, and students themselves can effectively evaluate using CBAs. This method allows ineffective adaptations to be more quickly redesigned.

1

❧   ❧   ❧

CBAs for Reading

In developmental curricula, the order of the lessons across the series and within book levels has been established by the publishers of the series. Each level of the series and each lesson within the series is intended to become progressively more difficult. The lessons are hierarchical, in that each lesson is built upon concepts and skills presented in previous lessons. Reading and spelling curricula are typical developmental curricula. Because these two curricula are taught in all school systems and each is uniquely different from the other, they have been selected as appropriate subject areas for which CBAs can be constructed.

The major reason for conducting a CBA in reading is to determine an instructional level for students within a reading series. This level should reflect the highest level at which students read proficiently. To determine this level, the teacher uses a reading CBA in the form of an informal reading inventory, with repeated testing across days. A student is required to read sample passages from each level of the reading series. The reading can be either oral or silent. With students who have serious word recognition and decoding problems, we recommend that the initial testing be conducted orally. In this procedure, the student reads three different sample passages from each level, one sample on each of three days of testing. Median scores for the three days are selected for three reading behaviors: accuracy, rate (reading speed), and reading comprehension. Mastery criteria are then established for each of the three reading

behaviors, and the student is placed for instruction at the highest mastery level.

This assessment procedure is identical to that used for informal reading inventories, in which sample passages are randomly selected to represent graded levels within a reading series. As noted by critics of informal reading inventories, the possibility of measurement error is reduced by obtaining repeated measures of performance (Epstein, 1980; Fuchs, Fuchs, & Deno, 1982; Elliott & Fuchs, 1997). This is accomplished by testing on three separate days from three separate passages from the first quarter of each book level. Testing over several days before making placement decisions is especially important in the case of learners with special needs. Often, such students have attentional problems, emotional problems, or school and home difficulties that contribute to sporadic test performance. Testing over several days helps to ensure that placement decisions are appropriate and valid.

Criterion levels of performance (mastery criteria) are set to determine appropriate curricular placement. The reading and literature-based CBAs in this chapter have criterion levels established for each of three oral reading behaviors (accuracy, rate, and comprehension). These criterion levels are presented in Table 1.1. Note that the criteria for oral reading rate are differentiated by the grade level of the materials being read. They are set low to provide initial incentive for problem readers. The rates are gradually increased as the students gain more confidence. The initial focus is on high mastery

Table 1.1. Initial Mastery Criteria for Graded Materials for Three Reading Behaviors.

Reading Behavior	Criterion Level	Materials Level
Accuracy	95% correct	All
Comprehension	83% correct (for 6 questions)	All
Rate	25 cwpm	Preprimer
	30 cwpm	Grades 1–3
	50 cwpm	Grades 4 & up
	100 cwpm	Upper level

Note. cwpm = correct words per minute.

of accuracy and comprehension with a steady rate of reading. The reader of this text may wish to set these initial levels higher so that they are closer to the average reading rate performance of average students in the target student's main-streamed classroom. In any case, it is important to note that the criteria in Table 1.1 are not dif-ferentiated with regard to the grade level of the student, but rather to the materials being read. For example, a student in the fourth grade read-ing at a preprimer level would be required to read at least 25 correct words per minute (cwpm), not 50 cwpm, the minimum rate for reading fourth-grade materials.

The rationale for this is that an assessment that uses curricular materials can provide teach-ers, administrators, and parents with more spe-cific and meaningful information than can be obtained from standardized tests. Students per-form or fail to perform in specific curricula used by individual schools. Therefore, the use of those same curricular materials to construct tests for assessment provides a more accurate way of describing how a student performs in comparison with other students in a particular classroom or school. In addition, the students can be placed for instruction in a graded reader that is commensurate with their reading skills.

Construction and Administration of a Reading CBA

In this section, we present a detailed descrip-tion of the procedures for constructing and administering a reading CBA. This material was adapted from the *Special Educator's Con-sultation Handbook* (Idol-Maestas, 1983, pp. 196–205).

Selecting and Marking 100-Word Passages

The reading test is constructed by selecting 100-word passages from the first quarter of each of the basal readers for Grades 1 through 6. The passages are randomly selected. The readers are ordered by difficulty and are referred to as book levels. In a traditionally constructed basal read-ing curriculum, there are five first-grade books (three preprimers, a primer, and a first-level book, levels 1 through 5), two second-grade books (levels 6 and 7), two third-grade books (levels 8 and 9), one fourth-grade book (level 10), one fifth-grade book (level 11), and one sixth-grade book (level 12).

Each student is tested on three separate days. Three separate 100-word passages should be selected from the first quarter of each of the basal readers. After identifying the selections to test, mark the beginning of the section with an arrow (→) and count off 100 words. A bracket (]) should be placed at the end of the 100-word passage. The slash (/) should be marked only on the teacher's copy.

If the last sentence in the passage is longer than 100 words, make a slash on the sheet to indicate the end of the 100-word sample (teacher's copy) and put a bracket at the end of the sentence (for both teacher's and student's copies). Sometimes you may have to have stu-dents read to the end of the paragraph to ensure that they read enough material for you to ask six comprehension questions.

Passages of 25 or 50 words must be taken from the preprimer and primer levels. If a 25- or 50-word passage is used, it is multiplied by four or two, respectively, to get a 100-word passage score.

Photocopying the pages for each 100-word passage will make administering the CBA easier. Comprehension questions should be included to accompany the passage. After photocopying the passages, label them with the book level number (1–12) and the day (1–3) and with a T (teacher) or C (child). For example:

B_6D_1C:

    Book 6 (Level 2.1)

    Day 1 (of testing)

    C (child's copy)

B_1D_3T:

    Book 1 (Preprimer)

    Day 3 (of testing)

    T (teacher's copy)

Measuring the Rate of Correct Words Per Minute

To get a rate measurement, you will need a stopwatch or the classroom clock with a second hand to time the student on each 100-word passage. Start the stopwatch when the student begins to read and stop it when the student finishes reading the 100th word (at the /). When the student finishes reading the 100-word passage, record in seconds the time required for him or her to read it. For example, 1 minute and 35 seconds would be recorded as 95 seconds. You will later convert this to cwpm by multiplying accuracy by 60 and dividing the result by total seconds. Thus,

$$\text{Rate (cwpm)} = \frac{\text{Accuracy} \times 60}{\text{Total Seconds}}$$

Procedures for Recording Errors

The following procedures for recording errors have been adapted from Haring, Lovitt, Eaton, and Hansen (1978):

1. Omissions
   If the student leaves out the entire word, mark one error. Example: The cat drinks milk. If the student reads "The drinks milk," mark one error.
   If the student omits the entire line, if possible redirect the student to the line and count the omission as one error. If you are unable to redirect the student, still count the omission as one error, not as an error for each word in the line. Subtract the number of words in the line from the total number of words read in the passage. Example: The cat drinks milk. If the student omits the sentence, count it as *one* error. The total number of words in the timed sample would be 96, not 100, words.

2. Substitutions
   If the student says the wrong word, mark it as one error.
   If the student mispronounces a proper noun, count it as an error the first time; accept as correct all subsequent presentations of the same noun. Example: John ran home. If the student says "Jan" instead of "John" four times, it is counted as only one error.
   If the student deletes suffixes such as -ed or -s in speech patterns, the deletion should not be counted as an error. You may, however, choose to make a note of it for subsequent oral language instruction.

3. Additions
   If the student adds a word or words not in the sample, mark it as one error.

4. Repetition
   Do not score repetition as an error.

5. Self-corrections
   Do not score a self-correction as an error.

6. Pauses
   After 5 seconds, supply the word and count the pause as an error.

Any help counts as an error. For example, redirecting students when they omit a line counts as only one error.

Be certain that the student says the whole word, not just a series of separate sounds in the word, before counting it as correct.

Do not prompt, praise, instruct, or encourage during the time sample. You may encourage the child after the sample is taken, but be non-specific. Do not praise for specific behaviors like reading fast or accurately.

Give the student directions along these lines: "I'd like to see what a good reader you are. Some of these words might be hard, but don't worry; read as well as you can. Begin reading here (→) and read all the way to here (]). Begin now."

Determining Accuracy

Subtract the number of errors from the total number of words read (the total number of words will be 100 unless the student has omitted a group of words).

Take the number of words read correctly and divide this number by the total number of words read in the sample to get a percentage. For example,

- 100 words read – 4 errors = 96 correct words;

$$\frac{96}{100} = 96\%$$

- 97 words read – 4 errors = 93 correct words;

$$\frac{93}{97} = 96\%$$

- 50 words read – 4 errors = 46 correct words (converted to a 100-word passage score: 46 × 2 = 92 correct words);

$$\frac{92}{100} = 92\%$$

Constructing Comprehension Questions

After each passage is read by the student, the teacher orally asks the student six comprehension questions. The student may respond either orally or in written form. The answers to the questions are usually derived from the 100-word time sample. However, the questions may cover information that extends to the end of a passage in order to generate a sufficient number of comprehension questions. The end of the entire sample is marked by a bracket (]).

For each of the passages, six questions are constructed: two *text-explicit (TE) questions* that are text-dependent, that is, the answers are explicitly found in the passage or picture; two *text-implicit (TI) questions*, whose answers are based upon two or more nonexplicitly connected details of the passage or picture; and two *script-implicit (SI) questions*, whose answers require integration of prior knowledge and one or more details of the passage or picture. Further guidelines to construct these questions can be derived from the writings of Johnston (1981), Pearson (1982), and Tuinman (1974).

Before administering the CBA, the teacher must write the questions and answers. It is important to write specific answers to minimize subjectively judgmental decisions regarding the student's comprehension skills. For implicit questions, feasible answers should be written, and the teacher should indicate which answers are acceptable.

The teacher may repeat a question if the student requests it or if the teacher thinks the student has not understood the question. However, the questions cannot be reworded or interpreted by the teacher. If a question is repeatedly missed by several students, the teacher may consider rewriting the question for future CBAs.

The wording of the questions should adhere as strictly as possible to the words used in the time sample. In instances where this is not possible, words of appropriate vocabulary level should be used (for example, from preprimer and primer books). After the comprehension questions are written, they should be attached to each 100-word passage. The acceptable criterion for comprehension is 83 percent, or five out of six questions answered correctly.

Using the CBA Performance Recording Form

The first step in using the CBA Performance Recording Form (Figure 1.1) is to determine the starting level of testing. Using information from informal observation, past performance records, and teacher recommendations, determine the book (level) immediately before the point at which the student is reading. This is the base point to begin testing.

Testing then continues through the point at which the student would be at the actual year-end grade level. For example, a third grader should read sample passages through the 3^2 book.

Enter the appropriate information at the top of the recording form. Now, with the 100-word passages prepared from the curriculum, you are ready to begin.

Begin with passages selected for Day 1. Enter the date on the Figure 1.1 form. The student and the teacher should read from separate copies. Have students read only the passages within their appropriate testing range (as determined previously). Skip the other sample passages that are not in the testing range. On the form, enter the number for each book level after "Book Number."

Using a stopwatch or minute hand on a clock, direct the student to read. Use tally marks on the record sheet to record errors as they occur. The students should read from ⟶ to]. Stop the stopwatch when the student reaches the slash mark (/), but allow the student to continue reading to the]. Read the stopwatch and record the number of seconds on the form in the space after "Seconds." Subtract the number of error tallies from 100 and record this number after "Correct/100."

Figure 1.1. Form for recording CBA performance. *Note.* Reprinted from *Reading Success* (p. 35) by L. Idol, 1997, Austin, TX: PRO-ED. Copyright 1997 by PRO-ED.

Some of the passages are only long enough for 25- or 50-word samples. In such cases, you need to double (for 50-word samples) or quadruple (for 25-word samples) the number of errors and seconds. Using the rate formula, determine the correct words per minute and record the number in the appropriate space ("Correct Words/Min") on the form.

At the end of each sample, ask the student the six comprehension questions you have prepared. Convert the number correct to a percentage and record it on the form (after "% Comprehension").

Proceed through all levels for Day 1. Repeat the procedure for Days 2 and 3. On the Figure 1.1 form, circle for each book level the median (middle) scores for accuracy (Correct/100), rate (Correct Words/Min), and comprehension (% Comprehension). For the three days of testing, you will then select a middle score for each skill area (accuracy, rate, comprehension), reflecting the most stable estimate of the student's performance.

Using the Placement in the Curriculum Form

The Placement in the Curriculum Form (Figure 1.2) is used to make a placement decision. It is designed to be used in conjunction with the CBA Performance Recording Form (Figure 1.1). After the median scores are circled on the recording form, they are plotted on graphs on the Placement in the Curriculum Form.

On the Figure 1.2 form:

1. Enter the name and grade of the student, the name of the school, the name of the examiner, and the type of curriculum used (at the bottom of the form).

2. Enter the dates of the three days of testing.

3. Plot the median scores for each tested level for correct words per minute, reading accuracy, and reading comprehension. (Note: The book levels are located at the top on the horizontal axis of the graph; the numbers reflecting measured performance appear on the vertical axis.)

4. Connect the data points (dots) representing each median score.

5. Place the student in a reader (book level). This is done by selecting the highest book level in which the student meets the following criteria:

   a. Reading accuracy is 95 percent or better.

   b. Comprehension is 83 percent or better.

   c. Correct words per minute is 25 cwpm or better if the student is reading on the preprimer level, 30 cwpm or better if the student is in Grades 1 through 3, 50 cwpm or better if the student is in Grades 4 through 6.

6. On the line following "Placement," write the name of the reader (book level) and the grade level of the book in which the student has been placed.

7. After "Comments," enter any additional behaviors that you observed that might be helpful for instructional purposes.

Once the reading assessment has been completed, the student is placed at the level at which the criteria are met, as described in the preceding section. The student is then ready to receive appropriate reading instruction.

Sample Reading CBA

In this section, we present a sample reading CBA from a basal reading series, *The Ginn Reading Program* (Ginn & Co., 1982). This example can be used as a model for preparing reading CBAs for any reading series that is developmentally sequenced. It is organized with sample reading passages from the Ginn series for Levels 5 through 15. Levels 1 through 4 were not used because they are prereadiness levels and do not contain exercises that require passage reading. The CBA provides three sample passages from each level. The passages are identified by the name of the book level and the pages in the text in which the passages appear. They are also labeled by level and by day of test administration. For example, the first three passages are labeled for Level 5, Day 1; Level 5, Day 2; Level 5, Day 3. The same pattern is repeated across each of the levels. Each passage is followed by a set of comprehension questions, with each question labeled as text explicit (TE), text implicit (TI), or script implicit (SI). A team of resource consulting teachers—Marguerite Gregory, Joan Kling, Kim Lagestee, and Lois Roelofs—wrote the comprehension questions for this CBA under the supervision of Patty Wayman and Dr. Lorna Idol.

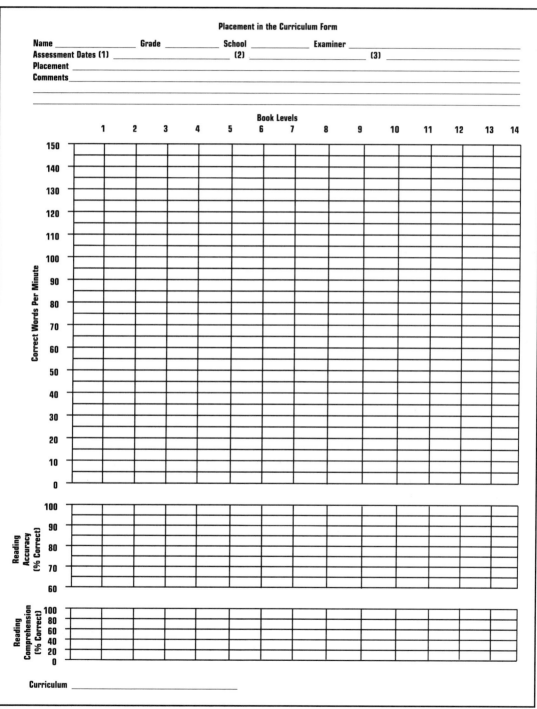

Figure 1.2. Placement in the Curriculum Form. *Note*. Reprinted from *Reading Success* (p. 37) by L. Idol, 1997, Austin, TX: PRO-ED. Copyright 1997 by PRO-ED.

Birds Fly, Bears Don't (pp. 12–13)

Day 1
Level 5

Passage

→ I did not go swimming yesterday. Yesterday was not a good day for swimming. But now it is a beautiful day.

"Mom, now may we go swimming?" I asked.

"It is a great day for swimming," Mom said. "But we are going for a train ride. We are going to see Grandpa. We can all go swimming another day."

"Listen, do you hear the bell?" asked Mom. "It's time for the train to go. What do you see out there?"

"I can see a little dog with a big bone," I said. "Look, Mom! There is a big man on/$_{100}$ a little bike."]

Comprehension Questions

(TE)   1. What kind of a day is it in the story?
(beautiful, nice)

(TE)   2. Who are Mom and the child going to visit?
(Grandpa)

(TI)   3. How did the child in the story know it was time for the train to leave?
(She heard the bell.)

(TI)   4. When did the child see the dog?
(when she was riding on the train)

(SI)   5. Why might yesterday not have been a good day for swimming?
(It was not sunny or nice; it may have been cold.)

(SI)   6. What do you think will happen when the train stops?
(Some people will get on the train, and some will get off; Mom and the child will see Grandpa.)

Note. This passage and the 32 that follow are from readers in *The Ginn Reading Program* by Ginn & Co., 1982, 1987, Lexington, MA: Author. Copyright 1982 by Ginn & Co.

Birds Fly, Bears Don't (pp. 21–23)

Passage

➔   "You stay there, Stanley. Stay in back of the fence. I don't care.

"I don't need you, Stanley. And I mean it, Stanley.

"I am making a great thing, Stanley. I know you will want to see it. Well, you can't. And I mean it, Stanley.

"I don't want you to see what I am making. Stay in back of the fence. Don't you look. Do you hear me, Stanley? This thing I am making is neat. It is all made now. It is the best thing I ever made.

"But don't look, Stanley. I don't want you to see/$_{100}$ it."]

Comprehension Questions

(TE)   1. Where was Stanley?
         (behind the fence)

(SI)   2. Who do you think Stanley is (say, to the child in the story, if necessary)?
         (the neighbor of the child in the story)

       3. Do you think the child in the story likes to play with Stanley? How do you know?
(TI)   (yes, because the child is trying to get him to play)
(TE)   (no, because the child says, "I do not want to play with you, Stanley.")

(TI)   4. Why do you think she says, "I am making a great thing"?

       5. What do you think might have happened in the story before the passage?
(SI)   (they had a fight) or
(SI)   (Stanley may have knocked down or broken something the child built before.)

Birds Fly, Bears Don't (pp. 29–31)

Passage

➔ Carlos said, "My grandma gave me a ball. It looked like this ball. I lost the ball at my grandma's house. Maybe my ball rolled here from my grandma's house!"

Carlos said, "My dog can find the way home. She can find the way home from my grandma's house."

"Yes, she can," Julia said. "But a ball is not a dog. Can a ball find the way home?"

Carlos wished and wished. He wished he did not know that Sammy lost that ball! He had to do something he did not want to do.

"Here," he said.

He looked at /₁₀₀ the big, beautiful ball. And he gave the big, beautiful ball to Sammy.]

Comprehension Questions

(TE) 1. What did Carlos lose at his grandma's house?
        (his ball)

(TE) 2. What else did he leave at his grandma's house?
        (his dog)

(TI) 3. How did Carlos get his dog back?
        (She found her way home.)

(TI) 4. Why couldn't Carlos get his ball back the same way?
        (A ball is not a dog; it can't find its way home.)

(SI) 5. Why did Carlos wish he didn't know Sammy lost the ball?
        (because he didn't want to return the ball to Sammy)

(SI) 6. Why did Carlos give Sammy the ball?
        (because Carlos knew the ball was not his but belonged to Sammy)

Across the Fence (pp. 18–19)

Passage

➔   They all ran to the Dog's house.

"Look at all the bones!" Fox cried.

"This place is a mess," said Bear.

"What game are we going to play?" asked Duck.

"I call it Bone-in-a-Hole. First, you must dig some holes. Then we will put all these bones in the holes."

"That is not a game," Duck said.

"Digging a hole is work. It's no fun!"

"Don't go," cried Dog. "If you help me, I'll make you a good lunch."

"No!" said Duck, Fox, and Bear. Then back they went to the pond.

Dog looked at his kitchen. / $_{100}$

He couldn't see the dishes. He couldn't see the floor.]

Comprehension Questions

(TE)   1.   Where were Dog, Fox, Bear, and Duck?
        (at Dog's house)

(TI)   2.   How do you play Bone-in-a-Hole?
        (You dig some holes, and then you put the bones in.)

(TI)   3.   Did Fox, Bear, and Duck want to play that game? Why or why not?
        (No, they thought that Bone-in-a-Hole was not a game or that it was work.)

(SI)   4.   Why does Dog want his friends to dig holes for his bones?
        (so he doesn't have to do it himself)

(TE)   5.   What did Dog promise his friends if they would help him?
        (a good lunch)

(SI)   6.   Why couldn't Dog see the dishes and the floor in the kitchen?
        (The kitchen was filled with bones.)

Across the Fence (pp. 32–33)

Passage

→ "Hello again," Dad said. "I have something that you may want to do. I made up some clues for you to read. First, you read the clues. Then you go where the clues tell you to go. You will find another clue there. Go from clue to clue. The last clue will take you to something you will like."

"Can we read the clues by ourselves?" I asked.

"Yes, you can," said Dad.

Dad gave me the first clue. It said:

I'm very tall.

Some of me is up in the air.

A bird can come home to me. What/$_{100}$ am I?]

Comprehension Questions

(TE)   1. What did Dad make up?
        (some clues)

(TI)   2. How will the children find the clues?
        (Read the clues, go where they say, and find another clue.)

(TE)   3. What will the last clue take them to?
        (something they will like)

(TI)   4. Why did they think the clue was telling about a tree?
        (because that is where a bird would go, or an answer from any other part of the clue, for example, tall, in the air)

(SI)   5. What is the answer to the clue?
        (a tree or a tall pole)

(SI)   6. Why do you think Dad made up the clues for them to read?
        (He wanted to give them something to do; he wanted them to have some fun; he wanted them to look for what he was going to give them—the "something you will like.")

Across the Fence (pp. 42–44)

Passage

→   Sue went down the road to find Jack.

"Hello, Jack," said Sue. "Will you play with me?"

"No," said Jack. "You know that I'm afraid of Puff."

"You don't have to be afraid now," said Sue. "I know where we can play by ourselves."

"Did you give Puff away?" asked Jack.

"No, I didn't," said Sue. "Come to my house. You don't have to be afraid."

Sue went down the road to find Gail.

"Hello, Gail," said Sue. "Will you play with me?"

"No, I will not play," said Gail. "I don't like Puff to kiss me."

"Puff will not/$_{100}$ kiss you," said Sue. "I have found a way that we can play by ourselves. Come to my house. You will see that it's OK."]

Comprehension Questions

(TE)   1.   What did Sue ask Jack to do?
(come play with her)

(TE)   2.   What didn't Gail like Puff to do?
(kiss her)

(TI)   3.   In what ways are Jack and Gail alike?
(They don't want to play near Puff, or they don't like Puff or are afraid of Puff.)

(TI)   4.   Why did Sue say that Jack didn't have to be afraid anymore?
(because she knew a place where they could play by themselves)

(SI)   5.   Describe Puff. What do you think he was like?
(a dog, perhaps fluffy as a puppy, perhaps big and scary—anything that makes sense for the story)

(SI)   6.   What would you do with Puff?
(tie him up or put him somewhere where he can't get loose or bother anyone; train him)

Glad to Meet You (pp. 15–16)

Passage

➔   Mom stopped. She said, "Call the police."

Dad stopped. He said, "Call the fire house."

Ruthy stopped. She said, "Call the zoo."

Mr. Pond stopped. He called the police. He called the fire house. He called the zoo.

Zoom! came the police.

Zoom! came the fire truck.

Zoom! came the woman from the zoo.

They all ran upstairs. "Look!" said Mom. "It is black."

"Look!" said Dad. "It is in the bed."

"Look!" said Ruthy. "It's a bear! Andrew said it was a bear. But nobody listens to Andrew."

The police said, "It must have come from the woods. It/₁₀₀ climbed up the tree. It climbed in the window."]

Comprehension Questions

(TE)   1. What did the people do to get help?
    (They called the police, the fire department, and the zoo.)

(TI)   2. Did the police, the firemen, and the zookeeper come quickly? How do you know?
    (Zoom means they came quickly.)

(TI)   3. What was in the bed?
    (a big black bear)

(TE)   4. Where did the bear come from?
    (from the woods)

(SI)   5. Why would a bear want to sleep in a human's bed?
    (It's soft, warm, or comfortable.)

(SI)   6. Who do you think will take care of the bear?
    (the lady from the zoo)

Glad to Meet You (pp. 20–21)

Passage

➔ "That is lunch," Polly answered. "It's stew."

"It looks like mud to me," Willie said.

"It is rock stew," said Polly.

Willie looked again. "It still looks like mud to me," he said.

"Oh, but it isn't," Polly said. "It is much better than mud. Would you like some?"

"OK," Willie answered. "Some rock stew, please."

Polly put some of the stew in a bowl.

"How much is that?" Willie asked.

"It's free to friends," answered Polly.

Willie put his spoon near his mouth and made a strange noise.

"What are you doing?" Polly asked.

"Eating," said Willie. "Now I/$_{100}$ am all done."]

Comprehension Questions

(TE) 1. What did Polly make for lunch?
      (rock stew)

(TE) 2. How did the stew look?
      (like mud)

(TI) 3. Were Polly and Willie friends? Why do you think that?
      (Yes, because after Willie asked how much it cost, Polly said the stew was free to friends.)

(TI) 4. Why did Willie make strange noises when he put the spoon near his mouth?
      (He said he was eating.)

(SI) 5. Why was the soup still in the bowl when Willie said he was done?
      (He was making believe.)

(SI) 6. Why do you think Willie didn't eat any of the stew?
      (It was actually made of rocks and mud, things people do not eat.)

Glad to Meet You (pp. 26–27)

Passage

→ Polly and Willie ran to see Mrs. Brimble.

"Do you know where the dictionary is, Mom?" Willie asked.

"I think it's in the kitchen," answered Mrs. Brimble.

Polly and Willie ran to the kitchen. The dictionary was there.

Polly stopped by the sink. "Here is my dark blue paint. I lost it this morning."

"Oh, your things get lost all the time," said Willie.

"Yes, but I find them again," Polly said.

"Let's find that word," said Willie.

They turned to the dictionary. When they came to the word serendipity, Willie stopped.

"Let me see," said Polly.

She began to/$_{100}$ read: " 'Serendipity—being able to find good things by accident.' Well, I found my bell, my train book, and my dark blue paint today—all by accident."

"Yes," Willie said, "and we found a good word, too."]

Comprehension Questions

(TE) 1. What are the children looking for?
       (the dictionary)

(TE) 2. Where did Mrs. Brimble think it (the dictionary) was?
       (in the kitchen)

(TI) 3. After the children found the dictionary, what did they find?
       (Polly's paints)

(TI) 4. Why is "serendipity" a good word to describe what happened to Polly?
       (It describes how Polly found her things by accident.)

(SI) 5. Why do you think Polly was always losing things?
       (She forgot where she put them, or she didn't put them back where they belonged, and so on.)

(SI) 6. Why do you think the paints were by the sink?
       (You need water to paint with or to clean up with.)

Day 1
Level 8

Give Me A Clue (pp. 12–13)

Passage

→ Jane came over to ask Elizabeth Ann to play baseball. Elizabeth Ann smiled and said, "Great!" She decided she would play. She liked playing baseball with her friends. She liked the crack of the ball on the bat. She liked the sound that showed she had made a good catch.

It was a hard game. First one team got a run. Then the other team did.

Elizabeth Ann worked hard trying to help her team. She forgot all about forgetting.

In the first inning, Elizabeth Ann just missed catching a ball. In the next inning, she hit a fly ball/$_{100}$ right to another player.

By the last inning, her team was still behind by one run. She had to get a run and tie the game!]

Comprehension Questions

(TE) 1. Who is this story about?
(Elizabeth Ann and Jane, or two little girls)

(TE) 2. What did Elizabeth Ann have to do to win the game?
(hit the ball, get a run)

(TI) 3. Why was it a "hard" game?
(They had a hard time getting ahead of the other team; it was hard for Elizabeth Ann because she had problems hitting and catching the ball.)

(TI) 4. How did you know that Elizabeth Ann was excited to play baseball?
(She smiled and said, "Great!")

(SI) 5. How do you think Elizabeth Ann felt in the last inning?
(nervous or scared that she wouldn't hit the ball)

(SI) 6. When Elizabeth Ann goes to bat, how might her team help her?
(cheer for her, wish her good luck)

Give Me A Clue (pp. 20–21)

Passage

➜ "You can't give a surprise party for yourself," said Albert. "You won't be surprised."

"I know I can't give a surprise party for myself," said Nicky. "But YOU can. You and Ann, and Jenny and Jan, and Morris and Doris, and Dan can give the party."

"How are we going to do that?" asked Albert.

"Easy," said Nicky. "You'll say, 'Nicky's birthday is coming; let's give him a surprise party.' Then they'll say, 'What a good idea. We love surprise parties. You can bring the cake. Ann can bring the paper plates."

"Oh, I get it," said Albert. "Everyone will/$_{100}$ bring something for the party. What a good idea."

"You can get the party ready at my house while I am out having a tuba lesson," Nicky said. "When I come home, you will yell, 'SURPRISE!' I'll be surprised even if this isn't the best surprise party ever."]

Comprehension Questions

(TE) 1. Whose birthday was coming up?
(Nicky's)

(TE) 2. What did Nicky want his friends to do for him?
(give a surprise party)

(TI) 3. Who was going to prepare the meal for the party?
(Nicky's friends)

(TI) 4. What instrument does Nicky play?
(tuba)

(SI) 5. Why is it funny that Nicky is planning his own surprise party?
(Because if he knows about it, it's not a real surprise.)

(SI) 6. Why does Nicky believe that Ann, Jenny, Jan, Morris, and Doris will like the idea of giving a surprise party for him?
(He assumes that they are good friends and that they like to help give parties. Albert agrees that it is a good idea.)

Give Me A Clue (p. 28)

Passage

➔ Nicky was walking home from his tuba lesson. He gave a little hop. His birthday had come at last. When Nicky got to his house, it was all dark. He practiced making a surprised face. He opened his front door. Nothing happened.

He went into the front room. Nothing happened. He turned on the light. Nobody was there.

"Where's the party?" he asked himself.

"They must be hiding." Nicky waited and waited. Nothing happened.

Then the doorbell rang.

"There they are!" Nicky thought. He practiced making surprised faces on the way to the door.

It was Albert, all by himself. /₁₀₀

"Where is my party?" asked Nicky.

"Oh, Nicky," said Albert. "It's too bad. Ann told everyone that you were going to a concert with your tuba teacher. They called off the party."]

Comprehension Questions

(TE) 1. Where was Nicky coming home from?
        (his tuba lesson)

(TI) 2. Who did he hope was waiting at his house?
        (his friends or people for the party)

(TE) 3. Who was waiting at his house when he got home?
        (nobody)

(TI) 4. When the doorbell rang, what did Nicky think?
        (The people for the party had arrived.)

(SI) 5. What kind of a party was Nicky expecting?
        (a surprise birthday party)

(SI) 6. How do you think Nicky felt when Albert told him they had called off the party?
        (disappointed, or sad, or angry)

Mystery Sneaker (p. 13)

Day 1
Level 9

Passage

➔   One day Charlie heard a "meow" up in a tree. That was the day he thought of a new way to get cats out of trees.

He went home and got a pail and a rope and a fish. He put the fish in the pail. Then he tied one end of the rope to the handle. He threw the other end of the rope over a branch up above the cat and pulled the pail up.

The cat smelled the fish and jumped into the pail. Then Charlie brought the pail down.

The cat had an elevator ride and /$_{100}$ a fish all at the same time.]

Comprehension Questions

(TE)   1. What did Charlie use to get the cat out of the tree?
            (a fish, a pail, and a rope)

(TE)   2. What made the cat jump into the pail?
            (the smell of fish)

(TI)   3. Why does the cat follow Charlie everywhere?
            (She likes Charlie—he got her out of the tree.)

(TI)   4. What did the cat do after she jumped in the pail?
            (ate the fish)

(SI)   5. Why is the ride like an elevator ride?
            (It goes up and down; it can carry someone/something.)

(SI)   6. Why does Charlie use a fish to get the cat out of the tree?
            (Cats will go after fish because they like to eat them.)

Mystery Sneaker (pp. 26–27)

Passage

➜ "There is something inside," Kate said. "It's a mystery smell." She stuck her nose inside the box and sniffed hard. Then she looked with the magnifying glass. Marsha and Nobby sniffed, too.

"I don't smell anything," Marsha said.

"Neither do I," said Nobby.

"I've lost it!" Kate cried.

"Never mind," Marsha said. "Tell us about it."

"You know that empty old house on Grizzly Hill?" Kate asked.

"The one that's haunted?" Nobby asked.

"That's it," Kate said. "Now lights are on in the house, and there's a funny smell around it."

Marsha laughed. "Maybe a wizard is in the/$_{100}$ haunted house making a brew of toads' ears and hairy spiders and crawly things."]

Comprehension Questions

(TE) 1. What did Kate say was in the box?
(a mystery smell)

(SI) 2. Why do you think she looked through a magnifying glass?
(to look for clues to the mystery; to see if she could see something inside)

(TI) 3. Who else smelled the mystery smell?
(nobody)

(TI) 4. What did Kate mean when she said, "I've lost it"?
(that she cannot smell the mystery smell anymore)

(TE) 5. Where did Kate smell the smell before?
(at the haunted house on Grizzly Hill)

(SI) 6. Why do you think Marsha laughed when she said, "Maybe a wizard is in the haunted house making a brew of toads' ears and hairy spiders and crawly things"?
(because she did not believe Kate's story about mystery smells in haunted houses)

Mystery Sneaker (p. 28)

Day 3
Level 9

Passage

➡   Nobby put his detective notebook, pencil, and magnifying glass in a bag. Kate led the way. They stopped in front of an old brown, tumbled-down house. The wind rustled dry leaves in the yard. The house looked empty and scary. A strange smell was all around. Kate sniffed.

"Here it is!" she yelled. "Can you smell it?"

Nobby took a long sniff. "That's interesting," he said. "There is a smell. It makes me hungry." He scribbled with his pencil in the notebook.

Marsha sniffed. "You're right, Kate. You always did have the best nose in the club." Kate rubbed her/$_{100}$ nose proudly.]

Comprehension Questions

(TE)   1. What did Nobby put in his bag?
            (detective notebook, pencil, magnifying glass)

(TE)   2. How did the house look?
            (old, brown, tumbled-down, empty, scary)

(SI)   3. What were Nobby and Marsha pretending to be?
            (detectives)

(TI)   4. After taking a sniff, how did Nobby feel?
            (hungry)

(TI)   5. Why did Kate rub her nose?
            (She was proud because Marsha said she had the best nose in the club.)

(SI)   6. What does it mean to "have the best nose in the club"?
            (to be able to detect smells the best)

Ten Times Around (p. 18)

Passage

➔ "And isn't this the third floor?" Ella asked.

"No. The third floor is downstairs, underneath my apartment. This is the fourth floor."

"But how could that be?" Ella asked. "We walked up three flights."

"Oh, I see." The woman nodded her head. "You didn't know that the ground floor is called the first floor. You should have walked up only two flights."

Ella could feel her cheeks turning scarlet. "Oh, we made such a dreadful mistake! I'm terribly sorry! You see, we thought we were in our aunt's apartment. Then we read the note . . . ," she ended lamely.

The woman shrugged/$_{100}$ her shoulders and chuckled. "Well, it's all right. What's done is done. Don't worry. A mistake can happen."

"But we ate up all your food!" Henny said.]

Comprehension Questions

(TE) 1. Where did Ella and Henny think they were?
(They thought they were in their aunt's apartment.)

(TI) 2. What was the "dreadful mistake"?
(They were in a stranger's apartment, one floor above their aunt's apartment.)

(TE) 3. What had Ella and Henny done in the stranger's apartment?
(They had eaten all the food.)

(TI) 4. What mistake did Ella and Henny make in climbing the steps to their aunt's apartment?
(They didn't know that the ground floor was also the first floor.)

(SI) 5. Did the woman seem angry with Ella and Henny? How do you know?
(She shrugged and chuckled; she wasn't yelling.)

(SI) 6. What emotion was Ella feeling when her cheeks turned scarlet?
(She was feeling embarrassed or very sorry.)

Ten Times Around (p. 26)

Passage

➔   Teresa turned around. She tried to walk down the escalator. She walked and walked. It seemed as if she were just standing still. Then she ran down the moving steps. It took a minute, but she finally reached the bottom.

Teresa found the keys on the floor. The key-ring held the car keys and the house keys. Her mother would be pleased Teresa had found them.

Teresa put the keys in her pocket and ran back up the escalator.

At the top she found hallways leading left and right. There were crowds of people rushing back and forth.

"Mom? Dad?" /$_{100}$ Teresa called.

There was no answer.]

Comprehension Questions

(SI)   1. Why did it seem as if Teresa were standing still?
(She was trying to walk down the up escalator.)

(TE)   2. What was Teresa looking for?
(keys, or her parents' key-ring)

(TE)   3. Where did Teresa find the keys?
(on the floor, or at the bottom of the escalator)

(TI)   4. After finding the keys, why did Teresa go back up the escalator?
(to look for her parents)

(TI)   5. What did Teresa do when she got to the top of the escalator?
(called, "Mom? Dad?")

(SI)   6. Where do you think Teresa is in this story, in what type of building?
(a department store, airport, any place with escalators)

Ten Times Around (p. 38)

Passage

➔ It is 10:26 A.M. Peg pulls her truck out of the firehouse. Luis Borjas, the butcher, jumps in next to her. Their fire gear is already on the truck. Luis will put on his big boots and heavy coat on the way to the fire. The team members have practiced many times. Each one knows just when to do every part of the job.

Gina Ortero and Bill Adams run to the Rescue Unit truck. Bill starts the engine just as Craig Scott gets in the back.

Gina is a druggist in town. As part of her work, she knows a/$_{100}$ lot about health. But to be in the Rescue Unit, Gina, Bill, and Craig had to take extra training.]

Comprehension Questions

(TE) 1. What were Gina, Bill, and Craig members of?
(the Rescue Unit)

(TI) 2. What do you think the Rescue Unit does?
(puts fires out)

(TI) 3. Did the members work full time at the Rescue Unit?
(no)

(TE) 4. What other jobs did some of them have?
(butcher, druggist)

(SI) 5. Why do you think they needed extra training before becoming members of the Rescue Unit?
(to learn exactly what to do)

(SI) 6. Why was it necessary to have several different kinds of people?
(For the various jobs, someone had to be trained in medical assistance, someone had to drive, some people who are strong were needed to carry the equipment and drag the hoses.)

Day 1
Level 11

Barefoot Island (p. 31)

Passage

➜   Huge waves crashed on the small rocky island. The wind whipped the rain against the lighthouse. Captain Hosea Lewis peered through the terrible storm. He could just barely make out the bobbing rowboat with its three passengers coming from the shore.

"Ida is coming," he told his wife. "I wish she had decided to stay on the mainland tonight."

"Don't worry," said Mrs. Lewis. "The children are safe enough." She wished her words equaled her feelings. She was as worried as her husband. But she didn't want to say so because the captain was not a well man.

The boat/$_{100}$ would be on the tip of a wave for a moment. Then it would slide down the hill of water and be lost from view.]

Comprehension Questions

(TI)   1. Where was the lighthouse located?
           (on a small, rocky island)

(TI)   2. Who was in the rowboat?
           (Ida and the children)

(TE)   3. What was the weather like?
           (There was a terrible storm.)

(TE)   4. What did Captain Lewis wish?
           (that Ida had decided to stay on the mainland tonight)

(SI)   5. Why was Captain Lewis very worried about the rowboat trying to get to his island?
           (He was afraid that the boat might sink in the storm.)

(SI)   6. The story said, "the captain was not a well man." What does that mean?
           (It means the captain was suffering from a severe illness of some sort.)

Barefoot Island (p. 44)

Passage

➔ It's very different on an island, and we live there all summer long.

In June my dad closes up his classroom, and my mom finishes painting winter things and packs her paint box full of summer colors. Then we drive away from the city. We drive all night and day until we come to the ocean, where we leave our car behind and ride on a ferryboat to the island. Grandma and her dog Shadow are already there, waiting with a wheelbarrow to carry our suitcases to our cabin.

There is a secret path through the woods between our cabin/$_{100}$ and hers.]

Comprehension Questions

(TE) 1. Where did the family live all summer?
(on an island)

(SI) 2. What does Dad do for a living?
(He is a teacher.)

(SI) 3. What kind of work does Mom do?
(She is a painter, artist.)

(TI) 4. Where do they live when it isn't summer and they're not on the island?
(in the city)

(TI) 5. Where did they have to drive to get to the island?
(to the ocean, or to the ferryboat)

(TE) 6. What does Grandma use to carry their suitcases?
(a wheelbarrow)

Barefoot Island (p. 57)

Day 3
Level 11

Passage

→ "After vacation time we get a lot of cats and dogs that people abandon when they go back to the city," the doctor said. "If they weren't brought here, most of these animals would get sick or starve."

Christopher held the puppy to his face. It felt silky and warm. He could hear how fast its heart was beating.

"How about it, Christopher. Would you like to keep him?" his father asked.

A big dog lying with its leg in a cast raised its head and thumped its tail. From another cage, a sheep dog with patches of hair shaved /$_{100}$ off was watching. It seemed as if the whole room were waiting for him to answer.

Christopher shook his head. "I don't really want to," he said slowly. "I'm sorry."]

Comprehension Questions

(TE) 1. How did the puppy feel?
(silky and warm)

(TE) 2. Who came to see the doctor?
(Christopher and his father)

(TI) 3. Why didn't the dogs have homes?
(Families came on vacations with the dogs and forgot about them and left them behind.)

(TI) 4. What did Christopher say when Dad asked him if he wanted the dog?
(Nothing; he just thought about it and looked at the cages.)

(SI) 5. What kind of doctor was the one in the story?
(a doctor who takes care of animals, a veterinarian)

(SI) 6. Why did Christopher say that it seemed that everyone was waiting?
(All the animals and the doctor were watching him to see if he decided to take the puppy.)

Ride the Sunrise (p. 12)

Passage

➔ "I don't want to swap," Walter said. "I've got almost a full set, only four more to go."

"It's up to you," Chester said. "I swapped a genuine compass for this yo-yo. It's made of real boxwood."

"Real boxwood? What's that?"

"It's what the best yo-yos are made out of," Chester said. "Take it or leave it."

"I'll take it," Walter said. Quick as a flash, the cards and the yo-yo changed hands. Chester had the cards, and Walter had the yo-yo.

"So long," Chester said, fanning out the cards and starting down the street, as Walter slipped the yo-yo/$_{100}$ cord over his finger and began to practice with it.]

Comprehension Questions

(TE) 1. What were the boys swapping?
(cards for a yo-yo)

(TI) 2. What did Chester say to convince Walter to swap?
(He told him that it was made from boxwood; that's what good yo-yos are made out of.)

(TI) 3. Why is Chester willing to give up the yo-yo?
(He would like the cards instead.)

(TE) 4. What did Walter do as he walked down the street with the yo-yo?
(practiced using the yo-yo; tried it out)

(SI) 5. Why would Chester want to get a full set of cards?
(It would be worth more; he might be able to make a better swap then.)

(SI) 6. Why does Chester tell Walter he swapped a genuine compass to get the yo-yo?
(to make it sound like a really good yo-yo, as if it were worth a lot, so that Walter would be convinced that it was a good swap)

Ride the Sunrise (p. 22)

Day 2
Level 12

Passage

➡ Belinda did have one nice trait. She took long naps. Right after lunch, she decided to go to sleep in the hammock in the backyard. She was sleeping soundly when my partner, Midge, came at one to take the afternoon shift. It seemed safe to leave her, so Midge walked to the road with me. We were trying to think of something to try next when Ruth Sebastian drove by in her little red car. When she saw us, she came to a stop and backed up.

"What's the matter? Has little Belinda disappeared and the famous Henry Reed Baby-Sitting/$_{100}$ Service can't find her?"]

Comprehension Questions

(TI)   1. What were Midge and the narrator (or the other person in the story) doing?
      (babysitting Belinda)

(SI)   2. Why is it a nice trait that Belinda takes long naps?
      (It is less work for babysitters.)

(TI)   3. Who babysat for Belinda during the morning shift?
      (the narrator, the other person in the story)

(TE)   4. What did Ruth Sebastian think when she saw Midge and the narrator walking together?
      (that Belinda had disappeared and that they were looking for her)

(TE)   5. What were the two babysitters trying to decide?
      (what to do next)

(SI)   6. Why did Ruth Sebastian think something was the matter?
      (It must have been unusual for both sitters to leave Belinda at the same time.)

Ride the Sunrise (p. 41)

Passage

➔ People made their own fun then. Families read stories aloud and played games together. They made their own music. They worked picture puzzles and held quizzes.

Because most entertainment took place in the home, people became excited when any kind of entertainment came to town. Sometimes a group of actors would appear, or perhaps a small circus. A showboat might stop to give a musical in a town near a large river. One of the most popular kinds of entertainment then was the medicine show.

The purpose of the medicine show was to sell medicine. A person who sold medicine/$_{100}$ attracted a crowd with a show. Then the salesperson gave a sales pitch. This approach was a great success. People enjoyed watching the free show so much they were happy to buy the medicines—even if they knew the medicines wouldn't work.]

Comprehension Questions

(TE)   1. How did people make their own fun?
(at least two of the following: read stories aloud, played games together, made music, worked picture puzzles)

(TE)   2. What were some kinds of entertainment that came to town?
(at least two of the following: groups of actors, a small circus, a showboat giving a musical, a medicine show)

(TI)   3. Before selling any medicine, what would the salesperson do?
(give a free medicine show)

(TI)   4. Why did the person who sold the medicine give a free show?
(People enjoyed the free show so much, they would spend their money on the medicine.)

(SI)   5. How is this story different from how things are today?
(Today we have TV and radios, but no medicine shows.)

(SI)   6. What do we call "medicine shows" on TV today?
(commercials, ads, advertisements for medicine, pills, etc.)

Flights of Color (p. 13)

Passage

➡ Emma Jane continued as if there had been no interruption. "Pa died in February. We left when the grass turned green. Ma drives the wagon with the little ones, while Marty and I herd the cattle."

The man squinted at her from under his hat brim. "But why did you bring the cattle along?"

"We're going back to Illinois to sell the cattle in Chicago and buy a farm."

The dark eyes blinked under the gray brows, and the man twanged softly, "Going to Chicago, she said—as if it were just over the next hill."

Emma Jane flashed him a grin./₁₀₀ "That's right. All we have to do is keep on walking, and one day that's where Chicago will be—over the next hill."]

Comprehension Questions

(TE)   1.   What kind of work do Emma Jane and Marty do?
(tend the cattle, herd the cattle)

(TE)   2.   Where is Emma Jane's family going?
(Chicago, Illinois)

(TI)   3.   When the man says, "Going to Chicago, she said—as if it were just over the next hill," to whom is he speaking?
(himself)

(TI)   4.   Why would Emma Jane and her family need to sell the cattle?
(to get money to buy a farm)

(SI)   5.   Who are the "little ones" that Emma Jane talks about?
(her mother's little children, Emma Jane's little brothers and sisters)

(SI)   6.   Why would the children need to work?
(Their father has died and they need the money, so now the children need to work.)

Flights of Color (p. 31)

Passage

➜   Old Ramon stepped to the burro and leaned his weight, pressing down on its back. It spread its legs a bit and braced them against the pressure. While the boy watched in wonder, Old Ramon climbed on his hands and knees on the burro's back and the two lashed packs that balanced each other on the two sides. The burro braced its legs, and they quivered some but held firm. Carefully Old Ramon steadied himself and rose upright. He peered all around into the distances, studying the land. He jumped down, and the burro, released from his weight, shook itself/₁₀₀ until the packs rattled in the stillness.]

Comprehension Questions

(TI)   1. What was Old Ramon trying to do?
(climb on a burro, a donkey, some animal)

(SI)   2. Why do you think the burro was having difficulties?
(Ramon was fat; or the donkey was not used to carrying people, or it didn't want to carry so much weight.)

(TE)   3. What did Ramon do when he was up on the burro?
(He crawled on hands and knees, and he stood up.)

(TI)   4. Why did Ramon stand up?
(to see the land, to be high up and see better)

(TE)   5. What did the burro do after Ramon jumped off?
(It shook itself.)

(SI)   6. What country could this story be taking place in?
(accept any Spanish-speaking country or the American Southwest)

Flights of Color (p. 48)

Passage

→   It seemed wise to try out the machine before attempting to cross the channel. For one thing, its controls were different from those of other planes I had flown. I arranged to have the monoplane shipped to Hardelot, a French seacoast village where Mr. Bleriot had a hangar.

Unfortunately, persistent harsh winds at Hardelot would not permit me to try out the machine. Time was flying—even if I was not. I had promised the *Mirror* editor to be at Dover promptly. So I arranged to have the monoplane shipped across to Dover at once. Nothing should be known of/$_{100}$ my projected journey. I wished to surprise the world. The machine was shipped secretly to the aerodrome on Dover heights, about three miles back from the channel.]

Comprehension Questions

(TE)   1. What did the person telling the story want to do before crossing the channel?
         (try out the plane)

(TE)   2. Where was the monoplane shipped to?
         (Hardelot, a French seacoast village)

(SI)   3. Why do you think the *Mirror* editor was going to be at Dover?
         (to watch the flight and report on it)

(TI)   4. What caused the flier to change his plans and ship the plane to Dover?
         (harsh winds and the fact that the editor was waiting in Dover)

(TI)   5. Why did he have the monoplane shipped secretly?
         (He wished to surprise the world.)

(SI)   6. How do you think the pilot felt during this time? Explain.
         (excited, because he was going to surprise the world by crossing the channel; or nervous, because he hadn't tried out the controls yet)

Green Salad Seasons (p. 16)

Passage

→   A big bus carried the thirty-five county champions from the dinner at the hotel to the high school. At eight o'clock the curtain parted revealing the audience to the boys and girls on stage. Thirty-five boys and girls on stage, thought Ellen, feeling a little bit sad, and thirty-four mothers in the audience. Henry was there, with his girl friend, Dorothy. Now that Father was gone, Henry was head of the family. It ought to be enough that her brother was in the audience.

The teacher said, "Botany," and smiled at Ellen. They had finished with the sixth-grade spelling books/$_{100}$ and were starting on the seventh. Twenty-eight girls and boys were still on stage.]

Comprehension Questions

(TE)   1. Where were the boys and girls?
   (at the high school or on stage)

(TI)   2. What kind of event was Ellen a part of?
   (a spelling bee)

(TE)   3. Since Ellen's father was gone, who had become the head of the family?
   (her brother, Henry)

(TI)   4. Ellen was feeling sad. Why was she feeling this way?
   (Her father was gone and/or her mother was not at the spelling bee.)

(SI)   5. When the teacher said the word *botany* to Ellen, what was Ellen supposed to do?
   (She was supposed to spell the word.)

(SI)   6. At the beginning of the story, there were 35 children on stage, but the last sentence says that 28 boys and girls were left. What happened to the other children?
   (They were eliminated from the competition by spelling a word incorrectly.)

Green Salad Seasons (p. 23)

Passage

➜   He walked to the back of the room, sat down, and then looked around at the field of suddenly upraised hands and said, "Go ahead, Getsinger. You go first."

A thin boy with wild blond hair and a red bow tie popped out of his seat and, carrying a sheet of paper, went to the front of the room and, in a fast, singsong voice, read, "He's So Understanding." Several of the boys turned in their seats and looked at one of the fathers and grinned as Getsinger went on, "When I ask for a dime he says he'll settle/₁₀₀ for a nickel, and I say you can't get anything for a nickel any more and he says that he'll settle for six cents. Then pretty soon Mom calls and says that supper is ready, and the fight goes on in the dining room. After a while Dad says he'll make it seven cents, and before supper is over I have my dime. That's why I say he is understanding."]

Comprehension Questions

(TE)   1. What did Getsinger raise his hand to do?
       (to get up and read his composition)

(TE)   2. How did Getsinger read his composition, what did his voice sound like?
       (fast and in a singsong way)

(TI)   3. For whom were the boys reading their compositions?
       (their fathers)

(TI)   4. Why did Getsinger say his father was understanding?
       (He would eventually give him the money he asked for.)

(SI)   5. Why do you think Mr. Getsinger gives his son what he asks for?
       (He is tired of fighting, or so he can eat his supper.)

(SI)   6. Are many boys eager to read their compositions?
       (Yes; there is a field of "suddenly upraised hands.")

Green Salad Seasons (p. 35)

Passage

➔   Each April, on Sunday afternoon, our family went up into the mountains in a picnic mood to observe a springtime ritual. Whenever my father decided the proper day had arrived, he shouldered an ax, my mother gave each of us children a teaspoon, and off we went, up the mountain to a spot where grew a grove of black birch trees. Father looked over the grove carefully, chose a sapling for the sacrifice, and chopped it down. Then, with his ax, he pried off the smooth bark in squares and gave a square to each of us. We sat about/$_{100}$ on stumps or on fallen tree trunks, and with our spoons scraped the inside of the bark for the sap that was both sweet and spicy, like wintergreen. This was the best of all spring days.]

Comprehension Questions

(TE)   1. What time of year was it?
         (spring)

(TE)   2. Where did the family go?
         (up the mountains to a grove of black birch trees)

(TI)   3. Why did the family go for a picnic in the mountains?
         (to eat the sweet sap from the birch trees)

(TI)   4. After father cut down the tree, what did he do?
         (gave each child a square of bark)

(SI)   5. Why did the author call this outing a springtime ritual?
         (because it was an outing that was important to the family, and they did it every year)

(SI)   6. Today, what do we use to get a wintergreen taste?
         (chewing gum)

Chains of Light (p. 17)

Passage

→   "I would have frozen to death, last night, had your hideout not been so well built; had it been less well hidden, the searchers who came by at dawn would have found me."

"Do you like it?" said Perdiccas, charmed. "It is good, isn't it?"

"Splendid!" the man said, suddenly smiling at us. "How did you make ivy grow on it?" We told him, both talking at once.

"And my fine young fellow, is that really a rabbit dangling from your bag? Are we having a feast? You are just in time. I haven't eaten for three days."

"You'd do/₁₀₀ better, you know," said Perdiccas, "to run away. You haven't really time for rabbit."]

Comprehension Questions

(TE)   1. When did the searchers come?
             (They came at dawn.)

(TE)   2. When was the last time the man had eaten?
             (three days ago)

(TI)   3. What was the man hoping to eat?
             (the rabbit)

(TI)   4. How was the hideout hidden from view?
             (It was covered with ivy.)

(SI)   5. If you could have a hideout, in what ways would it be like Perdiccas' hideout?
             (any appropriate answer: well-built, hidden from view, covered with ivy)

(SI)   6. Why did Perdiccas say the man hadn't really time for rabbit?
             (The man was trying to escape from the searchers.)

Chains of Light (p. 32)

Passage

➜   But all this—the mysterious, far-reaching hairline trail, the absence of sun from the sky, the tremendous cold, and the strangeness and weirdness of it all—made no impression on the man. It was not because he was long used to it. He was a newcomer in the land, a chechaquo, and this was his first winter. The trouble with him was that he was without imagination. He was quick and alert in the things of life, but only in the things, and not in the significances. Fifty degrees below zero meant eighty-odd degrees of frost. Such fact impressed him/$_{100}$ as being cold and uncomfortable, and that was all. It did not lead him to meditate upon his frailty as a creature of temperature, and upon human frailty in general, able only to live within certain narrow limits of heat and cold; and from there on it did not lead him to the conjectural field of immortality and humankind's place in the universe. Fifty degrees below zero stood for a bite of frost that hurt, and that must be guarded against by the use of mittens, warm moccasins, and thick socks. Fifty degrees below zero was to him just precisely fifty degrees below zero. That there should be anything more to it than that was a thought that never entered his head.]

Comprehension Questions

(TE)   1. What time of year is it; which season?
           (winter)

(TE)   2. How cold is it; what is the temperature?
           (50 degrees below zero)

(TI)   3. Why is the temperature important?
           (The man could freeze without even realizing how cold he was.)

(TI)   4. About how long had the man lived in that area?
           (less than a year, because it was his first winter there)

(SI)   5. What did the author mean when he said that the man did not think of the significance of the weather?
           (The man thought only about the immediate effects on how he felt, not about how important controlling his temperature was for his survival.)

(SI)   6. What does "human frailty in general" mean?
           (Any answer that indicates an understanding of the frailty of human beings or of survival skills is acceptable.)

Chains of Light (p. 53)

Passage

➜   Ishi was the last survivor of an American Indian tribe called the Yahi. For years, he and a few remaining tribespeople lived in hiding. They found it harder and harder to escape the notice of the changing civilization growing up around them, people with "firesticks" and "monsters" that moved through the land on iron tracks. One by one, Ishi's companions died, and he was left alone. There was no one who spoke his language. He was the last of his tribe.

For as long as Ishi could remember, the saldu, or white people, had been his enemies. Now, weakened and $/_{100}$ dazed from loneliness and starvation, Ishi stumbles into the saldu world.]

Comprehension Questions

(TE)   1. Who is Ishi?
            (last survivor of the Yahi Indian tribe)

(SI)   2. Why had Ishi and his companions lived in hiding?
            (They feared the white civilization, the "saldu.")

(SI)   3. What do you think "firesticks" were?
            (guns)

(TI)   4. Why did Ishi come into the "saldu" world?
            (All his companions had died, and he was starving.)

(TE)   5. What was Ishi like when he stumbled into the "saldu" world?
            (weak and dazed from loneliness and starvation)

(TI)   6. Why will Ishi still be lonely in the "saldu" world?
            (He speaks another language, all his companions have died, the saldu culture is very different, and so forth.)

Sample Literature CBAs

In this section, we present several samples of literature-based CBAs derived from classic literature as well as sample CBAs from the popular press, such as magazines and newspapers. These CBAs are included to illustrate several points. *One,* in elementary school programs where a literature-based approach to teaching reading is used, the CBAs can be constructed from sample passages taken from the literature stories in the same manner that they were taken from stories in a basal reading program. *Two,* this approach to developing reading CBAs can be applied most readily to the reading assignments given to secondary students because much of their reading in English classes is in the classical literature. Thus, some of the samples in this section are taken from secondary-level literature textbooks for Grades 7 and 9. *Three,* reading CBAs can be constructed for older students or for adults who are learning to read by deriving the reading materials from the popular press. Thus, this section also contains examples of CBAs from newspaper and magazine articles because these are typical of the types of materials appropriate for adult readers who are learning to read.

Another unique aspect of the CBAs in this section is that they are used to assess both oral and silent reading skills. Notice that the actual construction is identical to that used for the reading CBAs in the previous section. Each has the requisite 100-word sample, an extension beyond the 100-word mark to make the passage sufficiently long to glean comprehension responses, and six comprehension questions, two of each comprehension type: text-explicit, text-implicit, and script-implicit questions.

However, some are labeled to be used for oral reading samples and some for silent reading samples. Ordinarily, the oral sample is obtained first and then the silent right after, with the text for these two samples flowing from the oral sample to the silent sample. Thus, there is continuity in comprehension from the oral to the silent sample. But note that the entire oral sample is administered, including obtaining the comprehension responses, prior to beginning the silent reading sample.

A Sample CBA from a Seventh-Grade Literature Text

The following literature-based CBA is typical of the type of reading that middle-level secondary students are expected to read. This particular CBA contains different types of text: narrative, poetry, and fable literature. When constructing this type of CBA, teachers should select samples that reflect the variety of types of literature contained in the text. This CBA is a complete CBA with both oral and silent reading passages for Days 1, 2, and 3.

Prentice-Hall Literature: Bronze (p. 338)

Oral Passage

➔　Then Miss Hopley did a formidable thing. She stood up. Had she been standing when we entered she would have seemed tall. But rising from her chair she soared. And what she carried up and up with her was a buxom superstructure, firm shoulders, a straight sharp nose, full cheeks, slightly thin lips that moved like steel springs, and a high forehead topped by hair gathered in a bun. Miss Hopley was not a giant in body but when she mobilized it to a standing position she seemed a match for giants. I decided to like her.

She strode to/$_{100}$ a door in the far corner of the office, opened it and called a name. A boy of about ten years appeared in the doorway. He sat down at one end of the table. He was brown like us, a plump kid with shiny black hair combed straight back, neat, cool, and faintly obnoxious.

Miss Hopley joined us with a large book and some papers in her hand. She, too, sat down and the questions and answers began by way of our interpreter. My name was Ernesto. My mother's name was Henriqueta. My birth certificate was in San Blas. Here was my last report card from the Escuela Municipal Numero 3 para Varones of Mazatlan, and so forth. Miss Hopley put things down in the book and my mother signed a card.]

Comprehension Questions

(TE)　1.　What did Miss Hopley look like?
　　　　　(tall, buxom, firm shoulders, straight sharp nose, full cheeks, thin lips, high forehead, hair in a bun)

(SI)　2.　Why did the author decide to like her?
　　　　　(because of her formidable strength—or other reasonable answer)

(TI)　3.　How can you tell where the boy was born?
　　　　　(Spanish words in his address, Mazatlan, birth certificate, and so on)

(TI)　4.　Where did the incident take place?
　　　　　(in a school office)

(TE)　5.　What was the boy who came to the door like?
　　　　　(brown like the author, 10 years old, shiny black hair, faintly obnoxious, neat, cool)

(SI)　6.　Why were the author and her family meeting Miss Hopley?
　　　　　(to enroll in school)

Note. This passage and the five that follow are from *Prentice-Hall Literature: Bronze*, 1989, Englewood Cliffs, NJ: Prentice-Hall. Copyright 1989, 1996, by Prentice-Hall.

Prentice-Hall Literature: Bronze (p. 338)

Silent Passage

➔ As long as the questions continued, Dona Henriqueta could stay and I was secure. Now that they were over, Miss Hopley saw her to the door, dismissed our interpreter and without further ado took me by the hand and strode down the hall to Miss Ryan's first grade.

Miss Ryan took me to a seat at the front of the room, into which I shrank—the better to survey her. She was, too skinny, somewhat runty to me, of a withering height when she patrolled the class. And when I least expected it, there she was, crouching by my desk, her /$_{100}$ blond radiant face level with mine, her voice patiently maneuvering me over the awful idiocies of the English language.]

Comprehension Questions

(TE) 1. How long could Dona Henriqueta stay?
        (as long as there were questions)

(TI) 2. Why did she have to leave?
        (There were no more questions to be translated.)

(SI) 3. Who was Miss Hopley?
        (the principal, headmaster)

(TI) 4. What grade was the author in?
        (first grade)

(TE) 5. What did Miss Ryan look like?
        (tall, blond, radiant)

(SI) 6. Why did the author say that the English language had "awful idiocies"?
        (Compared to Spanish, which has lots of similarities, English has lots of differences.)

Prentice-Hall Literature: Bronze

Annabel Lee by Edgar Allan Poe (pp. 455–456)

Day 2
Grade 7

Oral Passage

➔ It was many and many a year ago,
　　In a kingdom by the sea,
That a maiden there lived whom you may know
　　By the name of Annabel Lee;—
And this maiden she lived with no other thought
　　Than to love and be loved by me.

She was a child and *I* was a child,
　　In this kingdom by the sea,
But we loved with a love that was more than love—
　　I and my Annabel Lee—
With a love that the winged seraphs of Heaven
　　Coveted her and me.

And this was the reason that, long ago,
　　In this/₁₀₀ kingdom by the sea,
A wind blew out of a cloud by night
　　Chilling my Annabel Lee;
So that her highborn kinsmen came
　　And bore her away from me,
To shut her up in a sepulcher
　　In this kingdom by the sea.]

Comprehension Questions

(TE)　1. What was the maiden's name?
　　　　(Annabel Lee)

(TE)　2. Where was the Kingdom?
　　　　(by the sea)

(TI)　3. How old was Annabel Lee?
　　　　(She must have been young, he referred to her as a child.)

(TI)　4. Explain this passage, "the winged seraphs of Heaven coveted her and me."
　　　　(The angels in heaven were jealous of the author's and Annabel's love for each other.)

(SI)　5. What happened to Annabel Lee?
　　　　(She died.)

(SI)　6. What do you think was the cause of her death?
　　　　(pneumonia, or the flu)

Prentice-Hall Literature: Bronze   **Day 2**
Annabel Lee by Edgar Allan Poe (p. 456)   **Grade 7**

Silent Passage

→   The angels, not half so happy in Heaven,
         Went envying her and me;—
      Yes! that was the reason (as all men know,
         In this kingdom by the sea)
      That the wind came out of a cloud, chilling
         And killing my Annabel Lee.

      But our love it was stronger by far than the love
         Of those who were older than we—
         Of many far wiser than we—
      And neither the angels in Heaven above
         Nor the demons down under the sea,
      Can ever dissever my soul from the soul
         Of the beautiful Annabel Lee:—

   For the moon never beams without
         bringing/$_{100}$ me dreams
      Of the beautiful Annabel Lee:
   And the stars never rise but I see the
         bright eyes
      Of the beautiful Annabel Lee;
   And so, all the nighttide, I lie down by
         the side
      Of my darling, my darling, my life
         and my bride,
   In her sepulcher there by the sea—
      In her tomb by the side of the sea.]

Comprehension Questions

(TE) 1. What brings dreams of Annabel Lee to the author?
          (moon)

(TE) 2. What causes the author to see Annabel Lee's bright eyes?
          (the stars)

(TI) 3. Where was Annabel Lee buried?
          (by the sea)

(TI) 4. Was the author married to Annabel Lee? Explain.
          (Yes; he refers to her as "my bride.")

(SI) 5. Why does the author lie by Annabel Lee's tomb at night?
          (He thinks of her and wants to be as close as possible.)

(SI) 6. Do you think the author will love again? Why or why not?
          (No; his feelings are too strong for Annabel Lee.)

Prentice-Hall Literature: Bronze

Day 3

The Fox and the Crow by James Thurber (p. 549)

Grade 7

Oral Passage

➔   A crow, perched in a tree with a piece of cheese in his beak, attracted the eye and nose of a fox. "If you can sing as prettily as you sit," said the fox, "then you are the prettiest singer within my scent and sight." The fox had read somewhere, and somewhere, and somewhere else, that praising the voice of a crow with cheese in his beak would make him drop the cheese and sing. But this is not what happened to this particular crow in this particular case.

"They say you are sly and they say you are/$_{100}$ crazy," said the crow, having carefully removed the cheese from his beak with the claws of one foot, "but you must be near-sighted as well. Warblers wear gay hats and colored jackets and bright vests, and they are a dollar a hundred. I wear black and I am unique." He began nibbling the cheese, dropping not a single crumb.]

Comprehension Questions

(TE)   1. Who were the two characters in this story?
         (fox, crow)

(TE)   2. What did the crow do with the cheese when he talked?
         (took it out of his mouth with his claws, put it under his claws)

(TI)   3. Why would the fox be surprised that the crow did this?
         (He expected the crow to drop the cheese so he would show how well he could sing.)

(TI)   4. Tell the difference between a warbler and a crow.
         (Warblers have gay hats, colored jackets, bright vests; crows are black.)

(SI)   5. Why did the crow think that the fox believed he was a warbler?
         (because the fox expected him to sing)

(SI)   6. What kind of story is this? Why?
         (fable—teaches a lesson)

Prentice-Hall Literature: Bronze **Day 3**

The Fox and the Crow by James Thurber (pp. 549–550) **Grade 7**

Silent Passage

➜   "I am sure you are," said the fox, who was neither crazy nor nearsighted, but sly. "I recognize you, now that I look more closely, as the most famed and talented of all birds, and I fain would hear you tell about yourself, but I am hungry and must go."

"Tarry awhile," said the crow quickly, "and share my lunch with me." Whereupon he tossed the cunning fox the lion's share of the cheese, and began to tell about himself. "A ship that sails without a crow's nest sails to doom," he said. "Bars may come and bars may go/₁₀₀ but crow bars last forever. I am the pioneer of flight. I am the map maker. Last, but never least, my flight is known to scientists and engineers, geometrists and scholars, as the shortest distance between two points. Any two points," he concluded arrogantly.

"Oh, every two points, I am sure," said the fox. "And thank you for the lion's share of what I know you could not spare." And with this he trotted away into the woods, his appetite appeased, leaving the hungry crow perched forlornly in the tree.]

Comprehension Questions

(TI)   1. What wasn't the fox so sure about that the crow claimed to be?
(unique)

(TI)   2. How do you know the fox wasn't crazy or nearsighted?
(The author says so.)

(TE)   3. Who tossed the lion's share of the cheese?
(the crow)

(TE)   4. What were the kinds of things the crow bragged about?
(crow's nest in a ship, crowbars, his flight)

(SI)   5. What did the fox mean by "Thank you for the lion's share of what I know you could not spare"?
(He knew the crow would be hungry for having given away most of the cheese.)

(SI)   6. What is the moral of the fable? What could be learned from this?
(Don't listen to flattery; don't brag; be funny by using puns; play with words.)

Sample CBA from a Ninth-Grade Literature Text

This second example of a literature-based CBA is more typical of the type of reading that secondary students are expected to read. The CBA was constructed from a ninth-grade text called *Man the Myth-Maker*. The text is considerably more difficult than the seventh-grade text, but the basic formatting is the same. It contains different types of text: nonfictional narrative and Greek myth. The following CBA is a complete CBA with both oral and silent reading passages for Days 1, 2, and 3.

Man the Myth-Maker (p. 174)

Oral Passage

➜ Our myths tell of the past, present, and future of the human race. We have already seen stories of our creation, our education by the gods, and our fall from innocence. However, there is one story pattern, or archetype, which tells in miniature the entire imaginative story of the human race. It is the story of the "flood"—a cycle of birth, death, and rebirth.

It is peculiarly human that we never imagine that people will be completely annihilated by the gods. Death is something we know we must face individually, but the pull of life is strong. So we/₁₀₀ create a vision that enables us to cope with the day of doom by imagining another birth and another chance.

The myth-makers often imagine the destruction of the world will be carried out by water, and that new life will arise from a cleansed earth.]

Comprehension Questions

(SI)   1. Why do we have myths?
(to learn about human nature and to pass on wisdom, folklore, etc.)

(SI)   2. What are they?
(a legend or a story usually involving gods or heroes—or other reasonable response)

(TE)   3. What is an archetype?
(story pattern)

(TE)   4. What does the story of the flood include?
(cycle of birth, death, and rebirth)

(TI)   5. What do myth-makers often imagine about floods?
(They cleanse the earth.)

(TI)   6. What would happen after the flood or the cleansing?
(New life would appear.)

Note. This passage and the five that follow are from *Man the Myth-Maker*, 2nd ed., edited by W. T. Jewkes and N. Frye, 1981, New York: Harcourt Brace Jovanovich. Copyright 1981 by Harcourt Brace Jovanovich.

Man the Myth-Maker (p. 174)

Day 1
Grade 9

Silent Passage

→ People, always symbol-makers, were quick to associate the natural world with the human and divine worlds, and so droughts and floods became signs of divine action. Why would the gods execute their power against people in these ways? Why would they want to destroy the creatures they had made? The imagination came up with several answers: to punish people for their corruption, to clean up the earth, to start a fresh new race, to remind us of a final day of doom.

The flood in literature, then, has been imagined as a destruction that enables a new creation to take/$_{100}$ place. It kills in order to cleanse. It washes away the order of earth so that a new order can be established. Perhaps people have used the image of water in this dual way because water is an element that not only is life-giving and life-threatening, but also is one that can take on different forms: it knows the dark depths of the ocean as well as the light ethereal spaces of the heavens.

Because water is a vehicle of destruction and fertility, of light and darkness.]

Comprehension Questions

(SI) 1. What does it mean when the author says people are always symbol-makers?
(Humans are able to think symbolically and use mythical stories to represent human nature—or any reasonable answer.)

(TE) 2. What did people associate with natural occurrences like droughts and floods?
(divine action)

(TE) 3. Why did the people think that droughts or floods occurred?
(to punish people; to clean the earth; to start a new race)

(TI) 4. Why has water been used as a symbol like this?
(Water is an element that gives life and threatens life; it can take on different forms.)

(TI) 5. What are some characteristics of water?
(destruction, fertility, light, darkness)

(SI) 6. What does it mean when the author says water is both life-giving and life-threatening?
(We need it to live, but we could also drown in it.)

Man the Myth-Maker

Atalanta's Race: A Greek Myth, Retold by Rex Warner (p. 100)

Day 2

Grade 9

Oral Passage

➡ The huntress Atalanta, whom Meleager, before he died, had loved, could run faster even than the fastest runners among men. Nor was her beauty inferior to her swiftness of foot; both were beyond praise.

When Atalanta asked the oracle about whom she ought to marry, the god replied [through the oracle]: "Do not take a husband, Atalanta. If you do, it will bring disaster on you. Yet you will not escape, and though you will continue to live, you will not be yourself."

Terrified by these words, Atalanta lived in the dark woods unmarried. There were many men who wished to marry her,/$_{100}$ but to them, in their eagerness, she said:]

Comprehension Questions

(SI) 1. What is a huntress?
      (female hunter)

(TE) 2. The huntress Atalanta, what was she like?
      (beautiful, fast runner)

(TI) 3. What is an oracle?
      (a person or thing through whom the gods speak)

(TI) 4. What did Atalanta ask the god?
      (whom should she marry)

(TE) 5. What did the god say?
      (A marriage would be disastrous.)

(SI) 6. Why did she consult a god?
      (The Greeks believed in many gods who could help them make decisions.)

Man the Myth-Maker

Atalanta's Race: A Greek Myth, Retold by Rex Warner (p. 100)

Day 2

Grade 9

Silent Passage

→ "No one can have me for his wife unless first he beats me in a race. If you will, you may run with me. If any of you wins, he shall have me as a prize. But those who are defeated will have death for their reward. These are the conditions for the race."

Cruel indeed she was, but her beauty had such power that numbers of young men were impatient to race with her on these terms.

There was a young man called Hippomenes, who had come to watch the contest. At first he had said to himself: "What/$_{100}$ man in his senses would run such a risk to get a wife?" and he had condemned the young men for being too madly in love. But when he saw her face and her body all stripped for the race—a face and a body like Venus's own—he was lost in astonishment and, stretching out his hands, he said: "I had no right to blame the young men. I did not know what the prize was for which they were running."]

Comprehension Questions

(TE) 1. If a man wanted to marry Atalanta, what must he do?
(beat her in a race)

(TE) 2. What would happen if he failed to beat her?
(He would die.)

(SI) 3. Why did the author say Atalanta was cruel?
(because many men would die)

(SI) 4. Why didn't her cruelty stop young men from wanting to marry her?
(She was beautiful.)

(TI) 5. Who was Hippomenes?
(a young man who had come to watch the contest, and who judged the other men as foolish)

(TI) 6. Why did he change his mind?
(He saw Atalanta's beauty.)

Man the Myth-Maker

The King Must Die, From the novel by Mary Renault (p. 248)

Day 3
Grade 9

Oral Passage

→ I rose at daybreak, waked by the herd's bleating, and washed in the stream; a thing my hosts beheld with wonder, having had their last bath at the midwife's hands. From there on, the road grew easier, and dropped seaward. Soon across a narrow water I saw the island of Salamis, and all about me a fertile plain, with fruit and cornlands. The road led down to a city on the shore, a seaport full of shipping. Some merchants I met on the road told me it was Eleusis.

It was good to see a town again, and be in/$_{100}$ a land of law; and better still that this was the last stop before Athens. I would have my horses fed and groomed, I thought, while I ate and saw the sights. Then, as I came to the edge of the town, I saw the road lined with staring people, and the rooftops thick with them.]

Comprehension Questions

(TE)   1. When did he wake up?
         (daybreak)

(TE)   2. What woke him up?
         (bleating of the herd)

(SI)   3. Why did he say his hosts had their last bath at the midwife's hands?
         (The sheep had an odor.)

(TI)   4. What form of transportation was he using?
         (horses)

(SI)   5. What did the author mean by "it's good to be in a land of law"?
         (area where laws were made and enforced perhaps made him feel safer)

(TI)   6. What did the author mean when he wrote "rooftops thick with them"?
         (Many people were on the roofs watching.)

Man the Myth-Maker

The King Must Die, From the novel by Mary Renault (p. 249)

Day 3

Grade 9

Silent Passage

→ Out of respect, I got down from my chariot and led the horses forward. Not only was she looking at me; I saw it was for me she waited. As I drew near and saluted her, all the crowd fell into a deeper silence, like people who hear the harper tune his strings.

I said, "Greeting, Lady, in the name of whatever god or goddess is honored here above the rest. For I think you serve a powerful deity, to whom the traveler ought to pay some homage or other, before he passes by. A man should respect the gods/$_{100}$ of his journey, if he wants it to end as he would wish."

She said to me in a slow Greek with the accent of the Minyans, "Truly your journey has been blessed, and here it ends."]

Comprehension Questions

(TI) 1. What was the first thing he did when he saw the lady?
(got down from his chariot)

(SI) 2. Who do you think the lady was?
(a queen; someone with high ranking)

(TE) 3. Who was the lady waiting for?
(this man)

(SI) 4. Why was there a crowd gathered? Why were they so silent?
(They were curious about what would happen; they wanted to hear what was said.)

(TE) 5. Why did the man think he should pay homage to the gods in this place?
(in order to have a good journey)

(TI) 6. How do you know Greek wasn't her native language?
(She spoke it slowly and with an accent.)

Sample CBA from the Popular Press: Newspaper

The third and fourth examples of literature-based CBAs are typical of what we would use for reading materials for adults who are learning to read or with older secondary students. The third example includes text derived from newspaper articles and the fourth is from magazine articles.

The newspaper CBA contains oral and silent reading samples for Days 1 and 2 and only a silent reading sample for Day 3. A complete CBA would include an oral sample for Day 3, as well; but we wanted to illustrate how a teacher might not construct the entire CBA depending on the needs of the student. With this particular example, the teacher found from obtaining the reading performance data from Days 1 and 2 that the student could read the oral passages at criterion for word accuracy, so he chose to focus only on silent reading for the remainder of the CBA (i.e., Day 3).

Newspaper: *Austin American-Statesman*   **Day 1**

Oral Passage

➜   CAPE TOWN, South Africa—On his first day of freedom in 27 years, black nationalist leader Nelson Mandela stepped back into the forefront of the anti-apartheid movement with a call to resume a campaign of defiance and armed struggle.

The stately, slim 71-year-old directed compliments to South African President Frederik de Klerk, the man who set him free. But Mandela made it clear he had not traded his hard political line for the opportunity to walk in freedom again before he dies.

"The mass campaigns of defiance and other actions of our organizations and people can only culminate/$_{100}$ in the best establishment of democracy," Mandela told a huge throng of cheering supporters within hours after being released from the Victor Verster Prison.]

Comprehension Questions

(TE)   1. Where in the world does this news take place?
             (Cape Town, South Africa)

(TE)   2. Who is it about?
             (Nelson Mandela)

(SI)   3. Who is he?
             (a black nationalist leader who had been jailed for 27 years)

(TI)   4. Why was he in prison?
             (because of his anti-apartheid beliefs, which were suppressed by the Whites in Africa)

(TI)   5. What does Mandela want?
             (democracy in South Africa)

(SI)   6. Why is he so determined in his quest for democracy?
             (He doesn't want all the efforts of his organizations to go unrewarded; he wants freedom for his people.)

Note. This passage and the one that follows are from "Unbowed, Unrepentant, and Unswerving" by M. Kunstel and J. Albright, 1990, February 15, *Austin American-Statesman*, pp. A1, A9.

Newspaper: *Austin American-Statesman*   **Day 1**

Silent Passage

➡ "The factors which necessitated the armed struggle still exist today. We have no option but to continue," he said in a confident voice, his bearing that of a long-time leader rather than a man who has just spent more than a third of his life in prison.

What was supposed to be a buoyant welcoming rally was deflated by repeated violent encounters between white police and black youths who smashed windows and looted stores.

The violence helped delay Mandela's presentation to the crowd by more than 2½ hours.

Aides said Mandela will fly this morning to Johannesburg, where most/$_{100}$ of the anti-apartheid groups have headquarters.]

Comprehension Questions

(TI)   1. How did he appear at the press conference?
         (confident)

(TE)   2. How much of his life has he been imprisoned?
         (more than one-third of his life)

(TI)   3. What happened to deflate the buoyancy of the rally?
         (violent encounters between white police and black youths who smashed windows and looted
         stores)

(SI)   4. Why did this violence occur?
         (racism and anger; or other reasonable response)

(TE)   5. What effect did the violence have on Mandela's speech?
         (It was delayed by more than 2½ hours.)

(SI)   6. What is anti-apartheid?
         (being against the separation of people based on race)

Newspaper: *Austin American-Statesman*   **Day 2**

Oral Passage

➔   If Congress amends the Clean Air Act as proposed, additional fees assessed on industry in Texas could generate up to $50 million a year for a comprehensive new statewide effort to control air pollution.

The proposal may mean that Texas Air Control Board officials, accustomed to having to scratch for modest budget increases, will enjoy a tripling of the agency's $16 million annual operation in the next few years.

The air board has already outlined a tentative budget for a $20-million-a-year toxic emission control program beginning in September 1992 that would add 512 new employees to the/$_{100}$ existing staff of 400.]

Comprehension Questions

(TE)   1. What law is discussed in this news item?
          (Clean Air Act)

(TI)   2. Is this a state or federal law?
          (federal)

(TE)   3. How much additional money would be generated by the new additional fees in Texas?
          ($50 million)

(TI)   4. Which agency administers this law?
          (Texas Air Control Board)

(SI)   5. Why are many new employees needed by this board?
          (to supervise the law)

(SI)   6. What does "having to scratch for modest budget increases" mean?
          (not having enough budgetary monies and using what exists by juggling funds)

Note. This passage and the one that follows are from "Air Board Budget May Triple" by B. Collier, 1990, February 12, *Austin American-Statesman*, p. B1.

Newspaper: *Austin American-Statesman*   **Day 2**

Silent Passage

→ Such growth would require legislative approval, but the U.S. Environmental Protection Agency would be holding a stick as well as its $50 million carrot. If the EPA finds the state's toxic pollution control program inadequate, the federal agency will move in, collect the fees and run the program itself.

"It is a massive project," said the air board's newly appointed executive director, Steve Spaw. "It is very ambitious, but we think it's a program that's needed in this state, and we plan to pursue it very aggressively with the Legislature."

Six hundred million pounds of toxic materials are emitted/$_{100}$ into Texas air every year, and until now the chief difficulty in controlling them has been a lack of information, Spaw said.]

Comprehension Questions

(TE)   1. What is required for this growth to occur?
           (legislative approval)

(TI)   2. What is meant by "the $50 million carrot"?
           (the new $50 million to be used to control air pollution)

(TE)   3. What would be needed in addition to this $50 million?
           (an adequate toxic pollution control program)

(TI)   4. If a company is in violation of this program, what would happen?
           (The federal agency would take over, collect fees, and run the program.)

(SI)   5. Why would it be necessary to have such a program as this?
           (to protect the environment)

(SI)   6. Why would lack of information be the chief difficulty in controlling a toxic pollution control program?
           (People in industry wouldn't know how to control it properly and/or there would be no standards or regulations.)

Newspaper: *Austin American-Statesman*   **Day 3**

Silent Passage

→ A federal grand jury is investigating whether tactics used to drum up campaign contributions for Agriculture Commissioner Jim Hightower and his right-hand man resulted in the misuse of public funds.

The grand jury and the Federal Bureau of Investigation have questioned people connected with the Texas Department of Agriculture about contracts the agency had with Associated Consultants Inc., headed by Bob Boyd, sources told the *Austin American-Statesman.*

The Austin consultant, who was a longtime employee of the Agriculture Department, has solicited campaign contributions for both Hightower and Deputy Agriculture Commissioner Mike Moeller from people regulated by the state agency, several/$_{100}$ sources said.

Moeller briefly geared up for a campaign for agriculture commissioner when it appeared Hightower would run for the U.S. Senate. However, when his boss changed his mind last year and decided to run for re-election, Moeller abandoned his campaign.]

Comprehension Questions

(TE)   1. Who is the Agriculture Commissioner?
       (Jim Hightower)

(TE)   2. Who is investigating him?
       (federal grand jury)

(SI)   3. What is a grand jury?
       (an impartial jury set up by the federal government)

(TI)   4. What possible problems are they investigating?
       (Tactics used to get campaign contributions resulted in misuse of public funds.)

(SI)   5. Why might the grand jury be questioning people about contracts with Associated Consultants?
       (private firm—need to know what activities the firm conducted for the public agency)

(TI)   6. Why did Moeller decide not to continue his campaign for Agriculture Commissioner?
       (Hightower changed his mind about running for U.S. Senate.)

Note. From "Hightower Consultant Investigated" by D. Graves, 1990, February 15, *Austin American-Statesman*, p. A1.

Sample CBA from the Popular Press: Magazine

For the fourth and final CBA, the sample passages were selected from *Audubon Magazine*. This magazine was chosen because an adult learner selected it as one he subscribed to and one for which he wanted to improve his reading speed and reading comprehension. You will find the CBA was used in a slightly different way with this example, combining oral and written expression, as an illustration of how flexible the basic format of the reading CBA can be to particular circumstances.

In this example, we constructed only one oral reading passage because we wanted to confirm that oral reading accuracy was not a problem for this person. His oral reading skills were sufficient, as he had indicated, so we used no more oral passages. Thus, the passages for Days 2 and 3 are for silent reading only. We were also interested in helping this adult learner to improve his written language skills. On both the oral and silent reading passages for Day 1, we asked him the questions orally. Thus, we had two samples of his skill in responding orally to comprehension questions. On Days 2 and 3, using silent reading, we asked him to write his responses to the comprehension questions. We then scored both types of comprehension responses (oral and silent) in the prescribed fashion; but we also scored his written responses using a subtest of the Quiz for Capitalization and Punctuation Skills, which is presented in Chapter 2. As an aside, we found that both the oral and reading comprehension skills of this adult learner needed considerable improvement, as he had indicated.

Magazine: *Audubon Magazine*   **Day 1**

Oral Passage

➔   Len McDaniel is a wildlife biologist in nominal charge of the Valentine National Wildlife Refuge, south of the Nebraska town that named it.

He grew up south of Rushville, in the western part of the Sand Hills, is forty-eight years old, and has been with the U.S. Fish and Wildlife Service for twenty-eight years, off and on. Lean, bearded, and outspoken, he's one of those mavericks that the Service has difficulty cataloging and who has worked as biologist, refuge manager, and even a rodent- and predator-control specialist. He likes to think he was one of the good/$_{100}$ ones, a gopher-choker with a white hat.

He wasn't wearing a white hat when I walked into his office one morning. It was nine o'clock, and he had already spent three hours in the saddle and put his horse up. Now he was relaxing, leaning back with feet up, a battered, nondescript old Stetson covering a stack of paperwork. The office smelled like horse.

"Maybe President Bush will buy you a new hat," I opened. "Part of his environmental commitment."

Len regarded the hat thoughtfully.

"Reckon he would? I had a better hat than this, but a guy in a bar over in Laramie thought it looked good enough to eat and tried to take a bite out of the brim. Tore half of it off. Damn, I was mad! It's one thing to grab one of those little plastic caps off a buddy's head when you're out hunting and shoot a hole through it. But that was a real good hat . . ."]

Comprehension Questions

(TE)   1. Who is Len McDaniel?
           (wildlife biologist)

(TE)   2. What is he in charge of?
           (the Valentine National Wildlife Refuge in Nebraska)

(SI)   3. What is a wildlife biologist?
           (a person who studies life in the wild)

(TI)   4. Why is he described as a maverick?
           (bearded, outspoken, thinks of himself as a "good guy")

(TI)   5. Why is he called a gopher-choker with a white hat?
           (He helps clear up rodents in the wild.)

(SI)   6. What type of a man do you think Len McDaniel is?
           (a hard-working nonconformist who likes wildlife, biology, and the outdoors)

Note. This passage and the one that follows are from "Yellow-Headed Blackbird" by D. Gulin, 1990, July, *Audubon*, p. 42.

Magazine: *Audubon Magazine*   **Day 1**

Silent Passage

➔   "A guy could get bruised, doing that."

"Sure could. But he was one of us wildlifers that were at a meeting. And you know how some of the boys are when they get to town."

Len would have to drive thirty miles to buy a new hat. As the crane flies, his office is about ten miles away from the main highway—and between the two is a tangled vastness of dunes, low meadows, lakes, and ponds that continues for miles on the east side of U.S. Highway 83. The Valentine National Wildlife Refuge sprawls over 71,516 acres of Sand Hills, and about 13,000 of those/$_{100}$ acres are wetlands, marshes, and lakes.]

Comprehension Questions

(TI)   1. What does this mean, "A guy could get bruised doing that."
             (He could get hurt or beat up.)

(TI)   2. What is a "wildlifer"?
             (a wildlife biologist)

(TE)   3. Where does Len reside?
             (at the Valentine National Wildlife Refuge)

(TE)   4. What is the terrain like there?
             (wetlands, meadows, lakes, ponds, dunes)

(SI)   5. Why is the land valuable?
             (preserves species of animals)

(SI)   6. Why would the land be less valuable if these wetlands were in a single lake?
             (There wouldn't be as much wildlife, especially birds that live in the marshes.)

Magazine: *Audubon Magazine*   **Day 2**

Silent Passage

➔   The water was pellucid; it looked as sterile as a Pre-Cambrian bay. No algae or higher plants, no fish or amphibians: just some mosquito larvae and the odd hell-granite or water bug. It was a young pond, no more than a year or two old.

The project had been decreed by my friend and landlord, Dave Steiner. (I had just moved into a small cabin on his property in Sonoma County, California.) He needed the reservoir to irrigate his twenty-five acres of Cabernet Sauvignon vines. He also needed a water source for the few cattle he raised. Steiner makes/$_{100}$ no money on the bovines; like many farmers, he simply fancies cows, especially Black Angus. "They're wilder and smarter than Herefords," he told me. "They like to wallow right up to their chins in the water, eating weeds, twitching their ears. I love it when they do that."]

Comprehension Questions

(TI)   1. What does "pellucid" mean?
            (sterile, little or no life in it)

(TE)   2. How old was the pond?
            (1 or 2 years old)

(TI)   3. Where was the pond?
            (Sonoma County, California)

(TE)   4. What kind of cattle did the property owner like?
            (Black Angus)

(SI)   5. Why is irrigation needed?
            (not enough rain)

(SI)   6. Why are grapes grown a lot in California?
            (favorable climate and soil)

Note. From "A Pond is Born" by G. Martin, 1990, July, *Audubon*, p. 64.

Magazine: *Audubon Magazine*   **Day 3**

Silent Passage

➔ Decades of such disdain have left us with a skimpy dossier of nutria natural history facts sprinkled with just enough intriguing tidbits to give us a yen for more. For starters there's the name. Nutria is actually a misnomer—it's Spanish for otter. Europeans favor its Indian name, "coypu," which means "water-sweeper," but—well, maybe the word sounds better on European tongues; would you want to raise coypu? Cajuns call it "nutra-rat," which sounds like a rodent caught in the basement of an organic food store.

Besides its dirty-orange teeth and its aptitude for procreation (females often mate again right after/$_{100}$ giving birth), the nutria's most distinctive feature is the female's mammary glands, which are on her back. While this might be awkward in some species, in nutrias it is thought to facilitate suckling while afloat. Nutrias divide their time between water and land, and they make their nests, either platforms or burrows, where land and water intersect. Valves on their ears and nose close when they're submerged.]

Comprehension Questions

(TE)   1. Nutria is a Spanish word. What is the English word for this animal?
            (otter)

(SI)   2. Why did the author say nutria is a misnomer?
            (It's really a coypu, a water-sweeper.)

(SI)   3. Why did the author say "nutra-rat" sounds like a rodent caught in the basement of an organic
            food store"?
            (Rat means a kind of rodent; "nutra" suggests nutrition.)

(TE)   4. What is the most distinctive feature of the nutria?
            (Females have mammary glands on their backs.)

(TI)   5. What is the advantage of the placement of nutria's mammary glands?
            (can suckle their young while floating)

(TI)   6. Describe the nests of nutria.
            (platforms or burrows where land and water intersect)

Note. From "Some Small Blue Places" by J. Madison, 1990, *Audubon*, p. 42.

2

✌   ✌   ✌

CBAs for Written Expression

The focus of this chapter is on the development of CBAs for analyzing various aspects of how students express themselves in writing. The contents center around examination of three samples of a student's writing—the compositions themselves as well as the mechanical aspects of the writing. Three types of mechanical skills are further elaborated upon by means of a sample spelling CBA from a third-grade spelling series and by a sample skills test that includes informal assessment of capitalization and punctuation skills.

Analysis of Compositional and Mechanical Writing Skills

A student's skill in writing can be organized into two categories of skills: (a) those pertaining to composition, or how the writer composes or organizes the composition, and (b) the mechanical skills of writing, or the correctness of how words are presented. Figure 2.1 is a form that lists these various skills organized into the two categories: compositional and mechanical skills.

After each skill is a place for the examiner to note how the student performed on that particular skill. This form is used to record your analysis of three written samples of a student's compositions.

Students are encouraged to write about any topic they like. For students who have difficulty getting started, give them a stem to help them begin. For example, you might give them a topic, a title, or a starter sentence. If you do so, indicate this on the analysis form.

It is important to allow a standard amount of time for each of the compositions to be written. For example, you might give the student 15 minutes to write the first composition. Then, at a subsequent time, allow a second 15-minute period in which to write a second composition, and then repeat the same process for the third composition. It is important to collect three different writing samples, because some students may take awhile to get used to writing or may have more difficulty writing on certain days.

Skill	Writing Sample 1	Writing Sample 2	Writing Sample 3
Total number of words[a]	_____	_____	_____
Title of composition	Yes/No	Yes/No	Yes/No
Title reflects contents	Yes/No	Yes/No	Yes/No
Compositional Skills			
Introduction	_____	_____	_____
Lead-in sentence to each paragraph	_____	_____	_____
Supportive sentences	_____	_____	_____
Transition sentences	_____	_____	_____
Number of paragraphs	_____	_____	_____
Summary	_____	_____	_____
Overall quality of composition	_____	_____	_____
Mechanical Skills			
Syntax	_____	_____	_____
Verb tense	_____	_____	_____
Parts of speech	_____	_____	_____
Contractions	_____	_____	_____
Number of words omitted[a]	_____	_____	_____
Punctuation	_____	_____	_____
Capitalization	_____	_____	_____
Number of misspelled words[a]	_____	_____	_____
Overall quality	_____	_____	_____

Use the following notations to appraise the quality of the writing samples:
　3 = Excellent quality
　2 = Needs improvement
　1 = Attempts made, but mostly incorrect
　0 = Totally incorrect responses or no attempt made

[a]For these items do not use number scale; write in actual number.

Figure 2.1. Analysis form for compositional and mechanical writing skills.

Test for Capitalization and Punctuation

Two very important mechanical skills for written expression are knowing when to capitalize certain words and knowing how to use proper punctuation. If the results of the analysis of a student's composition indicate that capitalization and punctuation skills are seriously lacking, the student could be given a simple test that covers all of the basic rules for capitalization and punctuation. If the test is too lengthy for a particular student, then subsections of the test can be given in separate testing sessions. The correct responses to each of the items can be found in the Appendix, The Mechanics of Composition.

This simple testing method leads to offering a more efficient instructional program. Rather than providing to a student information and instruction that covers all of the rules for capitalization and punctuation, only those skills that are targeted as needing improvement from the test results are pinpointed for instruction.

Quiz for Capitalization and Punctuation Skills

Student Name_____ Date_____

Grade Level_____ Age_____ School _____

Directions: For *each* of the following items, provide the correct capitalization and punctuation.

Capitalization

 1. the day was beautiful

 2. poems are made by fools like me
    but only god can make a tree   (two lines of poetry)

 3. the girl said wait for me

 4. resolved that the world is growing better   (formal resolution)

 5. i like summer better than winter

 6. my birthday is march 7 1947

 7. john is a senior at brown college he attended oak hill school

 8. the junior class invited ms smith to speak

 9. miss johnson sent the package c o d

10. we study history and english

11. he came from the south

12. he went south from town

13. he lives in the great northwest

14. is hutchinson northwest of wichita

15. i know he is the lord

16. jesus loves his friends as we know from reading the bible

17. he reads the wall street journal

Note. Designed and adapted from *Plain English Handbook* by J. M. Walsh and A. K. Walsh, 1951, Wichita, KS: McCormick-Mathers. Copyright 1951 by McCormick-Mathers.

(continues)

18. d h lawrence is one of my favorite authors

19. we think that captain smith would make a good school principal but he prefers to be a captain

20. the president of the united states spoke today

21. ann went with mother and me to see her mother

22. i went with mother to chicago

23. i went with my mother to chicago

24. will you help me father with this work

25. i went with my father to new orleans

26. come lovely autumn and make us glad   (line of poetry)

27. is lowell school near belmont park

28. does clifton avenue cross maple street

29. he lives near lake erie

Punctuation

Period

30. jean went to europe last summer   (declarative sentence)

31. let me see your book   (imperative sentence)

32. he saw principal john moore at the meeting of principals and superintendents

33. melissa jones she is president of our class will arrange the program

34. yes

35. the writings were probably made in 1800 b c

36. george f smith m d is our family physician

37. ben brown isnt here

38. a great battle was fought in the year 490 b c

39. he did his best yet he was never quite satisfied

40. the lake is 62 35 miles long

41. he arrived at 10 45 p m

Semicolon

42. the rain came in torrents we did not know what to do

43. he came he saw he went away

44. the day was very cold therefore we did not go for a ride

(continues)

45. john arrived last night i am told and on his arrival at the hospital he found his father still alive

46. the day was very cold therefore we did not go for a ride

47. we invited don webb the captain of the team sue mills the president of our class and joe wynn the chairman of our group

48. four boys were mentioned namely justin julio leo and mark

Colon

49. he brought the following fruits apples peaches pears

50. dear sir

51. he came at 6 15 this morning

Comma

52. robert entered the race but he did not win

53. she came she looked she went away

54. when my cousin came to spend the day with me she found me at work

55. if you expect to succeed you must prepare yourself

56. yes you may go

57. ah who can tell what may happen

58. edgar allen poe who wrote the raven is a great american poet

59. boys who study will learn

60. the girl who sells the tickets is a member of the class

61. jane gray who sells the concert tickets is a member of our class

62. the boy seeing the cloud hurried home

63. the girl holding the flag is margaret

64. wishing to see the parade we went to town early

65. the task being done we went home

66. will you help me harry with this work

67. nan gray my favorite cousin is here

68. tom came from dallas texas yesterday

69. mary jane was born on june 12 1992 in austin

70. that boy i believe is a dependable guy

71. edward the confessor was there

72. my cousin nell lives in arizona

(continues)

73. the girl said wait for me

74. wait for me the girl said

75. wait the girl said until i come

76. her cheerful greeting was always how do you do today

77. charles said he went to chicago

78. longfellow wrote the poem of life

79. they were married on tuesday may 6 1995

80. in august 1993 we were on vacation

81. it is time she said for me to go home

82. it is time to go she said it is very late

83. the farmer sold corn hay oats potatoes and wheat

84. they came from east from west from north and from south

85. he arose he smiled he began to speak

86. we saw tall slender graceful trees

87. a steep and narrow path led on

88. he is a courteous young man

89. ever since frank has been a better boy

90. the boy not the girl was to blame

91. whatever you do do well

Quotation Marks

92. he said he would go home

93. you may parse the word they in that sentence

94. he read wittiers maud miller

95. i read hawthornes the scarlett letter

96. do you know me he asked

97. i am not sure she replied

98. i am your old schoolmate edgar jones he explained

99. my friend shorty was there

100. his limousine was a model t

101. i was embarrassed mary admitted when i said i agree with shakespeare all the worlds a stage

(continues)

102. are you ill she asked

103. did father say wait until tomorrow

104. he gave a quotation from the raven

105. the music was beautiful she remarked

106. did elaine ask where have you been

107. come he said expecting to have a good time

108. you have delayed too long already he said success does not come to he who tarries

109. i have been wrong he admitted there is no denying that

Apostrophe

110. the man isn't here

111. she used two a s three b s two 8 s and two ands

112. that birds song is beautiful

113. the sales samples included mens hats

114. boys suits are on sale

115. the cat wants its dinner

116. its time to go home

117. one must do ones duty

Dash

118. the boy went where did he go

119. there is no time the speaker could not go on

120. smith told me but dont mention this that he was bankrupt

121. he planned he worked he sacrificed all these he did that he might succeed

122. for a thousand dollars a mere thousand dollars he betrayed his friend

123. shakespeare lived 1564 1616

124. have you seen captain h lately

Parentheses

125. if you come to see me and i hope you do come be sure to bring your case

126. when you receive your appointment and i hope you receive it soon you must tell me of your plans

(continues)

Brackets

127. it was this poem the raven that made poe famous

Question Mark

128. have you seen my new hat

129. when you come to see me why not come soon i will tell you of my trip to denver

130. did the coach inquire when did you return

131. he asked what the trouble was

132. will you please send the check at once

133. is this right he came here on may 5, 1928

Exclamation Mark

134. fire fire she yelled

Hyphen

135. he always had far flung ideas

136. his mother is self supporting

137. his mother is a well liked person

138. the ages of the members of the group ranged from twenty one to ninety nine

139. the recipe called for a half cup of water

3

ॐ   ॐ   ॐ

CBAs for History and Social Studies

Content area texts in social studies and history are read by students in all grade levels of instruction from Grades 2 through 12. The comprehension demands placed on the reader are somewhat similar to those required for reading literature and fiction, in that the same basic types of comprehension probes can be used: text-explicit comprehension, text-implicit comprehension, and script-implicit comprehension.

The comprehension demands are different, however, and somewhat more challenging, because students of history and social studies are required to retrieve significant "chunks" of factual information, as well as to draw conclusions about what can be learned from history. The social consciousness that is raised by being able to respond to text-implicit and script-implicit reasoning can be profound. Unfortunately, some novice teachers of history and social studies place too much emphasis on the retention of text-explicit, fact-based information, and not enough emphasis on the implications of what we can and should learn from the history of humans.

Purposes of the CBAs

The CBAs in this chapter can serve two primary purposes. A first purpose is they remind teachers of the "true" reason we teach history and social studies to our students—so they might be more socially conscious citizens. A second purpose is the CBAs provide a simple and explicit way for teachers to determine the match between text difficulty and skill levels of

the student targeted for individualized assessment and diagnosis.

Assessment of Comprehension and Written Skills

The CBAs in this chapter are used for four different assessments: (a) to assess oral reading comprehension, (b) to assess silent reading comprehension, (c) to assess listening comprehension, and (d) to assess written expression skills.

Oral Reading Comprehension

Oral reading comprehension is tested to determine if the student can decode the words in the passage, read at a reasonable oral reading speed, and understand and think about what he or she is reading as it is being read. The guides for obtaining oral reading samples and the rules for determining oral reading errors, which are described in Chapter 1, are used to obtain oral reading accuracy.

Silent Reading Comprehension

Silent reading comprehension is assessed to determine the silent reading speed of the students, as well as to check thinking and understanding. It is assumed that when a silent reading measurement is taken, the student can read the words, or at least a sufficient number of them, to understand and think about the content of the passage. It is recommended that the student first be given a single oral reading CBA. If the oral reading accuracy is at least 75 percent correct, then silent reading should be assessed as well. If the oral reading accuracy is above 90 percent, it probably isn't necessary to test oral reading on the second and third days but rather to test silent reading instead. The reasoning behind this is that by the time students are in about fourth grade, it is skill in silent reading that is most important. By this time, most of the textbook reading is done silently. We've also found many older students who read better silently than they do orally.

Listening Comprehension

For students with more limited reading skills, it can be useful to test their skill in listening comprehension, that is, how well they can understand a passage that is simply read to them. With these students, the examiner reads the selected passage and then orally asks the comprehension questions.

Written Expression Skills

For any of the three types of CBAs presented in this chapter (oral, silent, or listening), the teacher could write down the questions and give them to the student to complete as a written composition rather than orally asking them. This is an especially relevant technique for older students, where written responses are the primary means of assessing student understanding.

If the student is instructed to answer in complete sentences and to use proper capitalization and punctuation, then the accuracy of the mechanics of writing could be assessed as well. We ask some students to write a summary of what was in the passage and then have them respond, either orally or in writing, to the six comprehension questions. With either of these two methods (written responses to questions or written summaries), the examiner can then apply the methods described in Chapter 2 for checking written expression. In this way, both the compositional skills and the mechanical writing skills of the student can be assessed.

Sample CBAs for History and Social Studies

On the following pages are a series of sample CBAs for history and social studies. There are sample passages for oral, silent, and listening comprehension. The second passage in each set could be used for either silent reading or for listening comprehension. If both are needed, a third passage could be added. Included are sample CBAs from three different grade level texts: Grades 5 (Elementary Level), 7 (Lower Secondary Level), and 9 (Upper Secondary Level). This was done in order to illustrate that any difficulty level of text can be used to construct these CBAs.

The formatting and structure of these CBAs is identical to that of the reading CBAs presented in Chapter 1. They each represent a 100-word timed sample taken from a randomly selected page in the student textbook. The passage is extended beyond the 100-word mark in order to accommodate sufficient text for answering the six comprehension questions: two text-explicit, two text-implicit, and two script-implicit questions.

The World and Its People

Jacksonian Democracy (p. 140)

Day 1
Grade 5, Elementary Level

Oral Passage

➔ "Victory for the common man." Glass and china were smashed. Noses were bloodied. People fainted.

A riot? No. Another British raid on Washington? No. About 4 months earlier Andrew Jackson had been elected President. For weeks thousands of people had been coming to Washington, D.C., to see his inauguration. Jackson was their hero. His victory was seen as a "victory for the common man."

After Jackson was sworn into office, the crowd followed him to the White House. They jammed themselves in to get food and drink. Most of all they wanted to get closer to their hero. Muddy/$_{100}$ boots ruined expensive carpets and chairs as people pushed and shoved to see Andrew Jackson.]

Comprehension Questions

(TE) 1. Why were glass and china smashed and noses bloodied?
(People were trying to get into the White House to see Andrew Jackson.)

(TI) 2. Who was Andrew Jackson?
(a hero, a President)

(SI) 3. What is an inauguration?
(a ceremony where someone is sworn into office)

(SI) 4. Why was Jackson a hero?
(He fought in the Revolutionary War.)

(TE) 5. What did the people do after Jackson was sworn into office?
(They followed him to the White House.)

(TI) 6. Why did they do this?
(They wanted to get food and drink; they wanted to be closer to their hero, but mostly they wanted to see their hero inaugurated as President of the United States.)

Note. This passage and the five that follow are from *The World and Its People: The United States and Its Neighbors* by Silver Burdett, 1986, New York: Author. Copyright 1986 by Silver Burdett.

The World and Its People

Jacksonian Democracy (p. 140)

Day 1
Grade 5, Elementary Level

Silent Passage or Listening Passage

➔ "Old Hickory." To understand this deep love for Andrew Jackson, you have to understand who Jackson was and where he came from. Andrew Jackson was a fighter. At age 13 he was already fighting the Revolutionary War in the Carolinas. He and his brother were captured by the British, and taken to a prison camp. When ordered to clean a British officer's boots, Andy refused. The angry officer slashed Andy with a sword. Andy's brother was also badly cut.

The boys' wounds went untreated. Both caught smallpox. Andy's brother died. Andy was sick for months and carried scars for life./₁₀₀ Perhaps Jackson lived because of his fierce temper and stubborn nature.

Jackson had moved to Tennessee as a young man. He was just the kind of man the people of Tennessee liked. Westerners had to be tough , and Jackson was tough. His soldiers later called him "Old Hickory," because hickory wood was the toughest thing they knew.]

Comprehension Questions

(TE)   1. Who is this selection about?
        (Andrew Jackson and his brother)

(TE)   2. How old was he when he began fighting in the Revolutionary War?
        (13)

(TI)   3. Why did Andrew Jackson's brother die?
        (He was wounded by a British officer, and he caught smallpox.)

(SI)   4. Who were the opponents in the Revolutionary War?
        (Great Britain and The Thirteen Colonies in the Americas)

(TI)   5. Why did the people of Tennessee like Andrew Jackson?
        (He was tough.)

(SI)   6. What is hickory and where does it come from?
        (It's a tough kind of wood, from a hickory tree.)

The World and Its People
A Revolution in History (p. 206)

Day 2
Grade 5, Elementary Level

***

Oral Passage

→ Industry expands. A revolution took place in industry as well as in farming. In the Industrial Revolution, factory machines driven by waterpower—and eventually by steam power—replaced handwork, simple machines, and home crafts. As you read in Chapter 8, the revolution began with the textile mills started in New England by Samuel Slater. Other industries grew. The Civil War speeded up the growth of industry. It pushed the United States toward becoming the world's greatest industrial nation.

The United States changed as people moved from farms to cities and from hand labor to factory machines. There was an increase/$_{100}$ in the output of goods.]

Comprehension Questions

(TI) 1. What was the revolution that took place called?
         (Industrial Revolution)

(TI) 2. What two new sources of power were used?
         (water and steam)

(TE) 3. In what factories did the Industrial Revolution begin?
         (textile mills)

(SI) 4. What are textiles?
         (fabrics, cloth)

(TE) 5. What major event speeded up the growth of industries?
         (Civil War)

(SI) 6. Why would more people begin moving to the cities?
         (to work in the factories, to seek employment)

The World and Its People

A Revolution in History (p. 206)

Day 2

Grade 5, Elementary Level

Silent Passage or Listening Passage

→ Causes of industrial growth. What made these changes possible? The United States was blessed with a large supply of the natural resources needed to become an industrial power, such as coal and iron ore. Americans had the capital, or saved-up wealth, to invest in developing power machines and factories. There was a large labor force. Inventions greatly changed ways of doing things. Bold, daring, and sometimes ruthless business leaders put together the resources, capital, labor, and inventions to build the United States into an industrial giant. As a result, the nation grew in ways hardly imagined 100 years earlier.

Giant/$_{100}$ industries appeared. These were huge businesses that had nearly all the power and made great fortunes for their owners. One reason for the growth of these companies was the desire to do away with competition.]

Comprehension Questions

(TE)   1. What two natural resources did the United States have that were needed for a nation to become industrial?
(coal and iron)

(TE)   2. What is the word that means "saved-up wealth"?
(capital)

(TI)   3. Why is capital needed to have industrial growth?
(need capital to buy factory machines and to pay for labor)

(TI)   4. What is meant when the author says the United States was built into an industrial giant?
(The U.S. had a lot of large industries.)

(SI)   5. What changes would be made in an individual person's life by the industrial growth?
(maybe had to move from a farm to the city; maybe had to learn how to run a machine; could earn more money)

(SI)   6. What does competition mean?
(being against someone else in a win-lose situation)

The World and Its People (p. 178)

Oral Passage

➜   Near the end of the war Congress set up the Freedmen's Bureau. It helped the poor and the homeless. It gave food, blankets, and housing to freedmen, persons just set free from slavery, and to refugees, whites and blacks who fled from their homes because of the fighting. It also set up schools for black children.

Since the South was mainly a farming region and the soil was not hurt by war, rebuilding would not be hard. All that was needed were seeds, tools, and workers. However, it took money to buy seeds and tools and to pay workers. Confederate/$_{100}$ money printed during the war was worthless. Freeing the slaves left landowners, especially planters, without their workers. Freed workers, unlike slaves, had to be paid. But landowners had no money to hire anyone.]

Comprehension Questions

(SI)   1. What war had just ended?
        (Civil War)

(TE)   2. What did Congress set up near the end of this war?
        (Freedmen's Bureau)

(TI)   3. What was the purpose of the Freedman's Bureau?
        (helped poor and homeless; gave food, blankets, housing; set up schools for black children)

(SI)   4. What is Congress?
        (part of the government of the United States)

(TE)   5. Why was rebuilding not hard in the South?
        (mostly farming region; soil not hurt by war)

(TI)   6. What was needed to rebuild the South?
        (seeds, tools, and workers)

The World and Its People (p. 178)

Silent Passage or Listening Passage

➔ Planters and other large landowners could sell or rent land to the newly freed blacks and to landless whites. These blacks and whites, however, had no money to buy or rent land.

Sharecropping. New ways—sharecropping and crop lien—were found to solve these problems. In sharecropping, farmers, black and white, paid for the use of the land by giving the owner of the land a part of the crop. It was usually a fourth to a half. Storekeepers sold seeds, tools, supplies and other needs to landowners and sharecroppers on credit. In return, they got a lien, or first-claim,/$_{100}$ on the crop. The storekeepers sold the crops and took what was owed them. Any money left was shared by the landowners and farmers.

Comprehension Questions

(TE)   1. What is a sharecropper?
       (a farmer who pays for use of the land by giving owners a share of the crop)

(TI)   2. What races were the sharecroppers?
       (black and white)

(TI)   3. Who got first claim on the crop?
       (the storekeepers)

(TE)   4. Who actually sold the crops?
       (the storekeepers)

(SI)   5. Why would the storekeepers want to be the ones to sell the crops?
       (so they would get their money first)

(SI)   6. Why would people be sharecroppers instead of just renting the land?
       (Poor people didn't have enough money to rent the land.)

Texas and Texans (p. 346)

Oral Passage

➜ **Life of the Black Slaves.** The use of black slaves as laborers increased rapidly during the period of early statehood. In 1850, the first year the United States Census was taken in Texas, 58,161 slaves lived in Texas. Ten years later there were 182,466 slaves in the state. Three of every ten Texans in 1860 was a black slave. In 1860, most slaves lived in Harrison, Washington, Rusk, Grimes, Brazoria, and Smith counties where large amounts of cotton were grown.

The need for laborers to clear the fields, plant seed, and harvest crops caused a great demand for/$_{100}$ slaves during the 1850s. Field hands were sold for $1,200 to $2,000 each. Slaves with special skills, such as carpentry and blacksmithing, were even more valuable.

The treatment of slaves varied with each owner. Better owners cared for their slaves and provided them with adequate food and clothing. Other owners were cruel. They overworked their slaves, seldom provided them sufficient food or clothing, and often whipped them for punishment.]

Comprehension Questions

(TI)   1. Why were slaves valued in Texas?
        (the need for agricultural laborers)

(TI)   2. Why were there more slaves in certain counties?
        (Cotton was grown in those counties.)

(TE)   3. Why did the need for slaves increase in the 1850s?
        (the need for laborers to clear the fields, plant seed, and harvest crops)

(SI)   4. By 1860 what was the proportion of black slaves to whites?
        (approximately 30% blacks)

(TE)   5. What were examples of special skills slaves might have?
        (carpentry and blacksmithing)

(SI)   6. Why did some owners treat their slaves well while others treated them poorly?
        (different levels of ignorance; some more enlightened than others; or other reasonable answer)

Note. This passage and the five that follow are from *Texas and Texans* by A. N. Anderson, R. A. Wooster, J. R. Stanley, and D. G. Armstrong, 1987, 1993, Dallas, TX: Glencoe Publishing. Copyright 1987 by Glencoe Publishing.

Texas and Texans (p. 346)

Silent Passage or Listening Passage

➜   Slavery was inhuman, even under the best physical circumstances. Within the system of slavery, one human being was totally at the mercy of another. A slave was not allowed basic human rights. For example, families often were separated when a wife or child was sold.

Most slaves longed for freedom and a better way of life. The number who ran away increased during the 1850s. Most of them were either recaptured or returned voluntarily. Those slaves who did escape often found life difficult in frontier society. Many white settlers did not welcome them. Also, runaway slaves were constantly aware/$_{100}$ that they might be seized and again taken back to their owners.]

Comprehension Questions

(TI)   1. Why is slavery inhuman?
         (All humans are of equal value and should not own one another.)

(SI)   2. What are some examples of this inhumanity?
         (slavery, subjugation of women or certain classes of people, discrimination by income or social class)

(SI)   3. Why did the white Texans engage in slavery when it was inhuman?
         (They were more interested in making money and becoming prosperous.)

(TE)   4. What did most slaves long for?
         (freedom and a right to seek a better life)

(TI)   5. What did slaves often do to seek a better life?
         (They ran away.)

(TE)   6. What were the dangers to runaway slaves?
         (white settlers who didn't welcome them; others who might seize them and take them back to their owners)

Texas and Texans (p. 362)

Oral Passage

➔   **The Texas Secession Convention.** Sam Houston, governor of Texas at this time, opposed secession. He argued that Texas could better protect its interests by staying in the Union. He refused to call a special session of the legislature so that a convention to vote on secession could be called.

Judge O. M. Roberts, an associate justice of the Texas Supreme Court, John S. Ford, and other leaders who favored secession called a convention and urged people to elect the convention delegates. Those who opposed secession argued that the convention was illegal. Most of them refused to take part in such/$_{100}$ an election. As a result, most delegates chosen to the convention favored secession.

When Governor Houston realized that the convention was going to meet even without his approval, he called a special session of the legislature. He hoped the legislature would oppose the convention, but he was disappointed. The legislature supported the convention and gave it the authority to act for the people of Texas. The legislature also invited the convention to use the hall of the Texas House of Representatives for its sessions.]

Comprehension Questions

(TE)   1. Who was the governor of Texas at this time?
(Sam Houston)

(TE)   2. What was he opposed to?
(secession)

(TI)   3. What is secession?
(leaving the Union)

(SI)   4. Why could Texas protect its interests better by staying in the Union?
(to have a voice in national decisions that could affect Texas economy or other reasonable answer)

(TI)   5. What was the role of convention delegates?
(to vote on whether or not to secede from the Union)

(SI)   6. Did Texas leave the Union?
(Yes)

Day 2

Texas and Texans (p. 364)

Grade 7, Lower Secondary Level

Silent Passage or Listening Passage

→ **Removal of Governor Houston.** The Texas Secession Convention ordered all state officials to take an oath of allegiance to the Confederacy. When Governor Houston refused to do this, the convention declared the office of governor vacant. Houston declined President Lincoln's offer to send troops in order to help him hold the office. Lieutenant Governor Edward Clark, who had taken the oath to the Confederacy, assumed the duties of the governor.

Houston retired to his home in Huntsville where he lived quietly for the next two years. His oldest son joined the Confederate army and served in Tennessee.

Sam Houston died/$_{100}$ on July 26, 1863. Years later, the state of Texas erected a monument over his grave at Huntsville. The monument bears a tribute paid to Houston by his friend Andrew Jackson. It says, "The world will take care of Houston's fame."]

Comprehension Questions

(TE) 1. What were all state officials ordered to do?
(take an oath of allegiance to the Confederacy)

(TE) 2. What did Governor Houston do about the order?
(refused to obey)

(SI) 3. Why did he refuse it?
(He believed it was in Texas' best interest to be a part of the United States.)

(TI) 4. Why did they declare the governor's office vacant?
(so someone could replace Houston as Governor)

(TI) 5. Did Houston want to use violence to hold his office? (How do you know?)
(No; he declined Lincoln's offer to send in troops.)

(SI) 6. Why would the State of Texas erect a monument in memory of Houston?
(Later, Texans realized what a strong leader and hero he was.)

Texas and Texans (p. 403)

Oral Passage

→ **A Time of Trouble.** The end of the Civil War did not bring peace to all of Texas. For some 20 more years, Indian tribes and frontier settlers fought for control of western Texas. Enterprising pioneers, who were anxious to develop the land, settled wherever they had the opportunity. On the other hand, the Indian people fought to preserve their way of life.

Indian wars were not the only cause of trouble during these years. The border along the Rio Grande was frequently the scene of violence and destruction. Bandits and renegades from each side of the river plundered their $/_{100}$ own people and those across the border.

Frontier Indian raids became more troublesome as the Civil War ended. For several months, settlers had no organized defense against attacks. Many ranches and farms were abandoned. In some places, the frontier line of settlement was forced eastward 100 miles or more.]

Comprehension Questions

(TE)   1. Who fought for control of West Texas?
(Indian tribes, frontier settlers)

(TE)   2. How much longer after the end of the Civil War did they fight?
(20 years)

(SI)   3. Why were the pioneers anxious to develop the land?
(to plant crops, earn money)

(SI)   4. What two groups of people were fighting along the Rio Grande border?
(bandits, renegades)

(TI)   5. Why were the people fighting?
(to gain control of the land)

(TI)   6. Why was the frontier line of settlement forced eastward 100 miles?
(Pioneers were leaving the area because of Indian raids.)

Texas and Texans (p. 404)

Day 3
Grade 7, Lower Secondary Level

Silent Passage or Listening Passage

➔   **The Search for Peace.** In 1867 federal government agents and the chiefs of several Indian tribes signed a peace treaty called the Treaty of Medicine Lodge Creek. According to the terms of this agreement, Indians would live on reservations in Indian Territory, which is present-day Oklahoma. The government would provide them with supplies, but the army would not be allowed on the reservations. The Indians who signed the treaty agreed to stop warring with white settlers. This method of dealing with Indian affairs was known as the *peace policy.*

President Ulysses S. Grant tried to appoint federal Indian agents/$_{100}$ who would treat the Indians fairly and kindly. Many agents were members of the Society of Friends, who were also called Quakers. It was believed that kind, fair treatment would stop the Indian people from warring with settlers.

Peace still did not come to the western frontier. Some Indian leaders did not sign the treaty. About one-half of the Comanches and many Kiowas would not move to the reservations. Santa Ana, a Kiowa chief, insisted that West Texas belonged to the Comanches and Kiowas. Ten Bears, a Comanche chief, argued that his people must be allowed to roam free over the plains. Another capable Comanche chief, Quanah Parker, refused to sign the treaty. He was the son of a chief, Pet Nacona, and a white woman, Cynthia Ann Parker, who had been captured by the Comanches as a child. Quanah Parker grew up on the Texas high plains, a member of a roving band of Comanches. As a young man he joined in raids on military posts and white settlements. After he became chief, he spent ten years in a hopeless attempt to stop the spread of white settlements. Other Indians claimed that the government broke its promises, and that some Indian agents treated them badly.]

Comprehension Questions

(TE)   1. What happened in 1867?
        (A peace treaty was signed.)

(TE)   2. What were the terms of this agreement?
        (Indians would leave Texas and live on reservations in what is now Oklahoma.)

(TI)   3. Why was it important to sign the treaty?
        (to stop the war between the Indians and the settlers)

(TI)   4. How were Indians to get food and clothing?
        (government supplied them)

(SI)   5. Why would some Indians not sign the treaty?
        (They didn't want to give up their independent nations and be at the mercy of the American federal government.)

(SI)   6. Why did the Indians think the government broke promises?
        (because they did; there is a long history of this)

History and Life: The World and Its People
(p. 320)

Day 1
Grade 9,
Upper Secondary Level

Oral Passage

➔ Japanese culture developed during the Heian Era (794–1192). In 784, Nara ceased to be the emperor's court and, after two moves, the capital was located in 794 at Heian-Kyo, which was later renamed Kyo-to.

The founding of this new capital began what is known as the Heian period. During this time, Japan began to create its own kind of culture. It sent its last great embassy to Tang China in 838. By the early 900s, a distinct and new island civilization was being created in painting, architecture, and literature.

This flowering of cultural life was fostered by/$_{100}$ the emperor and his court in Heian-Kyo. These nobles lived a sheltered life and hardly ever went out of the capital except to visit Buddhist temples and Shinto shrines. They spent their days in ceremonies and festivities connected with court life and in endless pursuits of taste and culture.]

Comprehension Questions

(TE)   1. When did Japanese culture begin to develop?
(during the Heian Era, 794–1192)

(SI)   2. What does it mean, "Japan began to create its own culture?"
(a culture separate and distinct from the Chinese culture)

(TI)   3. Why would Japan have sent embassies to China?
(to maintain ties with China during the years of Japan's early development)

(TE)   4. What kinds of examples of culture began to develop?
(painting, architecture, and literature)

(TI)   5. How did the emperor encourage cultural development?
(by sheltering the lives of the nobles so they would have time to develop the culture)

(SI)   6. How do you know that Japan wanted to be separate from China?
(It stopped sending embassies to China and moved its capital; created its own culture; there are vast differences in beliefs between the two cultures.)

Note. This passage and the three that follow are from *History and Life: The World and Its People* by T. W. Wallbank, A. Schrier, D. Maier, and P. Gutierrez-Smith, 1984, 1993, Glenview, IL: Scott, Foresman & Co. Copyright 1984 by Scott, Foresman & Co.

History and Life: The World and Its People
(pp. 320–321)

Silent Passage or Listening Passage

➜   Some of Japan's earliest prose literature was produced at this time. It was written almost entirely by women. One reason was that men of the court were taught to write in Japanese by using the complicated and cumbersome characters of Chinese. For formal writing, educated Japanese men wrote only in Chinese (much like the scholars of medieval Europe who ignored their native languages and wrote only in Latin).

Japanese women, however, did not learn to write in Chinese. Instead, they wrote in their native language using *kana*. Kana was actually a kind of alphabetic representation of/$_{100}$ the 47 syllables of the Japanese language. Kana was developed in the 9th century.]

Comprehension Questions

(TE)   1. Who wrote Japan's earliest prose?
(almost entirely written by women)

(TE)   2. Why didn't the men write prose?
(They only wrote in Chinese, which was cumbersome and not amenable to prose writing.)

(TI)   3. How were the Japanese men like the medieval scholars in Europe?
(They both wrote in ancient languages—Chinese and Latin.)

(SI)   4. Why would this* be a problem? (*knowing only an ancient form of writing)
(The ancient languages were different than what the people actually spoke and prose is the language spoken in written form.)

(TE)   5. Which language did the women write in?
(in the native language, using kana, an alphabetic representation)

(SI)   6. Why would this be helpful to the people in learning about their culture?
(It would be written in the language they spoke.)

History and Life: The World and Its People (p. 454)

Silent Passage

→   **Napoleon became ruler of France.** A strong leader appeared—Napoleon Bonaparte—a lieutenant of artillery in Louis XVI's army. Because he belonged to the lesser nobility, Napoleon could not have hoped to rise much higher. But the revolution opened the door to fame and power.

In 1797, Napoleon was leading the French army in northern Italy. After several brilliant victories there, he crushed the Austrians. He was only twenty-eight years old and already a hero.

Napoleon's ambition had no limits. Well aware of the growing dislike for the Directory, he waited for an opportunity to seize power. Meanwhile he/$_{100}$ thought of a bold plan to hurt England by taking Egypt and then striking at India. Napoleon landed in Egypt in 1798, but the English fleet destroyed his transport ships and cut off his army.]

Comprehension Questions

(TE)   1. Who is described in this passage?
(Napoleon)

(TI)   2. Why could he not hope to rise higher than the rank of lieutenant?
(belonged to lesser nobility)

(SI)   3. What does nobility mean?
(kings, dukes, etc.)

(TE)   4. Where was he leading the French army?
(northern Italy)

(TI)   5. How old was he when he crushed the Austrians?
(28)

(SI)   6. Why did he want to hurt England?
(make him more of a hero)

Day 3
History and Life: The World and Its People (p. 451)
Grade 9,
Upper Secondary Level

Silent Passage

➜ **Points of Interest: Versailles.** Louis XIV's greatest creations were the Palace and park at Versailles, 12 miles (19 kilometers) southwest of Paris. After three centuries and four revolutions, Versailles is still a great wonder of the world.

Louis's purpose was to create the most splendid palace in Europe. To do this, he employed 36,000 workers for nearly 50 years. Finally, in 1682, some 21 years after construction had begun, Louis made Versailles his royal residence and thus the seat of French government.

The actual Palace of Versailles contains hundreds of rooms and is more than a half mile (0.8 kilometers) long. It is symmetrical/$_{100}$ in design and done in French Baroque style. Within the lavish central section are the royal apartments of the king and queen. These are separated by the Hall of Mirrors. It is decorated with marble, paintings, gilded statues, and 483 mirrors.]

Comprehension Questions

(TE)   1. What place does this passage describe?
       (Versailles, in France)

(TI)   2. Where is this place?
       (close to Paris)

(TI)   3. About how long ago was it built?
       (about 3 centuries)

(TE)   4. Who had this place built?
       (King Louis XIV)

(SI)   5. Why would he want to build the most splendid palace in Europe?
       (to show the importance of his country)

(SI)   6. Why would Versailles still be considered a great wonder of the world?
       (very large, very elaborate)

4

CBAs for Math

Mathematics and science are types of spiraling curricula. Spiraling curricula are those in which the concepts covered are repeated over time, usually becoming increasingly more difficult. For example, a graded math curriculum for Grades 1 through 6 might introduce two-place addition with regrouping in Grade 2 and then continue to review this concept in Grades 3, 4, and 5, although the problems in the upper levels would be more difficult than those in the lower levels.

There are at least five major problems one encounters with spiraling curricula—particularly math curricula—and each must be considered when assessing and teaching learners with special needs. One problem stems from the fact that spiraling curricula are usually paced fairly fast. Often there is not enough practice provided on a concept before students are introduced to a subsequent concept. A second problem is that sufficient practice is not always offered when concepts are presented, even though sufficient practice opportunities may be distributed throughout the book. A third problem arises if a given book has gaps in the developmental sequence of problem types. Thus, addition of one-digit numbers, for example, $n + n$ and $nn + n$ (where n = a numeral with no carrying or renaming) might be followed by addition of two-digit numbers with renaming, for example, $nc + nn$ (where c = a numeral that will require carrying or renaming). To aid a student with the transition to the more difficult problem, instruction and practice might be added for addition problems with more than one digit with no renaming. For all three of these prob-

lems, adjustments can be made in the curriculum itself—either by supplementing the curriculum with extra practice or by reordering student progression through the curriculum so that sufficient practices are offered after a concept is introduced. In the case of the third problem, gaps within the curriculum, supplementary lessons can be added. In such cases, adjustments will also need to be made on the CBA form so that the CBA content reflects the content of both the curriculum and the supplementary materials.

A fourth problem arises if the order of the concepts presented does not seem logical to the collaborating teachers. In this case, the teachers may choose to reorder the presentation of the concepts, for both curricular assessment and instruction. A fifth problem is posed when so many concepts are presented within a single level that the CBA becomes cumbersome. Particularly for learners with special needs, there may be too many concepts for the learner to master during the nine-month school year.

To streamline the assessment process, it is recommended that various CBA strands be developed within the curriculum with, for example, a CBA strand for addition, one for division, one for telling time, one for geometry, and so on. Examples of such strands can be found in Blankenship and Lilly (1981). If this option is chosen, each strand can be expanded to cover several levels within the curriculum, reflecting a progression from simple to more complex math problems. This procedure becomes quite operable when one considers that within a spiraling curriculum there is considerable repetition among the levels.

To minimize the instructional problem presented by curricula that contain too many concepts, teachers should project the number of concepts they want learners with special needs to master within the school year, even though this number will probably be less than the number of concepts contained in the level of the series. It is preferable to have mastered at least some concepts rather than have no mastery at all as a result of exposing the students to too many concepts.

The problem of too many concepts is compounded somewhat by the spiraling characteristic of the curriculum itself. If students are to be continuously exposed to the same concepts, it seems preferable to build a hierarchical progression in which students master one concept before progressing to subsequent concepts. Some practitioners have used this idea of hierarchical development of mathematics concepts for CBAs related to problem solving, mathematical reasoning, and critical thinking skills (see Parke & Lane, 1996, and Tindal & Nolet, 1996, for examples) instead of focusing only on computation skills.

Development of a Math CBA

The following procedural sequence—developed by Dr. Lorna Idol in the Resource/Consulting Teacher Program at the University of Illinois—has proven useful as a guide for developing curricular-based assessments in math, science, and social studies.

- Step 1: Use the table of contents, scope and sequence charts, placement tests, and review tests to determine the relevant concepts. All of these are excellent sources; however, placement tests are the best source if they are contained in the curriculum with which you are working. Most of the relevant concepts will be represented in these sources, even though, in our experience, there is not always perfect agreement between concepts in placement tests and those in review tests. Still, both types of tests are useful sources in constructing the CBA. For some curricula, the placement test will be comprehensive enough to serve with only minor changes as the CBA for the first day of testing. In this case, the tests for the second and third days of testing can be constructed by using the placement test as a sample and writing similar but different problems for the two remaining tests. Teachers should, however, be wary and check the contents of all of the sources cited previously to ensure development of a comprehensive CBA.

- Step 2: Make a list of the concepts identified within the curriculum.

- Step 3: Construct a raw data sheet containing concepts and page numbers. An example of this is the Scope and Sequence of Concepts (Figure 4.1). Note that the left column contains a listing of the concepts and the middle column contains a list of the pages with practice opportunities for the concept.

- Step 4: Reorder the concept list if the order is not progressive and logical. An excellent guide for determining the logical sequence of arithmetic can be found in Resnick, Wang, and Kaplan (1973). This source also provides a task analysis of math operations and includes a hierarchical sequence for teaching concepts and operations.

- Step 5: Determine if all of the concepts have enough practice. The right column of a scope-and-sequence raw data sheet should contain the total number of practice items for each concept.

- Step 6: Select complementary work materials when necessary. If the results of Step 5 indicate that there are insufficient practice opportunities for certain concepts that teachers want to include in the special program, auxiliary work materials should be added to the curriculum. These materials can be organized in manila folders and coded by concept and page number of the curriculum to indicate the point at which they should be used.

- Step 7: Organize the curriculum by concept, sequence, and page number. In some instances the collaborating teachers may decide upon a sequence of instruction that is different from that offered by the curriculum publishers. This reorganization should include the new order of concepts and the page numbers of practice opportunities.

- Step 8: Determine and code those concepts that can be taught simultaneously. Sometimes, different concepts may be so interrelated and complementary that they should be taught simultaneously. Teachers should determine in advance where this might occur.

- Step 9: Construct placement tests that are organized by concept. Three tests (one for each of three days of testing) should be written. Make certain that the important substeps within each concept are represented.

- Step 10: Administer the placement tests. Give only as many tests as the estimated skill levels of the student might indicate is appropriate; further testing can be done later. There is no reason to waste time testing at upper levels if it is evident that a student is functioning at a lower level. The test should be given on three separate occasions, using different forms of the test on each day. In the example of a math CBA for Level III of a Scott, Foresman and Company text presented in the following section, note that the types of problems are replicated across three days and that the order of the problems remains constant. It is recommended that the speed of computation (rate or correct problems per minute, cppm) as well as accuracy be measured. This can be done by recording the amount of time taken to complete the tests. For group testing, the students can be given a certain amount of time for test completion.

- Step 11: Enter the performance data on a student summary sheet at the end of each of the three testing sessions. Note that this sheet serves as a recordkeeping system for recording mastery and nonmastery of all concepts represented on the CBA form. An example of a student summary sheet is shown in Table 4.1.

- Step 12: Determine which concepts the student will begin to work on. It is recommended that median performance across the three days be used as the measure for each test item. A criterion level to determine test mastery must be established by the collaborating teachers. For the sample math CBA in this chapter, the criterion level was set at five out of six correct responses, or 83 percent correct, for mastery of each skill represented on the test.

- Step 13: Construct a yearly progress chart. The chart should include years spent in school (abscissa) and concepts contained within the curriculum (ordinate). This chart can be used for two purposes: (a) to record the placement of the student in the curriculum, and (b) to record monthly progress of the student through the curriculum. Examples of yearly progress charts as well as a basic framework for constructing progress charts can be found in Idol-Maestas (1983), Idol-Maestas, Paolucci-Whitcomb, and Nevin (1986), and Idol (1997).

- Step 14: Construct a daily progress chart to monitor daily progress of the student. Examples of behaviors that could be monitored are the percentage correct of the problems completed, correct problems per minute (cppm), and correct facts per minute (cfpm).

- Step 15: Use a lesson plan sheet to plan the procedures that will be used when beginning math instruction.

Testing Math Skills

This section contains two parts: (a) an example of the scope and sequence of concepts in a book level of a math curriculum, and (b) an example of the organization of a math CBA. The curriculum used for these examples is taken from a Scott, Foresman and Company text. Both the scope and sequence analysis and the organization of the math CBA were developed by Anita Andrews and Jill Cunningham while enrolled in the Resource/Consulting Teacher Program at the University of Illinois.

Scope and Sequence of Concepts

Figure 4.1 shows how to conduct an analysis of the concepts contained in a book level. In this particular book level, the skill areas included:

- Sets and numbers
- Place value
- Addition
- Subtraction
- Multiplication
- Division
- Measurement
- Geometry
- Fractions
- Money
- Time

The analysis is organized in terms of these 11 skill areas. The teachers examined the book and listed subskills in each of the skill areas. They recorded the page numbers at which the subskills appeared, and then determined the total number of items in the book that offer practice opportunities on each concept.

Organization of a Math CBA

A math CBA is organized to test a student's skill in a single math skill area or across several skill areas. The skill areas, as listed in Figure 4.1, are analyzed for frequency of occurrence in each book level. The CBA is then administered, and a summary sheet is used to record student performance data. Skill areas not mastered by the student are then selected and prioritized by the collaborating teachers, and appropriate instruction begins.

For example, administration of the following sample math CBA, organized by subskills within each skill area, requires three parts: (a) a summary sheet (Table 4.1) for recording student performance data, (b) directions for administering the CBA, and (c) the math CBA itself.

Summary Sheet

Table 4.1 presents a summary sheet of the analysis of the scope and sequence of concepts shown in Figure 4.1. The summary sheet lists the problem numbers for each subskill as they appear on the CBA. Space is provided for recording pupil achievement scores for each of the three days of testing. In this case, the teachers set the mastery criteria at five of six problems solved correctly for each subskill. A place is provided for recording the total score for each subskill, followed by a final column indicating whether or not the subskill was mastered.

Directions for Administering the CBA

The CBA (all or only a selected portion) is administered over a three-day period. The teachers pass out the CBA on Day 1, telling the students that it is a test on how much they know about math (or addition, subtraction, and so on). The students should be told that the CBA is not a test for a grade but rather a test designed to find out what the teachers need to know to improve their teaching of the students. The students should be told to do their best but, if they come to a problem they cannot solve, they should spend only a very few minutes on it and then move quickly to the next type of problem. On test Items 71 and 72 in the following CBA, a ruler must be provided for each student.

Similar instructions are given on Days 2 and 3. The CBA should be designed so that the teachers can give the entire test either as a placement tool (to a whole class, a small group,

Sets and Numbers

	Subskill	Pages	Total Items
1.	Sets xxx How many x's?	2, 3	6
2.	Counting, ordering	70, 71, 80, 81, 89T, 137, 125T, 126, 137, 187T, 189, 198, 207T, 236T, 237, 238, 325	83
3.	Comparison n_____n	4, 5, 6, 7, 82, 83, 84, 85, 89T, 126, 187T, 189, 346, 348	172
4.	Comparison (addition) n + n_____n	85, 101, 213, 239, 293	42
5.	Comparison (subtraction) n − n_____n	85, 225, 239, 288	28
6.	Comparison (multiplication) n × n_____n	145, 232, 248, 293, 302	63
7.	Comparison (division) n ÷ n_____n	293	7
8.	Odd–even	8, 9	27
9.	Ordinal numbers	72, 73, 89T	24
10.	Bar graphs	10, 11, 122, 147	17

Place Value

	Subskill	Pages	Total Items
1.	Hundreds, tens, ones	66, 67, 68, 69, 74, 75, 76, 77, 80, 89T, 125T, 126, 187T, 189, 238, 346, 348	131
2.	Thousands	194, 195, 196, 197, 207T, 236T, 238, 325, 346, 348	76
3.	Tens & hundreds, thousands	200, 201, 207T, 238, 396	32
4.	Millions	202, 203	16
5.	Expanded form	86, 89T, 199, 207T, 238	44

Addition

	Subskill	Pages	Total Items
1.	Basic facts 0–10	14, 15, 18, 19, 20, 21, 22, 23, 36, 45T, 62	140
2.	Basic facts 11–20	24, 25, 26, 27, 28, 29, 30, 31, 32, 35, 37, 45T, 61T, 63, 81, 87, 103, 189, 204	191
3.	Missing addends n + _____ = n	15, 18, 19, 20, 21, 24, 25, 34, 35, 36, 43, 45T, 63, 101, 127, 213, 239, 284	115
4.	Three or more numbers n + n + n = n	42, 43, 45T, 61, 102, 104, 105T, 125T, 127, 189	77
5.	Up to four digits nn nnn +nn +nnn nnnn +nnnn	93, 99, 100, 101, 105, 120, 121T, 125, 127, 187, 189, 205, 212, 219, 221T, 346, 348T	99

Addition (continued)

	Subskill	Pages	Total Items
6.	One renaming up to four numbers nc nc +xn +nn	91, 93, 96, 97, 98, 99, 100, 103, 105T, 120, 121, 125T, 127, 187, 189, 205, 212, 215, 217, 221T, 236T, 238, 284, 293, 346, 348T	211
7.	More than one renaming up to four numbers ncc ncc +nnn +nn	209, 212, 215, 217, 221T, 236T, 238, 239, 284, 293, 325, 346, 348T	79
8.	Story problems	38, 39, 45T, 94, 95, 105T, 119, 121, 125, 187, 210, 211, 213, 217, 221T, 236T, 347, 349	52

Subtraction

	Subskill	Pages	Total Items
1.	Basic facts through 10	16, 17, 18, 19, 20, 21, 22, 23	139
2.	Basic facts 11–20	24, 25, 26, 27, 28, 29, 30, 31, 33, 37, 63, 81	152
3.	Missing digit	20, 21, 24, 25, 213, 225, 239, 284	48
4.	2-digit (no borrowing) nn nn −n −nn	109, 110, 111, 116, 119, 121, 123T, 125T, 224, 346T, 348T	55
5.	3-digit (no borrowing) nnn nnn −nn −nnn	118, 120, 123, 125T, 127, 189T, 220, 224, 231, 232, 284, 293, 346	34
6.	2-digit (borrowing) nb nb −nn −n	106, 107, 109, 116, 117, 120, 121, 123T, 125T, 127T, 187T, 189T, 220T, 224, 232, 346T, 348T	95
7.	3-digit (borrowing) nbb nbb −nn −nnn	112, 113, 114, 115, 116, 117, 118, 119, 120, 121, 123T, 125T, 127T, 187T, 189T, 220, 222, 223, 224, 231, 232, 233, 235T, 236T, 239, 234, 293, 346, 348T	207
8.	4-digit (borrowing) nbbb nbbb −nnn −nnn	224, 325, 346	8
9.	Story problems	38, 39, 40, 41, 121, 225, 227, 228, 229, 335T, 347	35

Multiplication

	Subskill	Pages	Total Items
1.	Basic facts through 36 n × n ≤ 36	130, 131, 132, 133, 134, 135, 136, 137, 138, 139, 142, 143, 144, 145, 146, 163, 167T, 188T, 189, 190, 191, 199, 237, 248, 249, 250, 251, 270, 302, 346, 348	500
2.	Basic facts 40–54	242, 243, 244, 248, 249, 250, 251, 253, 257, 271T, 301T, 302, 346, 348	137

(continues)

Figure 4.1. Scope and sequence of concepts.

Multiplication (*continued*)

	Subskill	Pages	Total Items
3.	Basic facts 56–81	247, 248, 249, 250, 251, 253, 271T, 301T, 302, 346, 398	51
4.	Missing factors n × _____ = n	158, 167, 251, 256, 258, 271T, 284, 293, 301T, 302	51
5.	<, >, =	145, 237, 245, 302	57
6.	More than 2 factors n × n × n	257, 271T, 302	30
7.	number by 10, 100, & 1,000	272, 273, 285T, 301, 303, 325, 346, 349	66
8.	Multiply w/multiples of 10, 100, & 1,000 n × n0 n × n00	275, 285T, 301T, 303, 325, 349	49
9.	Multiply 2- or 3-digit by 1-digit nn × n nnn × n	276, 277, 280, 281, 282, 283, 285, 301T, 303, 346, 349	95
10.	Story problems	140, 141, 167T, 188T, 190, 245, 271T, 278, 279, 283, 283T, 301T, 303, 347, 349	43

Division

	Subskill	Pages	Total Items
1.	Basic facts through 36 (not zero)	148, 149, 150, 151, 152, 153, 154, 155, 159, 160, 161, 162, 163, 166, 167T, 188T, 189T, 190, 191, 225, 257, 259, 265	362
2.	Basic facts 40–54	254, 255, 256, 257, 259, 265, 271T, 302, 346, 348T	91
3.	Basic facts 56–81	258, 259, 265, 271T, 302, 346	53
4.	Zero division 0 ÷ n	264, 265, 271T, 301T, 302, 346, 348T	20
5.	Missing digits	284, 302	7
6.	2-digit division without renaming nn ÷ nn nnn ÷ nn	287, 298T, 301T, 303	18
7.	1-digit and 2-digit division with remainders	288, 289, 291, 292, 293, 294, 295, 296, 298T, 301T, 302, 303, 325, 346, 349T	118
8.	Story problems	156, 157, 167T, 188T, 191, 261, 262, 263, 268, 269, 271T, 285T, 286, 288, 290, 294, 296, 297, 298T, 301T, 303, 347, 349T	81

Measurement

	Subskill	Pages	Total Items
1.	Basic units	168, 169	2
2.	Inches	170, 171, 172, 173, 181T, 188T, 191	51
3.	Feet and yards	174, 175	21
4.	Metric	176, 177, 180, 181T, 188T	42
5.	Perimeter	179, 181T, 189T, 216	14
6.	Cups, pints, quarts, & gallons	326, 331T, 351	17
7.	Liters	327	6

Geometry

	Subskill	Pages	Total Items
1.	Shapes	46, 47, 48, 49	28
2.	Congruent figures	50, 51, 59T, 61	13
3.	Segments	52, 53, 59T	13
4.	Diagonals	54, 55, 59T	26
5.	Coordinates	182, 183, 184, 185, 186, 187T, 188T	64
6.	Radius & diameter	328, 329	21
7.	Angles	332, 333	8
8.	Similar figures	334, 335	6
9.	Area	336, 337, 344T, 345T, 349T, 351	23
10.	Volume	342, 343, 344T, 345T, 349T, 351	25

Fractions

	Subskill	Pages	Total Items
1.	Equal parts	306, 307, 308, 309, 317T	14
2.	Fractions = 1	311	6
3.	Shaded part (part of whole)	310, 317T, 345T, 350	35
4.	Part of set	312, 313	6
5.	Comparing fractions	314, 315, 317T, 345T, 350	32
6.	Fractions on number line	316, 317T, 350	8

Money

	Subskill	Pages	Total Items
1.	Writing ($, ¢) 2 dollars, 4 dimes, 6 pennies = n	78, 79, 126, 164, 165, 189, 191, 266, 267, 303, 325, 346, 348	93
2.	Addition of $n.nn + n.nn	118, 119, 218, 219, 201, 236, 293, 347	28
3.	Subtraction of $n.nn − n.nn	118, 293	16
4.	Story problems	119, 271T, 297, 298T, 303, 347	26

Time

	Subskill	Pages	Total Items
1.	To the hour	318, 331T, 345T, 350	21
2.	To the half-hour	319, 331T, 345T	10
3.	Quarter-hour	321, 350	11
4.	To five minutes	320, 331T, 350	21
5.	Story problems	322, 323	10

Note. T = test pages in the math book.

Figure 4.1. *Continued*

Table 4.1. Summary Sheet for a Math CBA

Concepts	Problem Numbers	Day 1	Day 2	Day 3	Total Score 5/6	Mastery 5/6	Concepts	Problem Numbers	Day 1	Day 2	Day 3	Total Score 5/6	Mastery 5/6
Writing digits	1, 2	/2	/2	/2	/6	/6	Mult. facts 56–81	43, 44	/2	/2	/2	/6	/6
Place value	3, 4	/2	/2	/2	/6	/6	Mult. > 2 factors	45, 46	/2	/2	/2	/6	/6
Comparing numbers	5, 6	/2	/2	/2	/6	/6	Mult. by 10, 100	47, 48	/2	/2	/2	/6	/6
Add basic facts 0–10	7, 21	/2	/2	/2	/6	/6	Mult. by multiples of 10	49, 50	/2	/2	/2	/6	/6
Add basic facts 11–20	8, 22	/2	/2	/2	/6	/6	Mult. 2 digit by 1 digit	51, 52	/2	/2	/2	/6	/6
Add 2 digits (no renaming)	9, 24	/2	/2	/2	/6	/6	Mult. 3 digit by 1 digit	53, 54	/2	/2	/2	/6	/6
Add 1 renaming	10, 26	/2	/2	/2	/6	/6	Div. facts thru 36	55, 56	/2	/2	/2	/6	/6
Add 3 digits (no renaming)	11, 28	/2	/2	/2	/6	/6	Div. facts 40–54	57, 58	/2	/2	/2	/6	/6
Add 2 renaming	12, 30	/2	/2	/2	/6	/6	Division by zero	59, 60	/2	/2	/2	/6	/6
Add 3 or more numbers	13, 32	/2	/2	/2	/6	/6	Div. facts 56–81	61, 62	/2	/2	/2	/6	/6
Add 4 digits (renaming)	12, 30	/2	/2	/2	/6	/6	Div. 2 digit by 2 digit (no remainder)	63, 64	/2	/2	/2	/6	/6
Subt. basic facts 0–10	15, 23	/2	/2	/2	/6	/6	Div. 2 digit by 2 digit (remainder)	65, 66	/2	/2	/2	/6	/6
Subt. basic facts 11–20	16, 25	/2	/2	/2	/6	/6	Div. 2 digit by 2 digit (remainder)	67, 68	/2	/2	/2	/6	/6
Subt. 2 digits (no renaming)	17, 27	/2	/2	/2	/6	/6	Missing factors (X,)	69, 70	/2	/2	/2	/6	/6
Subt. 2 digits (1 renaming)	18, 29	/2	/2	/2	/6	/6	Measuring in inches	71, 72	/2	/2	/2	/6	/6
Subt. 3 digits (no renaming)	19, 31	/2	/2	/2	/6	/6	Conversion to inches	73, 74	/2	/2	/2	/6	/6
Subt. 3 digits (1 renaming)	20, 33	/2	/2	/2	/6	/6	Perimeter	75, 76	/2	/2	/2	/6	/6
Missing addends (1)	35, 36	/2	/2	/2	/6	/6	Shapes	77, 78	/2	/2	/2	/6	/6
Sets in multiplication	37, 38	/2	/2	/2	/6	/6	Fraction for part of whole	79, 80	/2	/2	/2	/6	/6
Mult. facts thru 36	39, 40	/2	/2	/2	/6	/6	Writing money	81, 82	/2	/2	/2	/6	/6
Mult. facts 40–54	41, 42	/2	/2	/2	/6	/6	Writing time (hrs. & 5 min.)	83, 84	/2	/2	/2	/6	/6
							Story problem (+, −)	85, 86	/2	/2	/2	/6	/6
							Story problem (X,)	87, 88	/2	/2	/2	/6	/6

or an individual) or as a final assessment. It should also be possible to use only a part of the CBA to test specific skill areas. In giving the entire CBA, the teacher should allow for 30 to 45 minutes of work time in each day of testing.

Sample Math CBA: Elementary Level

The sample math CBA presented in this section contains problems for each of the subskill areas listed on the Table 4.1 summary sheet. The problem types are repeated across three days, with three different examples of the same type.

Math CBA

Give the number:

1. 9 tens, 6 ones   2.   3 thousand, 7 hundred forty-one

   _____   _____

Tell what place 7 holds:

3. 271 _____   4. 8,726 _____

Compare the numbers. Use > or < :

5. 32 _____ 49   6.   2 × 3 _____ 10

Add:

7.	2	8.	7	9.	42	10.	76	11.	231
	+6		+5		+21		+17		+243

12.   373   13. 7 + 2 + 5 = _____   14.   3692
      +147   +2345

Subtract:

15.	8	16.	11	17.	87	18.	76	19.	588	20.	349
	−7		−4		−43		−59		−164		−187

Add or subtract:

21.	4	22.	6	23.	9	24.	55	25.	15
	+3		+3		−4		+31		−8

26.	24	27.	79	28.	401	29.	82	30.	242
	+36		−25		+296		−37		+369

31.   865   32. 4 + 4 + 6 = _____   33.   824   34.   4654
      −321   −717   +1975

Fill in the missing number:

35.   3 + _____ = 9   36.   57 – _____ = 39

Look at the pictures of the x's and fill in the blanks for the problem:

Example: xx   xx
                  xx
              _3_ × _2_

37.   xxx   xxx   38.   x   x

      _____ × _____   _____ × _____

Multiply:

39.   6 × 3 = _____   43.   8 × 9 = _____

40.   5 × 7 = _____   44.   8 × 7 = _____

41.   6 × 8 = _____   45.   3 × 4 × 3 = _____

42.   9 × 5 = _____   46.   7 × 3 × 1 = _____

47.   10   48.   100   49.   70   50.   90
      ×6   ×3   ×8   ×8
      ___   ___   ___   ___

51.   45   52.   55   53.   672   54.   535
      ×2   ×5   ×5   ×2
      ___   ___   ___   ___

Divide:

55.   8 ÷ 2 = _____   59.   0 ÷ 3 = _____

56.   10 ÷ 5 = _____   60.   0 ÷ 4 = _____

57.   54 ÷ 9 = _____   61.   81 ÷ 9 = _____

58.   40 ÷ 8 = _____   62.   63 ÷ 7 = _____

63. 18)54   64. 12)24   65. 8)34   66. 6)31   67. 35)78   68. 17)39

Fill in the numbers:

69. _____ × 8 = 48   70. _____ ÷ 2 = 6

A   B   C   D   E   F

71. How long is the line from point A to D?

_____ inches

72. How long is the line from point C to F?

_____ inches

Convert to inches:

73. 1 foot = _____ inches   74. 1 foot + 8 inches = _____ inches

Find the perimeter:

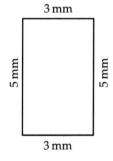

75. _____ millimeters   76. _____ millimeters

Count the number of shapes:

 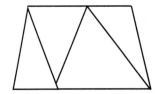

77. _____   78. _____

Give a fraction to tell how much is shaded:

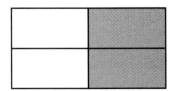 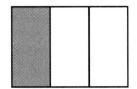

79. _____   80. _____

Use $ or ¢ to show the total value:

81.   3 dollars, 8 dimes, 3 pennies = _____

82.   7 nickels, 15 pennies = _____

Write the time shown on each clock:

83. _____   84. _____

Find each answer:

85. Marsha had 24 blocks. Mel had 38. How many blocks did they have in all? _____

86. 342 books in the library. 20 checked out. How many left? _____

87. 20 rows of stamps. 8 stamps in a row. How many stamps in all? _____

88. Pencils are 7¢ each. How many can you buy with 30¢? _____

Math CBA

Give the number:

1. 8 tens, 9 ones   2.   9 thousand, 2 hundred seventy-eight

   _____   _____

Tell what place 7 holds:

3.   937 _____   4.   7,453 _____

Compare the numbers. Use > or < :

5.   62 _____ 67   6.   6 + 4 _____ 9

Add:

7.	2 +5	8.	9 +6	9.	52 +36	10.	16 +27	11.	170 +325

12.   695
      +326

13.   8 + 1 + 9 = _____

14.   2342
      +5168

Subtract:

15.	4 −0	16.	12 −3	17.	59 −18	18.	67 −19	19.	385 −275	20.	931 −391

Add or subtract:

21.	5 +1	22.	5 +8	23.	9 −5	24.	63 +32	25.	17 −8

26.	39 +42	27.	63 −41	28.	555 +430	29.	51 −25	30.	578 +234

31.   497
      −352

32.   6 + 4 + 3 = _____

33.   125
      −117

34.   6234
      +3829

Fill in the missing numbers:

35. _____ + 5 = 7   36. 74 – _____ = 36

Look at the pictures of the x's and fill in the blanks for the problem:

Example: xx   xx
            _2_ × _2_

37.   xx   xx   38. x   x
   _____×_____   _____×_____

Multiply:

39. 4 × 5 = _____   43. 7 × 8 = _____

40. 6 × 6 = _____   44. 9 × 9 = _____

41. 7 × 6 = _____   45. 5 × 3 × 2 = _____

42. 7 × 7 = _____   46. 6 × 1 × 3 = _____

47. 10   48. 100   49. 80   50. 40
     ×4   ×7   ×4   ×6

51. 93   52. 35   53. 542   54. 156
     ×5   ×3   ×4   ×3

Divide:

55. 9 ÷ 3 = _____   59. 0 ÷ 6 = _____

56. 6 ÷ 3 = _____   60. 0 ÷ 2 = _____

57. 45 ÷ 9 = _____   61. 72 ÷ 8 = _____

58. 54 ÷ 6 = _____   62. 56 ÷ 7 = _____

63. 24)48   64. 30)90   65. 7)22   66. 9)23   67. 15)48   68. 26)49

Fill in the numbers:

69. 7 × _____ = 42   70. 32 ÷ _____ = 4

A _____ B _____ C _____ D _____ E _____ F _____

71. How long is the line from point C to G?   _____ inches

72. How long is the line from point B to G?   _____ inches

Convert to inches:

73. 1 yard = _____ inches   74. 1 foot + 3 inches = _____ inches

Find the perimeter:

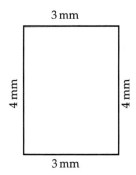

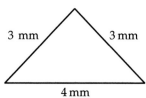

75. _____ millimeters   76. _____ millimeters

Count the number of shapes:

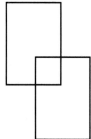

77. _____   78. _____

Math CBA

Give the number:

1. 7 tens, 1 one   2. 6 thousand, 4 hundred thirty-two

    _____   _____

Tell what place 7 holds:

3. 724 _____   4. 5,271 _____

Compare the numbers. Use > or < :

5. 75 _____ 85   6. 12 ÷ 2 _____ 8

Add:

7.   9   8.   6   9.   21   10.   59   11.   674
    +0   +5   +48   +16   +323

12.   276   13. 9 + 7 + 2 = _____   14.   5671
     +235   +4437

Subtract:

15.   8   16.   11   17.   64   18.   91   19.   745   20.   431
    −1   −9   −23   −37   −441   −234

Add or subtract:

21.   9   22.   7   23.   7   24.   41   25.   14
    +0   +4   −5   +18   −7

26.   61   27.   54   28.   123   29.   64   30.   495
    +39   −23   +736   −46   +326

31.   685   32. 5 + 2 + 3 = _____   33.   570   34.   2161
    −431   −248   +1847

Fill in the missing number:

35. 8 + _____ = 10   36. 81 − _____ = 63

Look at the pictures of the x's and fill in the blanks for the problem:

Example: x   x
                  x
          _3_ × _1_

37.   xx   xx   38. xxxx   xxxx

      _____ × _____   _____ × _____

Multiply:

39. 2 × 6 = _____   43. 7 × 9 = _____

40. 4 × 3 = _____   44. 8 × 8 = _____

41. 6 × 9 = _____   45. 4 × 2 × 1 = _____

42. 5 × 8 = _____   46. 4 × 3 × 2 = _____

47. 10   48. 100   49. 50   50. 30
     ×2   ×9   ×2   ×3

51. 32   52. 24   53. 833   54. 472
     ×6   ×2   ×3   ×2

Divide:

55. 8 ÷ 4 = _____   59. 0 ÷ 5 = _____

56. 12 ÷ 2 = _____   60. 0 ÷ 7 = _____

57. 48 ÷ 6 = _____   61. 56 ÷ 8 = _____

58. 48 ÷ 8 = _____   62. 64 ÷ 8 = _____

63. 13)‾52‾   64. 25)‾50‾   65. 5)‾43‾   66. 6)‾51‾   67. 68)‾93‾   68. 18)‾57‾

Fill in the numbers:

69. 6 × _____ = 48   70. _____ ÷ 2 = 9

A _____ B _____ C _____ D _____ E _____ F _____ G

71. How long is the line from point A to G?   _____ inches

72. How long is the line from point A to F?   _____ inches

Convert to inches:

73. 2 feet = _____ inches   74. 1 foot + 10 inches = _____ inches

Find the perimeter:

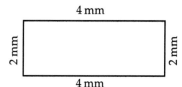

75. _____ millimeters   76. _____ millimeters

Count the number of shapes:

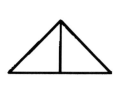

77. _____   78. _____

Give a fraction to tell how much is shaded:

   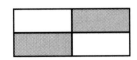

79. _____   80. _____

Use $ or ¢ to show the total value:

81. 2 dollars, 4 dimes, 6 pennies = _____

82. 5 dollars, 5 nickels, 5 pennies = _____

Write the time shown on each clock:

83. _____   84. _____

Find each answer:

85. Peter weighed 150 lbs. He gained 19 lbs. How much does he weigh now? _____

86. Sharon read 151 pages and Jane read 89 pages. How many more pages did Sharon read? _____

87. 8 cookies on a tray. 4 trays in all. How many cookies in all? _____

88. Newspapers are 10¢ each. How many can you buy with 55¢? _____

Sample Math CBA for Fractions

The CBA in this section is an example of one that might be developed for older students who need specialized work in a particular strand of math skills, in this case, fractions. For secondary students, it is unlikely that a teacher would develop a math CBA that covered all math skills. Rather, the CBA would be developed for particular types of math skills, such as algebra, geometry, and trigonometry, or for a particular strand of skills such as fractions or decimals or square roots. Because CBAs are primarily recommended for use with students with special learning needs or for students who are at risk for school failure, we believe use of the strand approach is the preferred method. Thus, the example in this section illustrates how a strand was developed for fractions, particularly because knowing how to calculate with fractions is an integral part of many higher math applications.

The sample math CBA for fractions was developed using a remedial mathematics book for teaching fractions, *Refresher Mathematics*. Using the guidelines explained earlier in this chapter, Tsivia Cohen developed this CBA while working on her Master's Degree in the Resource/Consulting Teacher Program at the University of Illinois.

The same procedures illustrated with the previously described math CBA for fourth grade were followed for the fractions CBA. Figure 4.2 reflects the scope and sequence of the contents of the remedial textbook on teaching fractions. If particular subskills were left out in the textbook scope and sequence, they have been added so that the increments of change in problem difficulty are logical and organized into relatively small steps of increasing difficulty. An instance such as this is indicated by the words *not in book* in Figure 4.2. Otherwise, the page numbers where each of the problem types occurred in the textbook are listed in the second column. The XXXXs indicate that that particular category of problems is broken down into smaller subskills of that problem type.

The sample math CBA for fractions follows and reflects the same order of difficulty of problem type as depicted in Figure 4.2. Following the prototype for the math CBA, there are sample problems for each of the problem types for three different days of testing. The problems for Day 1 were taken directly from the textbook; the problems for Days 2 and 3 were generated to give alternative examples of the same type of problem reflected in the Day 1 part of the CBA.

		Page	Score Day 1	Score Day 2	Score Day 3	Pass/ Fail
A	Naming fractions	(not in book)				
B	Reducing fractions to lowest terms	89				
C	Changing improper fractions	91				
D	Changing mixed numbers to simplest form	93				
E	Changing a fraction to higher terms	95				
F	Finding the lowest common denominator	97				
G	Changing fractions to equivalent fractions	93				
H	Addition of fractions		XXXX	XXXX	XXXX	
h-1	Like denominators	100				
h-2	Unlike denominators	102				
I	Addition of mixed numbers		XXXX	XXXX	XXXX	
i-1	Like denominators	102				
i-2	Unlike denominators	103				
J	Regrouping of fractions	106				
K	Subtraction of fractions (and mixed numbers)	108	XXXX	XXXX	XXXX	
k-1	Like denominators (no regrouping)	109				
k-2	Unlike denominators	110				
k-3	Like denominators (with regrouping)	110				
k-3a	Whole numbers on top	110				
k-3b	Mixed numbers on top	110				
k-4	Unlike denominators	110–111				
L	Comparing fractions	114				
M	Changing mixed numbers to improper fractions	116				
N	Multiplication of fractions					
n-1	Multiplication of simple fractions	118				
n-2	Multiplication of fractions and and whole numbers	118 121				
n-3	Multiplication of fractions and mixed numbers	122				
n-4	Multiplication of mixed numbers	122				
O	Division of fractions		XXXX	XXXX	XXXX	
o-1	Division of fractions by fractions	(not in book)				
o-2	Division of fractions by whole numbers	130				
o-3	Division of whole numbers by fractions	130				
o-4	Division of fractions by mixed numbers	130				
o-5	Division of mixed numbers by fractions	130				
o-6	Division of mixed numbers by mixed numbers	131				

Figure 4.2. Scope and sequence of contents—fractions.

Math CBA, Fractions

Day 1

Scoring Criteria for Math CBA

1. For Levels A–N, student must get 3 of 4 items correct (75%) for *each of 2 of 3 days*.

2. For *each* sublevel of Level O: (o-1, o-2, o-3, o-4, o-5, o-6), student must get 4 of the 6 total items correct (66%) for the *combined 3 days*.

   For example, under sublevel o-1, student must get 4 of the 6 o-1 problems correct over the 3-day testing period.

A. Write fractions for each of the following pictures. What portion is shaded?

1. _____ 2. _____ 3. _____ 4. _____

B. Reduce to lowest terms.

  1. $\frac{4}{8} =$ 2. $\frac{14}{20} =$ 3. $\frac{84}{100} =$ 4. $\frac{36}{45} =$

C. Change the following improper fractions to whole numbers or mixed numbers.

  1. $\frac{18}{6} =$ 2. $\frac{7}{3} =$ 3. $\frac{17}{4} =$ 4. $\frac{65}{9} =$

D. Simplify the following mixed numbers to their simplest form:

  1. $7\frac{4}{4} =$ 2. $9\frac{8}{4} =$ 3. $5\frac{4}{12} =$ 4. $7\frac{19}{8} =$

E. Change the following fractions to higher terms.

  1. $\frac{1}{6} = \frac{}{18}$ 2. $\frac{2}{3} = \frac{}{9}$ 3. $\frac{8}{9} = \frac{}{81}$ 4. $\frac{1}{2} = \frac{}{10}$

F. For each of the following sets of fractions, write the lowest common denominator.

  1. $\frac{1}{2}$ and $\frac{2}{4}$ _____   2. $\frac{2}{3}$ and $\frac{1}{2}$ _____   3. $\frac{9}{10}$ and $\frac{2}{5}$ _____   4. $\frac{5}{7}$ and $\frac{5}{8}$ _____

Note. Adapted from *Prentice-Hall's Refresher Mathematics* by E. I. Stein, 1989, Needham, MA: Prentice-Hall. Copyright 1989 by Prentice-Hall.

G. Change the following fractions so that they have the same denominators. An example is done for you.

Example: $\frac{2}{3} = \frac{16}{24}$

$\frac{5}{8} = \frac{15}{24}$

1. $\frac{2}{3} =$ 2. $\frac{1}{2} =$ 3. $\frac{1}{4} =$ 4. $\frac{4}{5} =$

$\frac{1}{6} =$ $\frac{4}{8} =$ $\frac{1}{3} =$ $\frac{1}{4} =$

$\overline{\text{don't add}}$ $\overline{\text{don't add}}$ $\overline{\text{don't add}}$ $\overline{\text{don't add}}$

H. Add the following fractions. Reduce your answer.

h-1   1. $\frac{1}{5}$ 2. $\frac{3}{7}$ 3. $\frac{5}{10}$ 4. $\frac{6}{9}$

$+\frac{1}{5}$ $+\frac{2}{7}$ $+\frac{3}{10}$ $+\frac{5}{9}$

h-2   1. $\frac{1}{2}$ 2. $\frac{2}{3}$ 3. $\frac{9}{24}$ 4. $\frac{6}{18}$

$+\frac{3}{4}$ $+\frac{1}{2}$ $+\frac{5}{8}$ $+\frac{5}{27}$

I. Add the following mixed numbers. Reduce your answers.

i-1   1. $2\frac{3}{10}$ 2. $7\frac{2}{18}$ 3. $25\frac{2}{3}$ 4. $7\frac{1}{2}$

$+5\frac{1}{10}$ $+6\frac{3}{18}$ $+16\frac{2}{3}$ $+3$

i-2   5. $17\frac{1}{3}$ 6. $8\frac{1}{2}$ 7. $15\frac{1}{4}$ 8. $24\frac{9}{10}$

$+ 6\frac{2}{6}$ $+7\frac{2}{14}$ $+13\frac{2}{5}$ $+17\frac{5}{8}$

J. Find the missing numbers.

1. $3 = \frac{}{2}$ 2. $1\frac{2}{3} = \frac{}{3}$ 3. $1 = \frac{}{8}$ 4. $5\frac{2}{5} = 4\frac{}{5}$

K. Subtract. Reduce your answer.

k-1   1. $\frac{2}{3}$ 2. $\frac{5}{6}$ 3. $\frac{8}{12}$ 4. $\frac{5}{9}$

$-\frac{1}{3}$ $-\frac{2}{6}$ $-\frac{3}{12}$ $-\frac{1}{9}$

k-2   5. $\frac{5}{6}$ 6. $\frac{7}{8}$ 7. $\frac{9}{16}$ 8. $\frac{5}{6}$

$-\frac{2}{3}$ $-\frac{1}{4}$ $-\frac{2}{24}$ $-\frac{5}{9}$

k-3a 9. 5 10. 7 11. 10 12. $9\frac{1}{6}$

$\underline{-2\frac{1}{3}}$ $\underline{-6\frac{1}{8}}$ $\underline{-4\frac{4}{5}}$ $\underline{-7}$

k-3b 13. $5\frac{1}{6}$ 14. $9\frac{1}{7}$ 15. $14\frac{4}{9}$ 16. $75\frac{7}{16}$

$\underline{-4\frac{4}{6}}$ $\underline{-5\frac{3}{7}}$ $\underline{-10\frac{8}{9}}$ $\underline{-71\frac{2}{16}}$

k-4 17. $9\frac{1}{6}$ 18. $17\frac{2}{8}$ 19. $26\frac{9}{17}$ 20. $48\frac{5}{7}$

$\underline{-3\frac{1}{3}}$ $\underline{-5\frac{4}{6}}$ $\underline{-13\frac{21}{34}}$ $\underline{-19\frac{2}{14}}$

L. Which is larger? Circle the larger fraction in each set.

1. $\frac{1}{3}$ or $\frac{1}{2}$ 2. $\frac{7}{8}$ or $\frac{1}{8}$ 3. $\frac{3}{4}$ or $\frac{5}{8}$ 4. $\frac{4}{6}$ or $\frac{5}{8}$

M. Change the following mixed numbers to improper fractions. An example has been done for you.

Example: $1\frac{1}{2} = \frac{3}{2}$

1. $1\frac{1}{3} =$ 2. $7\frac{1}{8} =$ 3. $9\frac{3}{5} =$ 4. $21\frac{2}{3} =$

N. Multiply. Cancel when possible. Reduce your answers.

n-1 1. $\frac{1}{5} \times \frac{2}{6} =$ 2. $\frac{1}{3} \times \frac{6}{8} =$ 3. $\frac{16}{10} \times \frac{5}{8}$ 4. $\frac{14}{64} \times \frac{24}{35} =$

n-2 5. $4 \times \frac{1}{6} =$ 6. $12 \times \frac{7}{8} =$ 7. $\frac{5}{11} \times 44 =$ 8. $\frac{9}{81} \times 27 =$

n-3 9. $5\frac{3}{6} \times \frac{3}{11}$ 10. $6\frac{1}{8} \times \frac{8}{14} =$ 11. $9\frac{1}{2} \times \frac{10}{36} =$ 12. $5\frac{1}{4} \times \frac{4}{7} =$

n-4 13. $5\frac{1}{4} \times 5\frac{1}{7}$ 14. $9\frac{1}{3} \times 3\frac{3}{4} =$ 15. $6\frac{1}{2} \times 4\frac{2}{3} =$ 16. $7\frac{3}{6} \times 9\frac{3}{5} =$

O. Divide. Cancel when possible.

o-1   1. $\frac{1}{2} \div \frac{1}{3} =$ 2. $\frac{4}{5} \div \frac{8}{10} =$

o-2   3. $\frac{1}{5} \div 5 =$ 4. $\frac{7}{19} \div 14 =$

o-3   5. $9 \div \frac{1}{2} =$ 6. $15 \div \frac{1}{3} =$

o-4   7. $\frac{1}{6} \div 2\frac{2}{3} =$ 8. $\frac{5}{7} \div 4\frac{1}{3} =$

o-5   9. $3\frac{1}{5} \div \frac{2}{15} =$ 10. $1\frac{4}{16} \div \frac{3}{8} =$

o-6   11. $3\frac{2}{5} \div \frac{2}{15} =$ 12. $2\frac{1}{8} \div 9\frac{3}{4} =$

Math CBA, Fractions

Day 2

A. Write fractions for each of the following pictures. What portion is shaded?

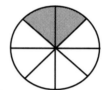

1. _____   2. _____   3. _____   4. _____

B. Reduce to lowest terms.

   1. $\frac{6}{9} =$ 2. $\frac{12}{18} =$ 3. $\frac{66}{80} =$ 4. $\frac{21}{35} =$

C. Change the following improper fractions to whole numbers or mixed numbers.

   1. $\frac{16}{10} =$ 2. $\frac{9}{5} =$ 3. $\frac{23}{5} =$ 4. $\frac{75}{8} =$

D. Simplify the following mixed numbers to their simplest form:

   1. $9\frac{3}{3} =$ 2. $8\frac{10}{5} =$ 3. $6\frac{14}{17} =$ 4. $5\frac{17}{7} =$

E. Change the following fractions to higher terms.

   1. $\frac{1}{9} = \frac{}{27}$ 2. $\frac{2}{5} = \frac{}{20}$ 3. $\frac{6}{8} = \frac{}{64}$ 4. $\frac{1}{3} = \frac{}{18}$

F. For each of the following sets of fractions, write the lowest common denominator.

   1. $\frac{1}{2}$ and $\frac{1}{5}$ _____   2. $\frac{4}{9}$ and $\frac{2}{3}$ _____   3. $\frac{2}{7}$ and $\frac{4}{21}$ _____   4. $\frac{2}{11}$ and $\frac{2}{3}$ _____

G. Change the following fractions so that they have the same denominators. An example is done for you.

Example: $\frac{2}{3} = \frac{16}{24}$

              $\frac{5}{8} = \frac{15}{24}$

   1. $\frac{2}{5} =$ 2. $\frac{1}{4} =$ 3. $\frac{1}{9} =$ 4. $\frac{2}{7} =$

        $\frac{1}{10} =$ $\frac{1}{12} =$ $\frac{1}{4} =$ $\frac{1}{5} =$

    _____   _____   _____   _____

    don't add   don't add   don't add   don't add

H.   Add the following fractions. Reduce your answer.

h-1   1. $\frac{1}{9}$ 2. $\frac{2}{5}$ 3. $\frac{4}{8}$ 4. $\frac{5}{7}$

   $+\frac{1}{9}$ $+\frac{2}{5}$ $+\frac{2}{8}$ $+\frac{6}{7}$

h-2   5. $\frac{1}{3}$ 6. $\frac{1}{3}$ 7. $\frac{8}{12}$ 8. $\frac{6}{49}$

   $+\frac{3}{6}$ $+\frac{3}{4}$ $+\frac{2}{3}$ $+\frac{4}{35}$

I.   Add the following mixed numbers. Reduce your answers.

i-1   1. $5\frac{1}{6}$ 2. $9\frac{4}{16}$ 3. $47\frac{5}{6}$ 4. $9\frac{1}{8}$

   $+2\frac{3}{6}$ $+6\frac{3}{16}$ $+18\frac{4}{6}$ $+6$

i-2   5. $19\frac{1}{4}$ 6. $4\frac{1}{4}$ 7. $18\frac{1}{5}$ 8. $26\frac{5}{7}$

   $+7\frac{3}{8}$ $+5\frac{3}{16}$ $+11\frac{2}{6}$ $+15\frac{4}{6}$

J.   Find the missing numbers.

   1. $4 = 3\frac{}{5}$ 2. $1\frac{2}{4} = \frac{}{4}$ 3. $1 = \frac{}{5}$ 4. $3\frac{4}{8} = 2\frac{}{8}$

K.   Subtract. Reduce your answer.

k-1   1. $\frac{2}{5}$ 2. $\frac{5}{9}$ 3. $\frac{16}{20}$ 4. $\frac{7}{14}$

   $-\frac{1}{5}$ $-\frac{2}{9}$ $-\frac{6}{20}$ $-\frac{2}{14}$

k-2   5. $\frac{5}{8}$ 6. $\frac{8}{12}$ 7. $\frac{10}{26}$ 8. $\frac{4}{5}$

   $-\frac{3}{4}$ $-\frac{1}{6}$ $-\frac{2}{18}$ $-\frac{2}{6}$

k-3a   9. 7 10. 5 11. 11 12. $8\frac{1}{9}$

   $-3\frac{1}{4}$ $-4\frac{1}{7}$ $-2\frac{5}{6}$ -3

k-3b 13. $11\frac{1}{8}$ 14. $4\frac{1}{6}$ 15. $19\frac{3}{7}$ 16. $45\frac{8}{15}$

       $-\ 3\frac{3}{8}$ $-2\frac{5}{6}$ $-11\frac{6}{7}$ $-40\frac{3}{15}$

k-4 17. $7\frac{1}{8}$ 18. $16\frac{2}{9}$ 19. $38\frac{5}{14}$ 20. $91\frac{7}{12}$

       $-5\frac{1}{4}$ $-\ 7\frac{4}{7}$ $-14\frac{11}{28}$ $-78\frac{3}{24}$

L.   Which is larger? Circle the larger fraction in each set.

    1. $\frac{1}{5}$ or $\frac{1}{4}$ 2. $\frac{9}{10}$ or $\frac{1}{10}$ 3. $\frac{2}{3}$ or $\frac{3}{6}$ 4. $\frac{6}{8}$ or $\frac{5}{7}$

M.   Change the following mixed numbers to improper fractions. An example has been done for you.

    Example: $1\frac{1}{2} = \frac{3}{2}$

    1. $5\frac{1}{6} =$ 2. $9\frac{1}{3} =$ 3. $7\frac{4}{5} =$ 4. $28\frac{3}{4} =$

N.   Multiply. Cancel when possible. Reduce your answers.

n-1   1. $\frac{1}{5} \times \frac{8}{9} =$ 2. $\frac{7}{15} \times \frac{5}{7} =$ 3. $\frac{9}{36} \times \frac{6}{27} =$ 4. $\frac{54}{72} \times \frac{16}{36} =$

n-2   5. $8 \times \frac{1}{4} =$ 6. $14 \times \frac{6}{7} =$ 7. $\frac{4}{13} \times 26 =$ 8. $\frac{6}{36} \times 24 =$

n-3   9. $4\frac{2}{10} \times \frac{5}{6} =$ 10. $4\frac{4}{7} \times \frac{7}{16} =$ 11. $\frac{9}{16} \times 1\frac{1}{3} =$ 12. $6\frac{3}{4} \times \frac{2}{3} =$

n-4   13. $5\frac{1}{3} \times 4\frac{1}{2} =$ 14. $2\frac{5}{8} \times 1\frac{5}{7} =$ 15. $1\frac{3}{4} \times 3\frac{1}{3} =$ 16. $4\frac{1}{8} \times 3\frac{13}{16} =$

O.   Divide. Cancel when possible.

o-1   1. $\frac{1}{3} \div \frac{1}{4} =$ 2. $\frac{2}{6} \div \frac{4}{9} =$

o-2   3. $\frac{1}{5} \div 7 =$ 4. $\frac{4}{9} \div 27 =$

o-3   5. $7 \div \frac{1}{3} =$ 6. $16 \div \frac{1}{4} =$

o-4   7. $\frac{1}{8} \div 3\frac{1}{5} =$ 8. $\frac{3}{11} \div 5\frac{1}{2} =$

o-5   9. $7\frac{1}{3} \div \frac{11}{12} =$ 10. $3\frac{2}{6} \div \frac{5}{12} =$

o-6   11. $5\frac{1}{3} \div 2\frac{4}{6} =$ 12. $2\frac{1}{10} \div 1\frac{2}{5} =$

Math CBA, Fractions

Day 3

A. Write fractions for each of the following pictures. What portion is shaded?

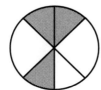

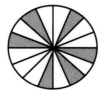

1. _____

2. _____

3. _____

4. _____

B. Reduce to lowest terms.

1. $\frac{6}{10}$ =   2. $\frac{16}{22}$ =   3. $\frac{46}{60}$ =   4. $\frac{32}{56}$ =

C. Change the following improper fractions to whole numbers or mixed numbers.

1. $\frac{14}{6}$ =   2. $\frac{8}{3}$ =   3. $\frac{15}{2}$ =   4. $\frac{57}{7}$ =

D. Simplify the following mixed numbers to their simplest form:

1. $5\frac{7}{7}$ =   2. $7\frac{16}{8}$ =   3. $3\frac{9}{18}$ =   4. $10\frac{21}{5}$ =

E. Change the following fractions to higher terms.

1. $\frac{1}{5} = \frac{}{15}$ 2. $\frac{2}{7} = \frac{}{24}$ 3. $\frac{7}{8} = \frac{}{56}$ 4. $\frac{1}{4} = \frac{}{16}$

F. For each of the following sets of fractions, write the lowest common denominator.

1. $\frac{1}{3}$ and $\frac{1}{4}$ _____   2. $\frac{1}{2}$ and $\frac{3}{8}$ _____   3. $\frac{2}{4}$ and $\frac{3}{24}$ _____   4. $\frac{4}{7}$ and $\frac{5}{6}$ _____

G. Change the following fractions so that they have the same denominators. An example is done for you.

Example: $\frac{2}{3} = \frac{16}{24}$

$\frac{5}{8} = \frac{15}{24}$

1. $\frac{1}{4}$ =   2. $\frac{2}{3}$ =   3. $\frac{1}{5}$ =   4. $\frac{2}{9}$ =

$\frac{3}{8}$ = $\frac{2}{9}$ = $\frac{1}{6}$ = $\frac{1}{6}$ =

don't add   don't add   don't add   don't add

H. Add the following fractions. Reduce your answer.

h-1 1. $\frac{1}{7}$ 2. $\frac{3}{16}$ 3. $\frac{5}{12}$ 4. $\frac{7}{9}$

  $+\frac{1}{7}$ $+\frac{2}{16}$ $+\frac{4}{12}$ $+\frac{3}{9}$

h-2 5. $\frac{1}{5}$ 6. $\frac{3}{5}$ 7. $\frac{9}{21}$ 8. $\frac{2}{15}$

  $+\frac{3}{10}$ $+\frac{1}{3}$ $+\frac{4}{7}$ $+\frac{6}{45}$

I. Add the following mixed numbers. Reduce your answers.

i-1 1. $4\frac{3}{8}$ 2. $6\frac{5}{19}$ 3. $32\frac{3}{4}$ 4. $13\frac{2}{3}$

  $+7\frac{3}{8}$ $+2\frac{1}{19}$ $+17\frac{3}{4}$ $+\ 4$

i-2 5. $14\frac{1}{2}$ 6. $9\frac{1}{3}$ 7. $21\frac{2}{3}$ 8. $17\frac{8}{9}$

  $+\ 3\frac{3}{4}$ $+2\frac{3}{12}$ $+18\frac{1}{2}$ $+45\frac{6}{7}$

J. Find the missing numbers.

  1. $9=8\frac{}{6}$ 2. $1\frac{3}{5}=\frac{}{5}$ 3. $1=\frac{}{9}$ 4. $7\frac{2}{6}=6\frac{}{6}$

K. Subtract. Reduce your answer.

k-1 1. $\frac{4}{7}$ 2. $\frac{6}{12}$ 3. $\frac{14}{18}$ 4. $\frac{8}{11}$

  $-\frac{1}{7}$ $-\frac{2}{12}$ $-\frac{5}{18}$ $-\frac{3}{11}$

k-2 5. $\frac{9}{10}$ 6. $\frac{8}{15}$ 7. $\frac{11}{21}$ 8. $\frac{7}{8}$

  $-\frac{2}{5}$ $-\frac{1}{5}$ $-\frac{2}{14}$ $-\frac{2}{10}$

k-3a 9. 9 10. 8 11. 14 12. $23\frac{1}{5}$

  $-2\frac{1}{5}$ $-7\frac{1}{6}$ $-\ 2\frac{4}{9}$ $-\ 2$

k-3b 13. $7\frac{1}{6}$ 14. $9\frac{1}{5}$ 15. $26\frac{4}{9}$ 16. $55\frac{9}{10}$

  $-4\frac{4}{6}$ $-4\frac{4}{5}$ $-17\frac{6}{9}$ $-52\frac{3}{10}$

k-4 17. $6\frac{1}{10}$ 18. $14\frac{2}{6}$ 19. $29\frac{8}{16}$ 20. $64\frac{6}{8}$

$\quad\quad\quad -3\frac{1}{5}$ $\quad -7\frac{4}{5}$ $\quad -12\frac{20}{32}$ $\quad -25\frac{2}{16}$

$\quad\quad\quad \overline{}$ $\quad \overline{}$ $\quad \overline{}$ $\quad \overline{}$

L. Which is larger? Circle the larger fraction in each set.

1. $\frac{1}{3}$ or $\frac{1}{5}$ 2. $\frac{6}{7}$ or $\frac{1}{7}$ 3. $\frac{5}{9}$ or $\frac{7}{18}$ 4. $\frac{7}{9}$ or $\frac{15}{27}$

M. Change the following mixed numbers to improper fractions. An example has been done for you.

Example: $1\frac{1}{2} = \frac{3}{2}$

1. $6\frac{1}{2} =$ 2. $4\frac{1}{8} =$ 3. $8\frac{5}{9} =$ 4. $26\frac{2}{6} =$

N. Multiply. Cancel when possible. Reduce your answers.

n-1 1. $\frac{1}{3} \times \frac{4}{5} =$ 2. $\frac{4}{6} \times \frac{5}{8} =$ 3. $\frac{8}{24} \times \frac{3}{4} =$ 4. $\frac{32}{81} \times \frac{27}{64} =$

n-2 5. $9 \times \frac{1}{2} =$ 6. $18 \times \frac{7}{9} =$ 7. $\frac{8}{12} \times 48 =$ 8. $\frac{7}{49} \times 21 =$

n-3 9. $6\frac{6}{8} \times \frac{4}{9} =$ 10. $7\frac{3}{6} \times \frac{6}{18} =$ 11. $\frac{5}{12} \times 2\frac{1}{4} =$ 12. $4\frac{5}{6} \times \frac{11}{16} =$

n-4 13. $2\frac{1}{3} \times 1\frac{1}{5} =$ 14. $2\frac{1}{6} \times 2\frac{2}{3} =$ 15. $3\frac{3}{4} \times 2\frac{7}{8} =$ 16. $2\frac{5}{6} \times 1\frac{1}{3} =$

O. Divide. Cancel when possible.

o-1 1. $\frac{1}{2} \div \frac{1}{5} =$ 2. $\frac{5}{8} \div \frac{10}{16} =$

o-2 3. $\frac{1}{9} \div 5 =$ 4. $\frac{8}{17} \div 16 =$

o-3 5. $11 \div \frac{1}{4} =$ 6. $18 \div \frac{1}{6} =$

o-4 7. $\frac{1}{7} \div 2\frac{1}{3} =$ 8. $\frac{5}{8} \div 4\frac{1}{6} =$

o-5 9. $4\frac{2}{3} \div \frac{7}{9} =$ 10. $6\frac{2}{5} \div \frac{8}{15} =$

o-6 11. $4\frac{1}{6} \div 2\frac{1}{12} =$ 12. $8\frac{1}{2} \div 2\frac{5}{6} =$

5

CBAs for Science

As in mathematics curricula, science curricula are based on a spiraling design, that is, different concepts are introduced and reintroduced again over time. This way students have opportunities to engage in more complicated and indepth investigations and understandings of basic science concepts as they progress in their schooling. Thus, science curricula are complex and multifaceted, presenting particular challenges to teachers interested in constructing science CBAs.

In this chapter are presentations of two different types of science CBAs. The first type of CBA takes a programmatic approach, where minimum goals and objectives have been determined for an entire fourth-grade science program. These objectives and goals reflect those competencies and skills that students meeting just the basic and minimal requirements would be expected to master. This type of CBA was designed to assist with students with special education needs who would have a curricular adaptation made in their program. This approach would be implemented with the understanding that only certain students with special needs would meet these minimal requirements and that this curricular modification would be described in the students' Individualized Education Program (IEP). Most students in such a science program would be expected to go well beyond the minimal requirements as exemplified in this sample CBA. This type of CBA actually serves well as a planning and monitoring instrument, as well as a means of assessing a student's entry-level skills. In most cases, this type of CBA would be used with students who have more moderate or

challenging learning needs, who are not likely to master the complete science program for a particular grade level.

The second type of CBA focuses on the student with more mild learning problems who, with some assistance in gaining skills in reading the textbook, could succeed in the complete science program. Thus, the science CBAs of this type, like the history and social studies CBAs presented in Chapter 3, are modeled after the reading CBAs presented in Chapter 1. The focus in these science CBAs is on assessing the student's skills in reading the science textbook itself.

Minimum Goals for a Grade 4 Science Program

The first science CBA presented in this chapter was prepared by collaborating teachers with a set of minimum objectives for a Grade 4 science curriculum. In the collaborative team, individual teachers were responsible for specific curricular goals at different grade levels. Classroom and consulting teachers at the Hinesburg Elementary School, Hinesburg, Vermont, worked with personnel from the University of Vermont Consulting Teacher Program to develop an alternative evaluation system based on the identification of minimum goals and objectives. Margaret Morse at the Hinesburg School took primary responsibility for the development of the CBA materials.

This resulting CBA can be used with various types of curricula—science, social studies, physical education, or spelling. The CBA has four components: (a) a delineation of the subareas of instruction for a curriculum, (b) a calendar of instructional activities for an academic year, (c) an analysis of the minimum objectives to be achieved by the students, and (d) an evaluation system.

Development of a Science CBA

In the development of a science CBA, three areas of instruction were identified: life science, earth science, and physical science. Subareas of instruction were then identified for each science area. The calendar of instructional activities covered the months of September through March. For each of the minimum objectives identified for each of the three science areas, the conditions under which the learning behavior would occur were specified or the behavior itself was defined, and the criteria for determining acceptable performance were established. Finally, a system of evaluation was developed for each of the science areas. The system included a minimum objective for each activity and a recording system for scoring the progress data for all students in the learning group. This evaluation system, based on the identification of minimum objectives, illustrates how goals and objectives are linked to the CBA.

Science instruction must be interpreted as a complete program, including math, language, and social studies. Elementary school children should be involved in the following two aspects of science learning:

1. Development of the scientific method, that is, the skills by which the student encounters and solves problems in all areas. This aspect is essential to the development of comprehension and computation by logical thinking.

2. Exposure to and interpretation of the disciplines of life science, earth science, and physical science. In today's world of science, awareness of and an ability to analyze in each of these areas is essential to an individual's development.

Curriculum Organization

Figure 5.1 shows the organization of a curriculum covering life science, earth science, and physical science. Each science is divided into the particular topics to be covered, and each topic is presented as a scientific question. This kind of organization allows the teachers to monitor each of the topics to be covered and also to focus on the primary target of instruction for each topic.

Testing and Instruction

Following the development of the science CBA, the students would be tested on each of the minimum objectives as they progress through the three subareas of instruction (life science, earth science, and physical science). Instruction would be offered in nonmastered areas. This would be followed by an evaluation to determine whether the appropriate skill had been mastered. In this procedure, the teacher should adhere to a test–teach–test paradigm.

Recordkeeping Systems

In the science CBA developed for this chapter, curricular progress was measured in various ways. A calendar of instructional activities was kept by the classroom teacher. The calendar was organized to document for each science the topics to be covered and the distribution of the topics over the school year (see Figure 5.2). An evaluation checklist was used for each student (see Figure 5.3). The checklist listed the CBA skills to be evaluated and provided space for marking off the time periods (November, January, March, and May) by which a student might be expected to master the skills.

Sample Science CBA

The sample science CBA presented in this section is organized in terms of the three sciences (life, earth, and physical), with a set of minimum objectives for each science. The objectives are organized by condition, behavior, and performance criteria. Following the listing of the objectives for each science, a system of evaluation is presented, which presents the minimum objective(s) and suggested procedures for measuring student mastery of them.

A—Grade 4		
Life Science	**Earth Science**	**Physical Science**
Pond Life	**Earth Materials and Interior**	**Microscope**
	Sizes, from planet to atom:	*Magnifying with a water drop:*
What do you think is in a pond?	How big and how small can you imagine?	What does a lens do?
Algae:	*Investigating rocks and minerals:*	*Types of microscopes:*
What makes the water green?	What are rocks made of?	Why do we have different types of microscopes?
Water insects:	*Elements in minerals:*	*Looking at pond water:*
Do insects live in the water?	What is an element?	What can you see with the microscope?
Protozoa:	*Atoms and molecules:*	*How to measure microorganisms:*
What are protozoa?	What is H_2O? What is H_2SO_4?	How long is a protozoan?
Regeneration of planaria:	*Conditions for formation:*	
Are planaria peculiar?	Could you make a rock?	Living or nonliving?
Plants:	*Volcanoes:*	
Can plants live under water?	Do you ever blow your top?	What is a cell?
Interrelations:	*Vermont rocks and minerals:*	*Larger organisms:*
Whose home is the pond?	What is Vermont marble?	How many segments are there in a grasshopper's leg?
	Elements in the atmosphere and hydrosphere:	*Stains:*
	What is a cycle?	Can you distinguish the cell's nucleus?
Field trip:		
Lake Iroquois		*(continues)*

Figure 5.1. Organization of a science curriculum.

B—Grade 4		
Life Science	**Earth Science**	**Physical Science**
What Makes Us Tick	**Mountain Buildup and Breakdown**	**Photography**
Skin: How does our skin protect us?	*The globe:* Where are the mountains?	*The camera:* How does the camera work?
Skeleton, muscles: What is your body framework?	*Heights, age of mountains:* How old are the Appalachians?	*Taking a picture:* What do you need to take a picture?
Digestion: Where does your food go after you close your mouth?	*Folding and faulting:* Does the earth move?	*Developing:* Will your picture come out?
Circulation: Do you have good circulation?	How is a mountain built?	*A new look at nature:* Have you photographed something from a new angle?
Lymphatic diseases: How does your body fight disease?	*Igneous rocks, the rock cycle:* What is the rock cycle?	*Sports and photography:* Can you capture the action?
Nervous: Why do we respond?	*Erosion and deposits:* What happens to eroded rocks?	*Close-up photography:* How do you take close-ups?
Sense organs: Have you any sense? Organs?	*Fossils:* Where do you find fossils?	*Patterns:* Can you photograph a pattern you see?
	Prehistoric life: Why did dinosaurs become extinct?	*Shadows:* Can you photograph a shadow?
Field trip: Health center		

C—Grade 4		
Life Science	**Earth Science**	**Physical Science**
Animal Adaptation	**Stars and Stargazing**	**Electricity**
Movement: Do all animals move?	*Stars:* What is a star?	*Simple circuit:* Can you light a bulb with a battery, bulb, and one wire?
Getting food: How do different animals get their food?	*Using a telescope:* What can you see with a telescope?	What's inside a bulb?
Breathing: Do we breathe like fish?	*The sun:* How far is the sun?	What is a battery?
Reproducing: Do all animals lay eggs?	*Life history of a star:* Will a star eventually burn out?	*Using more than one bulb, series, parallel:* Can you light more than one bulb?
		(continues)

Figure 5.1. *Continued*

Senses:	*Star pictures, constellations:*	*Symbols:*
How do we perceive the environment?	Where is the Big Bear?	What is a symbol?
Homes:	*The galaxy—parts, particles:*	*Mystery boxes:*
How are we adapted to our environment?	How many stars are there in the sky?	Can you figure out how the box is wired?
Communication:	What are stars made of?	*Conductors and insulators:*
Have you talked with a friend today?		What is a conductor?
	Theories of origin:	*Wires, thick and thin:*
	How did the universe begin?	Does the thickness make a difference?
Field trip:		
Looking for tracks		

D—Grade 4		
Life Science	**Earth Science**	**Physical Science**
Nature Trail	**Chemical Energy**	**Magnetism**
Types of trees:	*Chemicals in rocks:*	*Experimenting with magnets:*
What types of trees are in the school yard?	Are there chemicals in rocks?	What does a magnet attract?
Drawing and labeling:	*Investigating fire:*	*The compass:*
Can you draw and label a plant?	What is fire?	Why does the compass point north?
	Distillation of wood:	*Making a magnet with electricity:*
What is in the stream?	Can you break down wood chemically?	How can you make an electromagnet?
Pond ecology:	*Chemistry of a star:*	*Varying the coil:*
What lives in a pond?	What elements are in a star?	Does the number of coils make a difference in the strength of the magnet?
Forest ecology:	*Chemical changes:*	*Making a buzzer:*
What lives in the forest?	What happens in a chemical change?	Can you make a buzzer?
Field ecology:	*Chemical compounds, atoms and molecules:*	*Making a motor:*
What lives in the field?	What is a molecule?	Can you make a motor?
Insects:	*Interrelations of energy forms:*	*Making a meter:*
How many kinds of insects live around the school?	Does energy change?	How can you make a meter to measure your motor?
Field trip:		
Mt. Mansfield Nature Center		

Figure 5.1. *Continued*

Calendar of Instructional Activities Week of _____ Unit _____ Grade 4			
September	November	January	March
Life Science Pond Life (1)	What Makes Us Tick?	Animal Adaptation	Nature Trail Classification
Earth Science The Earth Materials & Interior	Mountain Building	Stars & Star Gazing & Breakdown	Chemical Energy
Physical Science Microscope	Photography	Electricity	Magnetism

Figure 5.2. Calendar form for measuring curricular progress in a science CBA.

Evaluation Checklist—Grade 4

Student _____

(Mark ✔ when ready / + if successful completion
→ if needs re-evaluation)

Skills To Be Evaluated	Dates			
	Nov.	Jan.	Mar.	May
Physical science:				
1. Observe and identify specimens				
2.. Draw microorganisms				
3. Answer questions about light and lenses				
4. Experiment with circuits				
5. Set up an experiment and describe the energy transformation				
6. Sequence objects				
7. Experiment for cause and effect				
8. Record results				
Earth science:				
1. Make predictions				
2. Record changes				
3. Describe using models				
4. Record effects caused by rate of change				
5. Interpret results from experimentation				
6. Estimate numbers and sizes				
7. Discuss library book				
8. Use 30 vocabulary words				
Life science:				
1. Classify organisms in environments				
2. Describe interdependence				
3. Hypothesize				
4. Answer questions about relation of structure and function				
5. Answer questions about adaptation				
6. Analyze size and types of populations				
7. Discuss library book				
8. Use 30 vocabulary words				

Figure 5.3. Checklist for evaluating skills in a science CBA.

Science CBA
Life Science Minimum Objectives

Grade 4

Condition	*Behavior*	*Criteria*
1. Given representatives of different ecological communities,	the student will classify the types of organisms and the types of environments...	with 80% accuracy.
2. Given a biological environment in the classroom,	the student will recognize and describe the interdependence of the organisms with their environment...	with 80% accuracy.
3. Given problems concerning the environment,	the student will hypothesize...	about three out of five possible solutions to the problems.
4. Given information about organisms and the environment,	the student will observe, read about, and answer questions orally or in written form about the relation of structure to function in eight out of ten organisms...	with 80% accuracy.
5. Given information about organisms and their environment,	the student will answer questions of deduction about the relation between structure and function as a causative factor in its adaptation to its environment...	with 80% accuracy.
6. Given organisms in the classroom and on school grounds,	the student will analyze quantitatively the size and type of population within the immediate environment...	with 80% accuracy.
7. Given a life science unit,	the student will read and discuss...	at least three major points from a library book related to the unit.
8. Given a life science unit,	the student will recognize and use in description at least 30 new operational vocabulary words...	with 95% accuracy.

Note. From "Minimum Objectives for Fourth-Grade Science" by M. Morse, Hinesburg, VT: Hinesburg Elementary School.

Systems of Evaluation
Life Science

Grade 4

1. Given representatives of different ecological communities, the student will classify the types of organisms and the types of environments with 80% accuracy.

Group the following organisms into their common habitat:

Habitats	Organisms
A. Pond	adult salamander
B. Field	grasshopper
C. Forest	dandelions
D. Sea	swordfish
E. Village	whale
	waterstrider
	algae
	dog
	people
	chipmunk

2. Given a biological environment in the classroom, the student will recognize and describe the interdependence of the organisms with the environment with 80% accuracy, as judged by the teacher.

Suggested oral questions:

1. How does the (organism) get food in its natural surroundings?
2. Can you think of any factors in the environment that could keep the (organism) from reproducing?
3. How does the (organism) get water?
4. How does the (organism) respond to various stimuli (choose one or two stimuli)?
5. How is the (organism) adapted to moving in its environment?

3. Given problems concerning the environment, the student will hypothesize about three out of five possible solutions to the problems.

Tape discussion of major environmental problems:

A. Litter
B. Sewage disposal

C. Water pollution

D. Air pollution

E. Soil conservation

F. Forest conservation

G. Conservation vs. recreation

H. Population

The student can hypothesize on the reverse side of the tape or on paper.

4. Given information about organisms and the environment, the student will read about and observe the relation of structure to function in eight out of ten parts.

Relate the proper part to the function it accomplishes in a diagram of the organ or organism:

Functions to consider:

Water to cells

Food to cells

Getting rid of waste

Reproduction

Responsiveness to environment

Breathing

Movement (cellulose and organism)

Possible diagrams:

Human body

Crayfish

Insect

Single-celled organism

Plant

Tree

5. Given information about organisms and their environment, the student will deduce the relation between structure and function as a causative factor in its adaptation to its environment.

Suggested procedure (oral evaluation):

Discuss the organism studied in terms of its adaptations:

Why is the (organism) adapted in its (special way) for each (life activity, function)?

food and water

reproduction

responsiveness

getting rid of water

For example, why do you think the woodpecker has its particular type of beak?

6. Given organisms in the classroom and on school grounds, the student will analyze quantitatively the size and type of population in the immediate environment with 80% accuracy.

Using an ant farm, fruit fly jar, terrarium, or sample square plot in the school yard, count and record the number of organisms of a specific type. Record all other observations made at the time. Do this at two different times.

Organism: _____

Number: _____

Date: _____

Other Observations:

Do you think this is a large population at this time? _____

How do the numbers of this population compare with the numbers of other organisms with which you are familiar? _____

_____

7. Given a life science unit, the student will read and discuss at least three major points from a library book related to the unit.

Oral evaluation:

8. Given a life science unit, the student will recognize and use in description at least 30 new operational vocabulary words with 95% accuracy.

The students will keep notebooks in which they can put new words as they are presented.

Earth Science Minimum Objectives

Grade 4

Condition	Behavior	Criteria
1. Given data on changes in earth science,	the student will make predictions based on past evidence...	with 80% accuracy.
2. Given demonstrations of physical changes in earth science,	the student will record at least four out of five changes...	with 80% accuracy.
3. Given materials and models in the classroom,	the student will describe and illustrate (using models) the movements of the actual material...	with 80% accuracy.
4. Given exploration of materials and experiments with changes,	the student will recognize and record...	four out of five different effects caused by the rate of change (e.g., crystallization).
5. Given experiments on energy forms,	the student will interpret verbally the interrelationship between matter and energy...	in two instances with 80% accuracy.
6. Given the dimensions of astronomical bodies,	the student will estimate numbers and sizes and consequently accept the idea of approximation...	as judged close enough by the teacher.
7. Given a unit in earth science,	the student will read and discuss...	at least three major points of a library book on the subject.
8. Given a unit in earth science,	the student will recognize and use in description...	30 new vocabulary words with 95% accuracy.

Systems of Evaluation
Earth Science

Grade 4

---

1. Given data on changes in earth science, the student will make predictions based on past evidence with 80% accuracy.

   Examples: Predict what will happen on the basis of the following evidence:

   Meteorologic data:

   1. There have been tornadoes in June in Texas every year in the period 1960–1970. What do you expect to happen in the next 10 years?
   2. The average annual precipitation in Vermont is _____. How much precipitation do you expect next year on the average?

   Astronomical data:

   3. The new moon appeared on: Jan. 12, 1950; Jan. 14, 1951; Jan. 17, 1952; Jan 19, 1953; Jan. 21, 1954. When would you expect a new moon in Jan. 1956?

2. Given demonstrations of physical changes in earth science, the student will record four out of five changes with 80% accuracy.

   Student chooses five demonstrations from the following:

   A. Experiment: Heating sulfur and iron

   B. Experiment: Heating sugar to get carbon

   C. Model: Faulting and folding

   D. Demonstration: Electrolysis of water

   E. Diagram: Inside of volcano

   F. Sedimentary rocks and fossils

   G. Spectroscope: Observation

   H. Telescopic observation of astronomical movements

   I.   Distillation of wood

   J. Breaking up compounds (e.g., apple)

3. Given materials and models in the classroom, the student will describe and illustrate (using models) the movements of the actual material with 80% accuracy.

Observation by teacher:

Check List:

Student_____

Materials Used	Described Movements
rocks	
sand	
models	
volcano	
fault	
fold	
the globe	
diagrams	
fossils	
telescope	
experiments	

4. Given exploration of materials and experiments with changes, the student will recognize four out of five different effects caused by the rate of change (e.g., crystallization).

How does the rate of change differ in an experiment?

Experiment	Condition	Rate of Change
1. Crystallization	hot	
	cold	
2. Pendulums	long	
	short	
3. Burning	open	
	closed	
4. Erosion	wind	
	no wind	
5. Electrolysis	catalyzed	
	not catalyzed	
6. Pendulums	heavy	
	light	

    7. Crystallization   seeded

                                    not seeded

    8. Burning   paper

                                    wood

5. Given experiments on energy, the student will interpret the interrelationship between matter and energy in two instances with 80% accuracy.

After doing at least two experiments, the student will draw conclusions, orally or on paper:

Matter	Energy	Possible Activities
Sun	Light	Fire
Stars	Heat	Distillation of wood
Bombs	Sound	Chemical Changes
Chemicals		Chemical compounds
Electricity		Rocks and minerals
Machines		Igneous rocks
		What is a star?
		The sun
		What are stars made of?

How can you relate the production of energy to the matter you are working with?

6. Given the dimensions of astronomical bodies, the student will estimate numbers and sizes and consequently accept the idea of approximation as judged close enough by the teacher.

                                                      How did you make your estimate?

1. How many peas are in the jar?   _____

2. How many stars are in the sky?   _____

3. How many stars are in a galaxy?   _____

4. How big is the moon?   _____

5. How big is the sun?   _____

7. Given a unit in earth science, the student will read and discuss at least three major points of a library book on the subject.

Oral evaluation:

8. Given a unit in earth science, the student will recognize and use in description 30 new operational vocabulary words with 95% accuracy.

Physical Science Minimum Objectives   Grade 4

Condition	Behavior	Criteria
1. Given lenses and several different types of microscopes,	the student will observe and identify...	five specimens with 80% accuracy.
2. Given microslides,	the student will draw one structure...	with two out of four functioning parts, accurately.
3. Given lenses, microscopes, cameras, and diagrams,	the student will answer questions of deduction about the relations of the lens to the bending of light rays in producing an image...	with 80% accuracy.
4. Given electrical materials,	the student will experiment to the point of discovery that a complete circuit requires a circle of conductors...	with 100% accuracy.
5. Given materials on electricity and magnetism,	the student will set up and describe the use of one energy form...	in two common problems.
6. Given a physical science unit,	the student will sequence ten objects in order of size and one other criterion of the student's own choosing...	with 100% accuracy.
7. Given a physical science unit,	the student will experiment to find the answer to three questions of cause and effect...	with 100% accuracy.
8. Given a physical science unit,	the student will record by tape, paper, or manipulative materials the results from exploration. . .	at least 80% of the time.

Systems of Evaluation
Physical Science

Grade 4

1. Given lenses and several different types of microscopes, the student will observe and identify five specimens with 80% accuracy.

   Student: *Specimens (check if completed successfully):*

   _____   _____   _____

   _____   _____   _____

   _____   _____   _____

   _____   _____   _____

   _____   _____   _____

2. Given microslides, the student will draw one structure with two out of four functioning parts, accurately.

   Student will diagram in notebook.

   Teacher checks when completed.

   Student: *Successfully Completed:*

   _____   _____

   _____   _____

   _____   _____

   _____   _____

   _____   _____

   _____   _____

   _____   _____

   _____   _____

3. Given lenses, microscopes, cameras, and diagrams, the student will deduce the relation of the lens to the bending of light rays in producing an image with 80% accuracy.

   Given a diagram the student will draw light rays through a lens from a light source.

   1.

   2.

   3.

   4. Do you need light to produce an image through a lens?

   5. What would you do to increase magnification?

4. Given electrical materials, the student will experiment to the point of discovery that a complete circuit requires a circle of conductors with 100% accuracy.

   Students will record results of experimentation in notebook.

Student:	*Date Completed:*
_____	_____
_____	_____
_____	_____
_____	_____
_____	_____
_____	_____

5. Given materials on electricity and magnetism, the student will set up and describe the use of one energy form in two common problems.

   Question: On the basis of your experiment, how is it related to our common problems?

Oral evaluation:

Student:	Experiment:	Description: one energy form in two common problems:

6. Given a physical science unit, the student will sequence ten objects in order of size and one other criterion of the student's own choosing with 100% accuracy.

   Check if completed successfully.

Student:	Chosen Criterion:	Sequencing Size:
_____	_____	_____
	_____	_____
	_____	_____
	_____	_____
	_____	_____
	_____	_____
	_____	_____
	_____	_____
	_____	_____
	_____	_____

7. Given a physical science unit, the student will experiment to find the answers to three questions of cause and effect with 100% accuracy.

   Teacher observation of student's experiment
   (check if experiment answers questions of cause and effect):

   Experiment:

   Does the student answer questions of cause and effect?_____

8. Given a physical science unit, the student will record by tape, paper, or manipulative materials the results from exploration at least 80% of the time.

Experiment:	Type of Record:
Example: Heating sugar	written

Sample CBAs for Science Textbooks

In this section are sample CBAs from two science textbooks from two different grade levels: (a) a fourth-grade science textbook and (b) a tenth-grade physical science textbook. In both sample sets, the CBA contains nine passages—one for each of three days for oral reading, silent reading, and listening comprehension. The formatting is identical to that used for the social studies and history CBAs in Chapter 3 and the reading CBAs in Chapter 1.

The intent of these textbook-based CBAs is to determine how well the student can actually read the textbook itself. It is important to recognize that even though the formatting is identical, the types of demands made by the textbook itself are quite different and more complex than those demands placed on a reader of literature.

The text of science books is usually comprised of a series of short sections, earmarked by titles, subtitles, and section headings. Most pages in the science book have figures, graphs, drawings, and illustrations. In the sample CBAs in this section, the comprehension questions have been derived solely from the text itself to circumvent publishing reproduction problems. However, in actuality, teachers might write some of the comprehension questions to address the content of the various illustrations rather than the text itself. Another aspect of science textbooks that makes them more challenging to the reader is that they contain a tremendous number of new vocabulary words. These words are usually typed in boldface type (and appear that way here on the sample CBAs) and reflect not only new vocabulary but also major concepts that are being introduced within the text.

In addition to asking the comprehension questions orally, the teacher could request written responses. The questions could be read to the student, but the student might be required to write his or her responses. Or, the student might read the questions silently and write the appropriate responses. The procedure for this is described more precisely in the introductory section of Chapter 3. Also in Chapter 3, it is suggested that some students might be asked to write a summary of the passage, as well as or instead of responding to the comprehension questions.

Another way to check the student's overall understanding of the passage is for the student to draw a diagram or illustration of the concept being described in the text. This type of probe is particularly useful for discerning if some students really do have sound understanding but are suppressed by their difficulty with choosing the right words to describe their understandings.

Physical Science (p. 69)

Oral Passage

➜   The changes that take place in a maple tree are a type of adaptation. How do these changes help the tree to survive? Maple trees are like most other types of green plants. Maple trees take in water from the ground through their roots. They lose water through their leaves.

    If maple trees kept their leaves during the winter, they would lose water through their leaves. But in most places where maple trees grow, water in the ground freezes during the winter. So the maple trees would not be able to replace the water they lost. Without water, the trees/$_{100}$ would soon die.]

Comprehension Questions

(TE)   1. How do maple trees lose water?
          (through their leaves)

(TI)   2. Why is it good that maple trees lose their leaves in the fall?
          (They will retain water through the winter months.)

(TI)   3. Why can't maple trees get water in the winter?
          (The ground freezes.)

(TE)   4. What do you call the changes that take place in a maple tree?
          (a type of adaptation)

(SI)   5. Can you think of another type of adaptation that occurs in nature?
          (Trees grow leaves in the spring; rabbits' fur turns white in the winter; or some similar answer.)

(SI)   6. Why do leaves appear on the maple tree in the spring?
          (The trees can now take in water through their roots.)

Note. This passage and the two that follow are from *Physical Science* by Silver Burdett, 1985, 1990, New York: Author.

Physical Science (p. 59)

Oral Passage

→   As you know, plants and animals live close to one another. All the plants and animals in an area make up a **community**. A **food web** shows how all the animals in a community get their energy.

A food web can be thought of as being like a spider web. All the threads of a spider web are connected to each other. All the living things in a food web are also connected to each other.

Study the drawing of the food web. Look at the hawk. As you can see, hawks eat snakes, mice, and rabbits in this food/$_{100}$ web. Look at the mouse. Mice eat insects and green plants in this food web. What do bears eat in this food web?]

Comprehension Questions

(TE)   1. What is a food web?
        (It shows how all the animals in a community get their energy.)

(TE)   2. What do all the plants and animals in an area make up?
        (a community)

(TI)   3. In this passage, what is converted into energy?
        (food)

(TI)   4. How are spider webs and food webs alike? How are they different?
        (They both have connecting threads. A spider web connects threads and a food web connects animals.)

(SI)   5. The passage says plants and animals live close to one another. Where do they often live?
        (woods, fields, etc.)

(SI)   6. What do you think would happen if *part* of the food web disappeared?
        (Some of the animals would begin to starve.)

Physical Science (p. 48)

Oral Passage

➔   Have you ever tried to work or play when you have not had enough to eat? You get tired easily when you have not eaten enough food. You need food to give you energy.

All living things need energy. Living things need energy to move and grow. Living things die if they do not get enough energy.

Where do green plants get their energy? Like other living things, green plants get energy from food. But green plants are different from other living things. Green plants can produce, or make, their own food. Green plants use sunlight, water, and air / $_{100}$ to produce food in their leaves. Plants store some of this food in their roots, stems, and leaves. Because plants produce their own food, they are often called **producers**.]

Comprehension Questions

(TI)   1. Why do you eat food?
         (for energy)

(TI)   2. What would happen if you didn't eat enough food?
         (die or too tired to work or play)

(TE)   3. Where do green plants get energy?
         (from food)

(TE)   4. What do green plants use to make food?
         (sunlight, water, and air)

(SI)   5. Where do plants get the water to make food?
         (It rains, this is often collected in the ground, and the roots pick it up and take it into the plant.)

(SI)   6. What do you think would happen if there was an eclipse? Explain.
         (Plants wouldn't be able to produce food and they would die.)

Physical Science (p. 588)

Oral Passages

→   Most of the energy you use every day comes from **fossil fuels.** Fossil fuels formed hundreds of millions of years ago when layers of dead plants and animals were buried beneath sediments such as mud, sand, silt, or clay. Over millions of years, heat and great pressure changed the sediments into rocks and the plant and animal remains into fossil fuels. **The three main fossil fuels are coal, oil, and natural gas.**

The reason fossil fuels are so useful as energy sources is due to their chemical makeup. Fossil fuels are rich in **hydrocarbons.** Hydrocarbons are substances that contain the/$_{100}$ elements hydrogen and carbon.]

Comprehension Questions

(TE)   1. What is the source of most energy?
        (fossil fuels)

(TE)   2. What are the three main fossil fuels?
        (coal, oil, natural gas)

(TI)   3. What does chemical makeup mean?
        (the chemicals that are in something)

(TI)   4. Explain how fossil fuels are formed.
        (layers of dead plants and animals buried beneath sediments; pressures changed sediments into rock; plants and animals changed into fossil fuels)

(SI)   5. Where would the sediments (mud, silt, sand, and clay) come from?
        (rain and wind action)

(SI)   6. What other kinds of fossils are there?
        (shells, bones, dinosaurs—any buried animal life)

Note. This passage and the eight that follow are from *Prentice-Hall Physical Science* by Prentice-Hall, 1988, 1997, Englewood Cliffs, NJ: Author.

Physical Science (p. 588)

Silent Passage

→ Coal

Coal is a solid fossil fuel. There are four types of coal, each of which represents a different stage in the development of coal. Each can be used as a fuel.

The first type of coal is **peat.** Peat is a soft substance made of decayed plant fibers. When peat undergoes pressure from rocks piled above it, it is converted into **lignite.** Lignite, the second type of coal, is soft and has a woody texture.

If even more pressure is applied to lignite, it turns into bituminous coal. Bituminous coal, the third type of coal, is often called soft/$_{100}$ coal. Bituminous coal is the most plentiful type of coal on the earth. It takes tremendous pressure to change bituminous coal into anthracite, the fourth type of coal. Anthracite is very hard and brittle. Few deposits of anthracite are located in the United States.]

Comprehension Questions

(TE) 1. How many types of coal are there?
          (four)

(TE) 2. What is the first stage or type of coal?
          (peat)

(TI) 3. What causes the different stages or types of coal?
          (pressure)

(TI) 4. What is coal made from?
          (decayed plant fibers)

(SI) 5. What will cause the development of the fourth stage of coal?
          (more pressure)

(SI) 6. Which types of coal would be best to heat a house? Why?
          (lignite, because it's like wood, or bituminous coal, because it's plentiful)

Physical Science (p. 589)

Listening Passage

→   **Oil and Natural Gas**

Unlike coal, the plants and animals from which oil and natural gas formed probably lived in the earth's oceans. When they died, they sank to the ocean floor and were covered by sediments. In time, the layers of sediments changed into sandstone, limestone, or shale. Pressure from these rock layers, in addition to great heat and the action of certain bacteria, changed the plant and animal remains into oil and natural gas.

Rocks such as sandstone and limestone have tiny pores through which oil and gas can seep. When oil and natural gas were first formed, /₁₀₀ they probably seeped through the sandstone and limestone layers. In time, the oil and gas that were covered by harder rocks through which they could not seep formed pools. The oil and gas became trapped in natural "pockets" under the harder rocks.

Oil that is drilled from beneath the earth is called crude oil, or petroleum. Some of the fuels that can be obtained from petroleum are gasoline, kerosene, heating oil, and jet fuels.]

Comprehension Questions

(TE)   1. Where did the plants and animals live from which oil and natural gas were formed?
(oceans)

(TE)   2. These plant and animal remains were changed into oil and natural gas by three forces. One was pressure. Name the other two.
(heat, and action of certain bacteria)

(TI)   3. Are all oil and gas deposits found under only one kind of rock? Explain.
(No, it depends on the types of sediments deposited.)

(TI)   4. How could people locate where oil or gas might be found?
(by types of rock found there)

(SI)   5. What is meant by certain rocks having "pores"?
(They have small open spaces in them.)

(SI)   6. What kinds of things can seep?
(liquids)

Physical Science (p. 591)

Oral Passage

→   Life on earth could not exist without the energy given off by the sun. Without this solar energy, plants would not grow, rain would not fall, and wind would not blow. Planet Earth would be so cold and dark that nothing could survive.

Scientists estimate that the amount of solar energy falling on a 200-square-kilometer plot near the equator is enough to meet the world's energy needs! As you can see, tapping this solar energy certainly would help conserve fossil fuels. Solar energy can be used directly from the sun or indirectly, such as using wind or water/$_{100}$ power to produce usable energy.]

Comprehension Questions

(TE)   1. What could not exist without the energy given off by the sun?
(life on earth)

(TE)   2. What would happen to planet Earth if solar energy didn't exist?
(cold and dark)

(TI)   3. Explain the direct and indirect ways that solar energy can be used.
(from sun/from wind and water)

(TI)   4. What does it mean when it says that the amount of solar energy falling on a 200-square-kilometer plot near the equator is enough to meet the world's energy needs?
(A relatively small amount of area has enough solar energy to meet the needs of the whole world.)

(SI)   5. What does conserve mean?
(saving, using resources carefully or wisely)

(SI)   6. How does using solar energy help people conserve?
(don't have to use so many fossil fuels)

Physical Science (p. 591–592)

Silent Passage

➜ **DIRECT SOLAR ENERGY**   Direct solar energy means taking energy straight from the sun and using it. The main problem with direct solar energy is that it is difficult to collect, convert, concentrate, and store.

   PASSIVE SOLAR ENERGY   Direct solar energy can be either passive or active. An example of passive use would be positioning windows in a house so that the amount of sunlight absorbed would be enough to heat the house. The obvious problem with passive solar energy for home heating is that when the sun stops shining, the source of heat is removed.

   ACTIVE SOLAR ENERGY   Active solar/$_{100}$ energy involves collecting the sun's energy in a device called a **solar collector.** In a typical solar collector, a large, dark surface covered with glass or plastic absorbs energy from the sun. Water is actively pumped through pipes or a large, flat surface inside the collector. The water is warmed by the sun's energy. The warm water is then stored to provide heat and hot water for some future time. What advantage does active solar heating have over passive solar heating?

   Although the use of passive and active solar heating has been successful in many homes, it has not gone far to meet the energy needs of society as a whole. In order to provide energy for offices, schools, factories, hospitals, and apartment complexes, some type of central solar power plant must be designed.]

Comprehension Questions

(TE)   1. What is the meaning of direct solar energy?
         (taking energy straight from the sun and using it)

(TE)   2. What are the two kinds of direct solar energy?
         (passive and active)

(TI)   3. Imagine a picture of solar collectors on a school. Are they an example of direct or indirect use of solar energy?
         (direct)

(TI)   4. How does active solar energy differ from passive solar energy?
         (Water inside the collector is warmed by the sun, collector takes energy from the sun.)

(SI)   5. What advantage does active solar heating have over passive solar heating?
         (Heat can be stored in the form of warm water.)

(SI)   6. If you want to use passive solar energy in your home would you open or close the curtains during sunlight hours? Why?
         (open—so more sunlight could come in)

Day 2
Grade 10

Physical Science (pp. 592–593)

Listening Passage

→ **SOLAR CELLS**   A solar cell, or **photovoltaic cell,** is a device that converts sunlight directly into electricity. Most solar cells are "sandwiches" of very thin layers of silicon and metal. When sunlight strikes the surface of this sandwich, electrons flow across the layers. This flow of electrons is electric current, which can be used to do work. Unfortunately, the amount of electricity produced by a single solar cell is very small. Huge numbers of cells are needed to produce useful amounts of electricity.

Solar cells were first used on a large scale in/$_{100}$ 1959 to generate electricity aboard the United States space vehicle *Vanguard I.* Since then, they have been used to generate electricity on most spacecraft. Can you think of a reason why solar cells would be especially effective in space?

One disadvantage of solar cells has been their cost. In 1959, electricity from solar cells cost about $500 per watt. Now it is down to $6 per watt. Although the efficiency of solar cells has been greatly improved, energy experts say that the cost will have to be lowered to $1 per watt in order to compete with the cost of electricity obtained from fossil fuels.]

Comprehension Questions

(TE)   1. What is another name for photovoltaic cell?
            (solar cell)

(TE)   2. Where were solar cells first used?
            (on space vehicle)

(TI)   3. Why are solar cells called "sandwiches"?
            (have layers of different materials)

(TI)   4. Why are huge numbers of solar cells needed to be useful?
            (One cell produces very little electricity.)

(SI)   5. Why are solar cells especially useful in space?
            (more sunlight there)

(SI)   6. Why has the cost of electricity from solar cells decreased?
            (Efficiency has been improved.)

Physical Science (p. 497)

Oral Passage

➔ **Waves Through a Medium**

A **medium** is any substance or region through which a wave is transmitted. Water is a medium for ocean waves. Air is a medium for sound waves. All phases of matter can act as a medium. For certain waves, a medium of matter is not required. These waves can be transmitted through a vacuum. Light is such a wave. Light from the sun, for example, travels to the earth through the vacuum of space.

A medium transfers wave energy but has no overall motion itself. The particles of the medium vibrate, or move, in small circles./$_{100}$ The energy is transmitted from one place to another. But there is no movement of matter between these places. In other words, energy is transmitted *without* the movement of the medium as a whole.]

Comprehension Questions

(TE)   1. What is a medium?
(any substance, matter)

(TE)   2. Tell two substances that are mediums.
(air, water)

(TI)   3. Some waves don't need a medium; instead, how are they transmitted?
(through a vacuum)

(TI)   4. How does light travel from the sun to the earth?
(through space, a vacuum)

(SI)   5. In your own words, explain how a medium transfers energy.

(SI)   6. Give another example of waves moving with the medium remaining stationary or relatively still.
(object floating on the waves)

Physical Science (p. 497)

Silent Passage

➜ If you ever watched an object floating on water, you will understand wave motion and the transfer of energy. As the waves move past the object, the object bobs up and down. The waves continue to move forward, but the object remains in approximately the same place. Energy is transmitted, but matter is not.

Two properties of a medium affect the speed of the wave. One property is density. A wave moves more slowly in a denser medium. As the density of the medium increases, the speed of a wave decreases. Why? A denser medium has more inertia to overcome. It is harder to get/$_{100}$ the particles of a denser medium to respond to the energy of the wave and to start moving.]

Comprehension Questions

(TE)   1. What happens to a floating object when waves move past it?
(It bobs up and down.)

(TE)   2. What do the waves do?
(move forward)

(TI)   3. How is the energy transmitted?
(by moving waves)

(SI)   4. Why does a wave of energy move more slowly in a denser medium?
(Denser medium has more inertia to overcome.)

(TI)   5. What is density?
(thicker; more molecules)

(SI)   6. What is inertia?
(the tendency for matter to remain at rest)

Physical Science (p. 496)

Listening Passage

➔ **Waves and Energy**

When a pebble is dropped into a still pond, the surface of the water is disturbed. The disturbed surface moves outward along the surface of the water in a series of **waves.** The disturbance is caused by energy traveling through the water. What is the cause of this energy?

The pebble that is dropped into the water has kinetic energy because it is moving. Kinetic energy is energy of motion. When the pebble hits the surface of the water, some of its kinetic energy is transferred to nearby particles of water. These particles start to move/$_{100}$ as a result of this energy. Their movement transfers energy to neighboring water particles, which in turn move. As the water particles move, a wave is produced across the surface of the water. Energy is transferred from one place to another.]

Comprehension Questions

(TE)   1. What happens when you drop a pebble in still water?
(Surface of the water is disturbed.)

(TE)   2. What causes the disturbance in the water?
(energy traveling through the water)

(TI)   3. What does kinetic mean?
(motion or movement)

(TI)   4. What happens to the kinetic energy of a pebble when it is dropped in water?
(It transfers to other parts of the water; it makes waves.)

(SI)   5. How are waves produced?
(kinetic energy transmitted to water particles from something in motion)

(SI)   6. How is energy transmitted in a hurricane?
(Disturbed air transfers to disturbed water.)

6

CBAs for Dictionary Skills

When working with students with special needs, teachers often find it necessary to offer instruction in a curricular area that has not been previously established in the classroom. In this case, the task is to develop the curriculum in a sequential fashion, covering all essential skill areas. An expedient way to accomplish this is to construct a CBA as part of the process of developing the sequence. The source of the curriculum itself may vary. The curriculum might be based on teacher ideas, on a combination of various curricula, on outside reading, on courses taken by the teachers, or on some combination of these sources.

In developing a CBA for a previously unestablished curriculum, you can use the same procedures that are used in the development of a spiraling curriculum. An example of this type of CBA, a dictionary skills CBA, is presented in this chapter. In Chapter 7, we present a second example of a CBA for an unestablished curriculum: a CBA for study skills and following directions. Both of these CBAs were developed by consulting teachers and represent skill areas that were problematic for students experiencing academic difficulty in the classroom.

Development of a Dictionary Skills CBA

The dictionary skills CBA presented in this chapter was developed by Margie Heinz while preparing as a consulting teacher in the Resource/Consulting Teacher Program at the University of Illinois. To establish the concepts for the CBA, this consulting teacher referred to three different sources used in the school where she was working (Fisher Elementary School, Fisher, Illinois). These sources were (a) the basal reading program, (b) the spelling program, and (c) the phonics program. To supplement and fill gaps in the material from these sources, she added concepts from her own experience. The result was a CBA that covers skills in alphabetization, guide words, pronunciation, and word meanings.

The dictionary skills CBA has three parts: (a) a scope and sequence chart, (b) a recording form, and (c) the CBA itself. The CBA is designed for skill areas taught in Grades 2 through 6. It provides similar tests for three different days of testing.

The CBA's scope and sequence chart is organized by the four skills tested and by grade levels 2 through 6 (see Figure 6.1). A raw data sheet is provided to record student performance on the CBA (see Figure 6.2). The data sheet is also organized by grade level and skill area across each of the three days of testing.

As with previously described CBAs, the Figure 6.1 scope and sequence chart is used to organize and analyze the contents of the dictionary skills CBA. The CBA is then constructed and administered to students, using the recording form to store student performance data. Instruction would then be offered on unmastered areas. The general format and procedures of this CBA could be applied to any subject area taught in the classroom. Teachers are encouraged to develop the assessment instruments in collaboration, combining their knowledge of curricula, task analysis, and measurement techniques.

Dictionary Skills Assessment Test—Scope and Sequence Chart

Dictionary Skills	Grade 2	Grade 3	Grade 4	Grade 5	Grade 6
Alphabetizing	1. S. fills in 14 missing letters of alphabet. 2. S. lists 6 words in ABC order by 1st letter only. 3. S. lists 2 groups of 3 words in ABC order by 2nd letter (1st letters the same).	1. S. identifies section of dictionary in which particular words are found. 2. S. numbers 4 words in ABC order by 1st letter and also by 2nd & 3rd letters (with 1st & 2nd letters the same), e.g., train, tried, trumpet.	1. Same as Grade 3. 2. Same as Grade 3, except ABC order by 4th letter; also some previous letters are not the same, e.g., again, agate, arm.	From 4 groups of 3 words S. identifies 2 groups that are in ABC order (ABC order by 2nd, 3rd, 4th, & 5th letters required).	Same, except ABC order to 6th & 7th letters required.
Guide Words	None	Given 5 words & 2 guide words, S. identifies words that would & would not be found on that page in a dictionary. Knowledge of ABC order by 1st, 2nd, & 3rd letters required.	Same as Grade 3, except knowledge of ABC order by 1st, 2nd, 3rd, & 4th letters required.	Given 5 words and 2 guide words, S. identifies words that would & would not be found on that page (ABC order by 4th letter required).	Given 2 guide words & 4 groups of 3 words, S. identifies the group that would be found between the guide words (ABC order by 5th & 6th letters).
Pronunciation Key	None	1. Given 8 correctly spelled words and 7 pictures accompanied by a dictionary spelling, S. must write the correctly spelled words next to dictionary spelling. 2. S. must read aloud to tester a sentence written in dictionary spelling.	1. Given 8 correctly spelled words and 6 words spelled with dictionary spellings, S. must write the correctly spelled words next to dictionary spellings. 2. Given 4 words, accompanied by their dictionary spellings, S. will answer 4 questions relating specifically to knowledge of the pronunciation key.	1. Same as Grade 4, except 6 correctly spelled words & 3 dictionary spellings. 2. Given 4 words, their dictionary spellings, & actual dictionary definitions, S. will answer 5 questions relating specifically to the pronunciation key.	1. Same as Grade 5. 2. Same as Grade 5, except 7 questions.
Word Meanings	None	1. Given one word with 4 dictionary definitions & 4 sentences using the word, S. will identify which meaning goes best with each sentence. 2. Given 2 words, each having 3 definitions and 3 sentences using the target words, S. will identify which meaning goes best with each sentence.	Given 4 words, each having multiple meanings and 7 sentences using these words, S. will identify which meaning goes best with each sentence.	Given 2 words with multiple meanings and 9 sentences using the target words, S. will identify which meaning goes best with each sentence.	Given 1 word with 6 different meanings & 1 word with 3 meanings, with 7 sentences & 2 sentences respectively, S. will identify which meaning goes best with each sentence.

Figure 6.1. Scope and sequence chart for dictionary skills CBA.

Dictionary Skills Assessment Record Form

Student's name _____

Age _____ Grade _____

Classroom teacher _____

Tester _____

School _____

Dates _____

	Grade 2	Grade 3				Grade 4				Grade 5				Grade 6			
	Alphabetizing	Alphabetizing	Guide Words	Pronunciation Key	Word Meanings	Alphabetizing	Guide Words	Pronunciation Key	Word Meanings	Alphabetizing	Guide Words	Pronunciation Key	Word Meanings	Alphabetizing	Guide Words	Pronunciation Key	Word Meanings
Day 1 # correct / total %	/17	/13	/15	/15	/7	/9	/15	/10	/7	/6	/12	/8	/9	/4	/2	/10	/9
Day 2 # correct / total %	/17	/13	/15	/15	/7	/9	/15	/10	/7	/6	/12	/8	/9	/4	/2	/10	/9
Day 3 # correct / total %	/17	/13	/15	/15	/7	/9	/15	/10	/7	/6	/12	/8	/9	/4	/2	/10	/9
X% correct																	

Figure 6.2. Recording form for dictionary skills CBA.

Sample Dictionary Skills CBA

The sample dictionary skills CBA presented in this section, like other CBAs in this book, consists of three tests of similar content to be administered on three separate days. The CBA is organized by grade levels (2 through 6) and subdivided by skill areas within each grade level.

Dictionary Skills Assessment

A. Alphabetizing

1. Fill in the missing letters:

   a b _____ d _____ _____ g _____ _____ j _____ _____ m _____ _____ _____

   q r _____ _____ u _____ w x _____ z

2. Write these words in ABC order:

a. wear	clear	year	b. berry	basket	bowl

   a. wear   clear   year

      near   hear   bear

   (1) _____

   (2) _____

   (3) _____

   (4) _____

   (5) _____

   (6) _____

   b. berry   basket   bowl

   (1) _____

   (2) _____

   (3) _____

   c. bunk   bitter   blank

   (1) _____

   (2) _____

   (3) _____

17

Dictionary Skills Assessment

A. Alphabetizing

1. Fill in the missing letters:

____ ____ c ____ e f ____ ____ i ____ k l ____ n o ____ ____

____ s t ____ ____ w ____ y ____

2. Write these words in ABC order:

a. far	part	tart	b. grand	glance	gum
hard	mar	dark	(1) _____		

(1) _____   (2) _____

(2) _____   (3) _____

(3) _____   c. picture   paints   poem

(4) _____   (1) _____

(5) _____   (2) _____

(6) _____   (3) _____

17

Dictionary Skills Assessment

A. Alphabetizing

1. Fill in the missing letters:

a _____ c _____ e _____ g h _____ _____ k _____ _____ _____ o p _____

r _____ t _____ v _____ _____ _____ z

2. Write these words in ABC order:

a. third   curl   serve   b. chase   crumb   clap

bird   girl   hurt   (1) _____

(1) _____   (2) _____

(2) _____   (3) _____

(3) _____   c. tiny   think   tell

(4) _____   (1) _____

(5) _____   (2) _____

(6) _____   (3) _____

Dictionary Skills Assessment

A.   Alphabetizing

1.   1st   2nd   3rd

                      A—G   H—Q   R—Z

After each word, tell if it would be found in the first (1st), second (2nd), or third (3rd) part of the dictionary.

sign _____   every _____   police _____

wolf _____   dance _____   under _____

ivy _____   merry _____   fool _____

2. Number each group of words in ABC order.

a. _____ maybe   _____ thought   b. _____ begin   _____ blanket

   _____ people   _____ cold   _____ ball   _____ big

c. _____ snowstorm _____ stretch   d. _____ angry   _____ answer

   _____ swim   _____ soap   _____ anywhere _____ animal

                                                              _____
                                                                13

B. Guide words

Read the guide words. Then cross out the words that would not be found on that page.

1. *mitt   mold*

   mix   moan   mood   noise   model

2. *goad   going*

   goblin   gnu   gobble   gloom   goggle

3. *peppermint   perfect*

   pineapple   penny   percent   pep   pad

                                                              _____
                                                                15

C. Pronunciation key

1. Read the dictionary spellings. Then write each word the correct way.

avoid   hammer   curtains   whiskers

barrel   entrance   currants   ostrich

a. /kėrt′ənz/ _____

b. /hwis′kərz/ _____

c. /bar′əl/ _____

d. /ham′ər/ _____

e. /en′trəns/ _____

f. /ôs′trich/ _____

g. /ə void′/ _____

$$\overline{}$$
7

2. Read this sentence aloud to the person giving you this test.

h w a r   d u z   yər   m u th′ér   kēp   thė

v a k′ yu̇ m   k l ė n′ė r?

$$\overline{}$$
8

D. Word meanings

Read each sentence and find the meanings in the dictionary entry for the underlined word. Next to each sentence, write the numeral of the meaning that goes best with that sentence.

play·er (pla′ər) 1. a person who takes part in a game or sport. 2. an actor. 3. a person who plays a musical instrument. 4. a phonograph.

_____ 1. She is a <u>player</u> in the movie.

_____ 2. Turn the <u>player</u> up louder.

_____ 3. The tennis <u>player</u> is a star.

_____ 4. He is a <u>player</u> in the school band.

cir·cle (sėr′kl) 1. a ring. 2. to make a ring around something. 3. a figure that is round.

horn (hôrn) 1. a hard growth on the heads of some animals. 2. a thing to honk as a sign to look out for something.

_____ 1. The dog jumped when it heard the car's <u>horn</u>.

_____ 2. <u>Circle</u> all the right answers.

_____ 3. The bull has one broken <u>horn</u>.

7

Dictionary Skills Assessment

A. Alphabetizing

1. | 1st | 2nd | 3rd |
    |---|---|---|
    | A—G | H—Q | R—Z |

    After each word, tell if it would be found in the first (1st), second (2nd), or third (3rd) part of the dictionary.

    edge _____   donkey _____   very _____

    potato _____   blanket _____   jacket _____

    traveler _____   number _____   yellow _____

2. Number each group of words in ABC order.

    a. _____ zoo   _____ edge   b. _____ tend   _____ tail

        _____ father   _____ glide   _____ turtle   _____ trap

    c. _____ mix   _____ mend   d. _____ cauliflower   _____ carrots

        _____ mud   _____ moist   _____ cashews   _____ cabbage

    _____
    13

B. Guide words

    Read the guide words. Then cross out the words that would not be found on that page.

    1. *was*   *wind*

        web   wrong   who   won't   wide

    2. *pipeline*   *pitch*

        pink   pirate   pole   pixie   pistol

    3. *loan*   *lock*

        lobster   loan   lone   lobby   lock

    _____
    15

C.　Pronunciation key

　1.　Read the dictionary spellings. Then write each word the correct way.

antlers	awhile	banner	blanket
insect	insert	laundry	ribbon

 a. /rib'ən/ _____

 b. /ban'ər/ _____

 c. /ant'lərz/ _____

 d. /lôn'drē/ _____

 e. /in'sekt/ _____

 f. /blang'kət/ _____

 g. /ə hwīl/ _____

$$\overline{\qquad 7 \qquad}$$

　2.　Read the riddle and the answer aloud to the person giving you this test.

　　hwuts　blak　ənd　whīt　ənd　red　ôl　o'vər?

　　　　　　ɹed ͵ɐd ͵znu　ɐ

$$\overline{\qquad 8 \qquad}$$

D.   Word meanings

Read each sentence and find the meanings in the dictionary entry for the underlined word. Next to each sentence, write the numeral of the meaning that goes best with that sentence.

de·liv·er   (dĭlĭv'ər)   1. to take (letters, packages, etc.) to the persons to whom they are addressed. Deliver a package.   2. to send against; aim; strike. Deliver a blow.   3. to give or utter. Deliver a speech.   4. to rescue; save. Deliver us from our enemies.

_____ 1. Dan <u>delivered</u> a great book review to the class.

_____ 2. The mail carrier is often late <u>delivering</u> our mail.

_____ 3. The life guard <u>delivered</u> the boy safely to the beach.

_____ 4. Mother otter <u>delivered</u> a sound spanking to her naughty pup.

piece   (pēs)   1. one part of something.   2. a section of land.   3. something moved as part of a game.

sight   (sīt)   1. thing seen.   2. a person's sense of seeing.   3. something that looks odd.

_____ 1. The nicest <u>sight</u> we saw on our trip was the mountains.

_____ 2. My grandfather gave me a big <u>piece</u> of pie.

_____ 3. Carmen has better <u>sight</u> in her left eye than in her right.

7

Dictionary Skills Assessment

A. Alphabetizing

1.

	1st	2nd	3rd
	A—G	H—Q	R—Z

After each word, tell if it would be found in the first (1st), second (2nd), or third (3rd) part of the dictionary.

kitchen_____   cactus _____   octopus _____

fancy _____   lemon _____   x-ray _____

wonder _____   turkey _____   books _____

2. Number each group of words in ABC order.

a. _____ rose   _____ subway   b. _____ who   _____ wish

_____ order   _____ pepper   _____ well   _____ wrong

c. _____ top   _____ teddy bear   d. _____ tricycle   _____ trumpet

_____ turnips   _____ throw   _____ troop   _____ train

13

B. Guide words

Read the guide words. Then cross out the words that would not be found on that page.

1. *lamp*   *live*

most   like   listen   leave   love

2. *foliage*   *food*

fond   force   fondle   fancy   foal

3. *wasn't*   *window*

water   well   wish   wide   was

15

C. Pronunciation key

1. Read the dictionary spellings. Then write each word the correct way.

athlete	awoke	coffee	hardware
pillow	turkey	turnip	turtle

a. /härd'wār/   _____

b. /ath'lēt/   _____

c. /tėr'kē/   _____

d. /tėr'nəp/   _____

e. /kôf'ē/   _____

f. /pil'ō/   _____

g. /ə wōk'/   _____

7

2. Read this riddle and the answer (printed upside down) aloud to the person giving you this test.

hwī did ŦHə chik'ən kros ŦHə rōd?

sed,ɹə d ʇnoɟ uıns ɹeʃ

8

D. Word meanings

Read each sentence and find the meanings in the dictionary entry for the underlined word. Next to each sentence, write the numeral of the meaning that goes best with that sentence.

march   (märch) *v* 1. to walk at a steady rate, as in a parade: With song we cheerfully march along.   2. to walk in a determined manner: He marched right up to the police officer and asked the name of the street. —*n* 3. a journey by foot: A march of ten miles.   4. music written to accompany marching.

_____ 1. He played a lively <u>march</u> on the piano.

_____ 2. The soldiers went on a long <u>march</u>.

_____ 3. Elephants <u>marched</u> to the music at the circus.

_____ 4. She <u>marched</u> up to the driver and asked what was wrong.

mine   (mīn) 1. a place where coal, gold, or such things are found.   2. to dig into.

pa·tient (pā′shənt) 1. willing to wait or to put up with something.   2. one being taken care of by a doctor.

_____ 1. The doctor was worried about her young <u>patient</u>.

_____ 2. Ten people were trapped in the <u>mine</u>.

_____ 3. The <u>patient</u> dog waited for his dinner.

──────
7

Dictionary Skills Assessment

A. Alphabetizing

Number each group of words in ABC order.

	1st	2nd	3rd
	A—G	H—Q	R—Z

1. _____ solid _____ gas _____ vapor _____ liquid

In what part of the dictionary would each group be found?

2. _____ blink _____ brick _____ bench _____ bank

2. _____

3. _____ think _____ throw _____ three _____ thank

3. _____

4. _____ arm _____ agate _____ area _____ again

4. _____

5. _____ hectic _____ horse _____ headlong _____ headquarter

5. _____

_____
9

B. Guide words

Read the guide words. Then cross out the words that would not be found on that page.

1. *objections*   *October*

obvious   object   oak   occasional   occur

2. *empress*   *encircle*

emit   empty   enchant   endanger   emperor

3. *offal*   *old*

official   off   offspring   ocean   offside

_____
15

C. Pronunciation key

Read each dictionary spelling. Then write each word the correct way.

| continue | minute | question | remember |
| machine | syllable | sensible | ketchup |

/ m i n' ə t /　　　　　_____

/ m ə s h ē n' /　　　　_____

/ s i l' ə b ə l /　　　　_____

/ k w e s' c h ə n /　　　_____

/ k ə n t i n' ū /　　　　_____

/ r ē m e m' b ə r /　　　_____

ăr·cade　　/ ä r k ā d' /

auk　　　　/ ô k /

de·tect　　/ d ĭ t ĕ k t' /

gar·bage　/ g ä r' b ĭ j /

Pronunciation Key

ă pat / ā pay / â care / ä father / ĕ pet / ē be / ĭ pit / ī pie /
î fierce / ŏ pot / ō go / ô paw, for / oi oil / o͝o book / o͞o boot /
ou out / ŭ cut / û fur / *th* the / th thin / hw which / zh vision /
ə ago, item, pencil, atom, circus

1) Which word in the pronunciation key has the same vowel sound as the one in <u>auk</u>? _____

_____

2) How many syllables are there in <u>arcade</u>? _____

3) Which two letters represent the short i sound in <u>detect</u> and <u>garbage</u>? _____

4) Which word has the accent on the first syllable?_____

____

10

D. Word meanings

In front of each sentence, write the numeral of the correct definition for the underlined word.

b a r k / b ä r k /	*n* 1. the tough outside covering of the trunk, branches, and roots of trees. 2. the short sharp sound a dog makes.
f i e l d / f ē l d /	*n* 1. land with few or no trees. 2. all persons in a game, contest, or outdoor sport —*v* 3. to stop a ball or catch it and return it.
p e r c h / p ė r c h /	*n* 1. a bar, branch or anything else on which a bird comes to rest. 2. a small, fresh water fish. —*v* 3. to alight and rest on.
s t a r / s t ä r /	*n* 1. any heavenly body other than planets, moons, comets, or mete-orites. 2. a famous person. —*v* 3. have the main part in a per-formance.

_____   Sue was able to <u>field</u> the fly ball.

_____   A giant oak stood in the middle of the <u>field</u>.

_____   Roy wants to be a country-music singing <u>star</u>.

_____   Venus is often called a <u>star</u>.

_____   The bird likes to <u>perch</u> on his shelf.

_____   I fish for <u>perch</u> every spring.

_____   <u>Bark</u> from trees is used to make canoes.

7

Dictionary Skills Assessment

A. Alphabetizing

Number each group of words in ABC order.

	1st	2nd	3rd
	A—G	H—Q	R—Z

1. _____ peculiar   _____ record

    _____ filed   _____ tricked

In what part of the dictionary would each group be found?

2. _____ row   _____ risk

    _____ rank   _____ rut

2. _____

3. _____ pry   _____ produce

    _____ present   _____ price

3. _____

4. _____ banker   _____ bang

    _____ banish   _____ bend

4. _____

5. _____ meeting   _____ meditate

    _____ medium   _____ medial

5. _____

_____
9

B. Guide Words

Read the guide words. Then cross out the words that would not be found on that page.

1. *yawn*   *yonder*

    x-ray   yen   yarn   yes   yield

2. *glob*   *grotesque*

    glory   gate   guest   greet   going

3. *bought*   *bowl*

    boss   bounce   brace   boulder   bower

_____
15

C.   Pronunciation key

Read each dictionary spelling. Then write each word the correct way.

plentiful	action	tomato	stomach
enough	anxious	wonderful	wander

/ s t u m' ə k / _____

/ ə n u f' / _____

/ a k' s h ə n / _____

/ p l e n' t ə f ə l / _____

/ t ə m ā' t ō / _____

/ w u n' d ə r f ə l / _____

Pronunciation Key

de·tect	/ d ĭ t e k t' /
fiend	/ f ē n d /
hab·er·dash·er	/ h ă b' ə r̠ d ă s h' ə r /
ma·caw	/ m ə k ô' /

ă pat / ā pay / â care / ä father / ĕ pet / ē be / ĭ pit/ ī pie / î fierce / ŏ pot / ō go / ô paw, for / oi oil / o͝o book / o͞o boot / ou out / ŭ cut / û fur / *th* the / th thin / hw which / zh vision / ə ago, item, pencil, atom, circus

1)   Which word in the pronunciation key has the same vowel sound as the third syllable of <u>haberdasher</u>?

_____

2)   Which word has only one syllable?

_____

3)   Which word in the pronunciation key tells you how to pronounce the first syllable of <u>macaw</u>?

_____

4)   Which word has no accent mark?_____

10

D. Word meanings

In front of each sentence, write the numeral of the correct definition for the underlined word.

light / lĭt /   *n* 1. thing that gives light.   2. pale in color. —*v* 3. set fire to.

plant / plănt /   *n* 1. a young tree, vine shrub or herb planted or suitable for planting.
                          2. put in the ground to grow.   3. set firmly; place.

ring / rĭng /   *n* 1. circle.   2. thin circle of metal worn on the finger. —*v* 3. to sound
                          or cause to sound.

trunk / trungk /   *n* 1. the main stem of a tree.   2. an elephant's snout.   3. a big box
                          for holding clothes.

_____ Ella packed her <u>trunk</u> for the long journey.

_____ Ella used her <u>trunk</u> to pick up the peanuts.

_____ My coat is <u>light</u> blue.

_____ Please <u>light</u> the candles.

_____ Did the telephone <u>ring</u>?

_____ She wants to buy a gold <u>ring</u>.

_____ Where will you <u>plant</u> the seeds?

_____
7

Dictionary Skills Assessment

Day 3
Grade 4

A. Alphabetizing

Number each group of words in ABC order.

	1st	2nd	3rd
	A—G	H—Q	R—Z

1. _____ fundamental   _____ garage

_____ oily   _____ hemp

In what part of the dictionary would each group be found?

2. _____ notch   _____ hinge

_____ king   _____ heavy

2. _____

3. _____ school   _____ scent

_____ scoop   _____ square

3. _____

4. _____ plural   _____ plant

_____ plastic   _____ plow

4. _____

5. _____ fortune   _____ forecast

_____ forlorn   _____ former

5. _____

_____
9

B. Guide Words

Read the guide words. Then cross out the words that would not be found on that page.

1. *mend*   *mesa*

menial   messy   mercy   memory   meet

2. *sprung*   *squeeze*

square   squid   stadium   squeak   spring

3. *ghost*   *grow*

grateful   gypsy   gift   glow   group

_____
15

C. Pronunciation key

Read each dictionary spelling. Then write each word the correct way.

| attention | action | jealous | animal |
| echo | nation | possible | nature |

/ j e l′ ə s /   _____

/ e k′ ō /   _____

/ n ā′ s h ə n /   _____

/ p o s′ ə b ə l /   _____

/ a n′ ə m ə l /   _____

/ ə t e n′ s h ə n /   _____

el·bow	/ĕlbō/	Pronunciation Key
fiend	/fēnd/	ă pat / ā pay / â care / ä father / ě pet / ē be /
scal·lion	/skăl′yən/	ĭ pit / ī pie / î fierce / ŏ pot / ō go / ô paw, for /
		oi oil / o͝o book / o͞o boot / ou out / ŭ cut / û fur /
taut	/tôt/	*th* the / th thin / hw which / zh vision /
		ə ago, item, pencil, atom, circus

1) How many syllables are there in <u>scallion</u>?

_____

2) Which word in the pronunciation key has the same vowel sound as the one in <u>taut</u>?

_____

3) Which syllable is accented in <u>scallion</u>, first or second?

_____

4) Which word in the pronunciation key has the same vowel sound as the one in the first syllable of <u>elbow</u>?

_____

10

D. Word meanings

In front of each sentence, write the numeral of the correct definition for the underlined word.

b a r k / b ä r k / *n* 1. tough outside covering of the trunk, branches and roots of trees. 2. short, sharp sound a dog makes.

b r a n c h / b r ă n c h / *n* 1. part of a tree. 2. a local office apart from the main office. 3. part of a river.

s p e l l / s p ĕ l / *v* 1. to write or say the letters of a word in order. —*n* 2. word or words having magic power. 3. a period of work or duty.

t i e / t ī / *v* 1. to fasten; bind. —*n* 2. fabric that fastens around the neck or waist.

_____ We hiked along the west <u>branch</u> of the river.

_____ I stopped at the <u>branch</u> post office for stamps.

_____ The <u>spell</u> of the magician was broken.

_____ I don't know how to <u>spell</u> those words.

_____ Please help me <u>tie</u> this knot.

_____ He took off his <u>tie</u>.

_____ My dog has a loud <u>bark</u>.

7

Dictionary Skills Assessment

A. Alphabetizing

Which groups of words are in alphabetical order? Circle the correct groups.

1. strength   rap   trip   strait

    strip   right   triple   strain

    strap   rodeo   tripod   straight

2. fantastic   potash   national   hurtle

    frantic   possible   nearby   hydrogen

    frivolous   porpoise   nation   hyena

3. player   poem   plaque   plant

    platter   point   plaid   plane

    plaza   poet   plain   plan

_____
6

B. Guide Words

Which word or words would you find between the given guide words below? Cross out the words that do not belong.

1. *mob*   *mogul*

    modern   motor   modish   mohair   moreover

2. *slash*   *sleepy*

    slap   slate   sled   sleek   slave   sling   sleeve

_____
12

C.   Pronunciation key

Read the dictionary spellings. Then write each word the correct way.

company   officer   official   companion   general   genuine

/ j e n' y ủ ə n /   _____

/ k u m' p ə n ē /   _____

/ o f' ə s ə r /   _____

Use the four dictionary entries below to answer the next five questions.

chrome (krōm)   *n* a kind of metal. —*v* to cover with chrome.

ed i ble (ed' ə bl *or* bəl)   *adj* fit to eat.

ram i fy (ram' ə fī)   *v* to divide into branches.

mys ter i ous (mĭs tēr' ē əs)   *adj* full of mystery; hard to explain.

1. Which word has only one syllable? _____

2. Which words are neither nouns nor verbs?

_____   _____

3. Which word does not have a *schwa* sound (ə) in it?

_____

4. Which letter spells the *schwa* sound (ə) in *edible* and *ramify*?   _____

5. Which word has a long ō sound in it? _____

_____
8

D.   Word meanings

For each sentence, select and write the number of the definition of the underlined word in the space provided.

clear (k l i r) *adj* 1. not cloudy.   2. not confused; easily understood.   3. certain; sure.   —*v* 4. to make empty or free.   —*adv* 5. completely; entirely.

_____ It is <u>clear</u> that we won't play ball today since it is raining so hard.

_____ The sky was <u>clear</u> and the sun shone brightly.

_____ The horse jumped <u>clear</u> over the fence.

_____ He <u>clears</u> the table of all the dishes.

_____ She gave a <u>clear</u> explanation of the answer to the math problem.

_____ Please <u>clear</u> a space on the deck.

trip (t r ĭ p) *n* 1. a journey; a voyage. —*v* 2. to stumble and fall. 3. to stop lightly and quickly. 4. to start or set free.

_____ He <u>tripped</u> and dropped the boxes.

_____ We took a three-week <u>trip</u>.

_____ The children <u>tripped</u> down the street to the ice cream truck.

9

Dictionary Skills Assessment

A. Alphabetizing

Which groups of words are in alphabetical order? Circle the correct groups.

1. plastic	guess	scale	bright
play	guest	scallop	brittle
place	guide	scar	brisk
2. came	obey	puppet	crisp
camel	object	pupil	cracker
camp	oboe	puppy	chorus
3. clam	submarine	stress	concern
clambake	sublet	strong	cope
clamor	sublime	struggle	compute

———
6

B. Guide words

Which word or words would you find between the given guide words below? Cross out the words that do not belong.

1. *waitress*   *wander*

    waist   wash   walrus   wampum   when

2. *wood*   *worse*

    worth   wool   won't   woe   wolf   word   worst

———
12

C. Pronunciation key

Read the dictionary spellings. Then write each word the correct way.

presence   present   muscular   money   cinnamon   singular

/ m u s′ k y ə l ə r / _____

/ p r ē z e n t′ / _____

/ s i n′ ə m ə n / _____

Use the four dictionary entries below to answer the next five questions.

gentle (jĕn'tl)   *adj* 1. mild; not rough.   2. soft; low.   3. kind; friendly.

geography (jē og' rə fē)   *n* 1. study of the earth's surface, climate, continents, countries, peoples, industries and products.   2. the surface features of a place or region.

gnat (năt)   *n* small, two-winged insect or fly.

laxity (lak' sə tē)   *n* looseness.

1. Which word has only one syllable? _____

2. Which two words begin with the same sound?

   _____   _____

3. Which word is not a noun?

   _____

4. Which word has its accent on the second syllable?   _____

5. Which letter spells the *schwa* sound (ə) in *geography*?   _____

_____

8

D. Word meanings

For each sentence, select and write the number of the definition of the underlined word in the space provided.

draw (d r ô)   *v* 1. to pull; to drag.   2. to make a picture of.   3. to attract.   4. to cause to come out; to take out.   5. to inhale.   —*n* 6. to tie in a game.

_____ Accidents often <u>draw</u> a large crowd.

_____ The horse will <u>draw</u> the carriage.

_____ He couldn't <u>draw</u> his breath because the smoke was so thick.

_____ She will <u>draw</u> ten dollars from the bank.

_____ The teams were equally matched and the game ended in a <u>draw</u>.

_____ Do you like to <u>draw</u> with crayons?

_____ A turtle can <u>draw</u> its head in and out of its shell.

sight (sī t)   *n* 1. the power of seeing.   2. a device on an instrument that aids the eye in aiming.   3. something worth seeing.

_____ The mountains are a magnificent <u>sight</u>.

_____ For a moment after the flash, I lost my <u>sight</u>.

_____

9

Dictionary Skills Assessment

A. Alphabetizing

Which groups of words are in alphabetical order? Circle the correct groups.

1.	chip	brought	than	place
	chat	broke	that	plan
	chose	brood	thaw	plaque

2.	waist	wampum	walnut	Wales
	wait	wand	waltz	wake
	waiter	wash	walrus	wane

3.	begun	becloud	indigo	scorch
	began	become	indirect	school
	begin	believe	indiscreet	screen

—————
6

B. Guide words

Which word or words would you find between the given guide words below? Cross out the words that do not belong.

1. *glamour*   *glove*

   glad   glimpse   good   glower   glass

2. *blurry*   *book*

   blunt   blue   boom   boot   blush   blind   bloom

—————
12

C. Pronunciation Key

Read the dictionary spellings. Then write each word the correct way.

odious   contain   continue   century   audience   sentinel

/ ô′ dē ə n s /   _____

/ k ə n t i n′ ū /   _____

/ s e n′ c h ə r ē /   _____

Use the four dictionary entries below to answer the next five questions.

beggary (beg′ ər ē)   *n*   great poverty.

cloture (klō chər)   *n*   a procedure for ending debate.   —*v*   to end debate by means of cloture.

kleptomania (klep′ tə mā′nē ə)   *n*   the compulsion to steal.

knead (nēd)   *v*   to press and squeeze.

1. Which word has only one syllable? _____

2. Which word can be used as both a noun and a verb?   _____

3. Which two words begin with the same sound?

   _____   _____

4. Which word contains two *schwa* sounds (ə)? _____

5. How many syllables are there in *kleptomania*?   _____

____

8

D.   Word meanings

For each sentence, select and write the number of the definition of the underlined word in the space provided.

just (j u s t)   *adj* 1. fair; not partial.   2. well-deserved; earned.   —*adv* 3. exactly.   4. barely.   5. only; merely.

_____   He is just a baby and cannot talk yet.

_____   Jim was mad that his arrow came so close to the target and then just missed it.

_____   The umpire made a just decision.

_____   Debbie is such a just person that she is usually asked to resolve arguments among the other children.

_____   Mandy received a just reward for her honesty.

_____   Fred is just seven years old; today is his birthday.

press (p r ĕ s)   *v* 1. to push with steady force.   2. to make smooth.   —*n* 3. a printing machine.   4. urgency; hurry.

_____   Have you learned how to run the press?

_____   You have to press on that tag to make it stick.

_____   You do not have to press no-iron shirts.

____

9

Dictionary Skills Assessment

A. Alphabetizing

Which groups of words are in alphabetical order? Circle the correct groups.

1. material   parody   guarded   chorale

    maternal   partake   guardian   chore

    maternity   partial   guardsmen   chord

2. realism   precise   energy   choroid

    reality   precision   enemy   chorus

    realize   preclude   enormous   chortle

_____
4

B. Guide words

Which groups of words would you find between the guide words below? Cross out the words that don't belong.

1. *grill*   *groove*

    grace   grim   groom   grind

    gift   grief   grind   grip

    grim   gross   grouch   grizzly

2. *hear*   *hurdle*

    heard   hunger   heaven   hurt

    heal   hunt   heel   here

    height   hurl   honey   heron

_____
2

C. Pronunciation key

Read each dictionary spelling. Then write each word the correct way.

terrible   colonel   colonial   terrified   scenery   scientific

/ sī'ən t i f'ik /   _____

/ ter'ə b əl /   _____

/ k ə lō'nē əl /   _____

Use the four dictionary entries below to answer the next seven questions.

confront (kən frunt') *v* to meet head-on.

cruise (krüz) *v* to sail from place to place. —*n* the act of sailing.

emancipation (ĭ man' sə pā' shən) *n* freedom.

irony (ī rə nē) *n* a way of saying one thing and meaning the opposite.

1. Which word has only one syllable? _____

2. Which words have only one *schwa* sound?

_____   _____

3. Which word has two *schwa* sounds? _____

4. Which word begins with a long vowel sound? _____

5. Which word may be used as either a noun or a verb? _____

6. Which words begin with the same sound?

_____   _____

7. How many syllables does *emancipation* have? _____

_____

10

D. Word meanings

For each sentence, select and write the number of the definition of the underlined word in the space provided.

gather (g a ᵀH' ə r)   *v* 1. bring into one place or group. 2. come together; assemble. 3. conclude; infer. 4. pull together into folds and stitch. 5. pick; glean or harvest. —*n* 6. one of the little folds between the stitches when cloth is gathered.

_____ A crowd may <u>gather</u> at an accident.

_____ Just let me <u>gather</u> my books and we will go.

_____ I <u>gather</u> from what he said that he will not go.

_____ You must <u>gather</u> the skirt and then sew on the waistband.

_____ The farmers will soon begin to <u>gather</u> their crops.

_____ From what he said, we <u>gathered</u> that he was very upset.

_____ The <u>gathers</u> in her blouse were ripped.

fair (f ã r)   *adj* 1. clear and sunny; not stormy. 2. free of bias; impartial. 3. moderately good.

_____ The weather in June is usually <u>fair</u>.

_____ Carla's performance at the concert was <u>fair</u>.

_____

9

Dictionary Skills Assessment

A. Alphabetizing

Which groups are in alphabetical order? Circle the correct groups.

1. personnel   charge   group   refresh

    personal   charity   grouping   refund

    person   charm   grouper   retake

2. clover   floatage   wallaby   color

    clown   floatable   wallet   colony

    cloy   floatation   wallop   colossal

———
4

B. Guide words

Which group of words would you find between the guide words below? Cross out the words that do not belong.

1. *mansion*   *mariner*

    marathon   mantle   manner   map

    manual   margarine   maple   manifest

    mark   marigold   march   margin

2. *lament*   *lapel*

    lake   lap   languid   lark

    lame   lapse   lamp   landing

    lance   lane   lap   lance

———
2

C. Pronunciation key

Read each dictionary spelling. Then write each word the correct way.

preserve   altogether   preservation   politician   olive oil   political

/ôl′təgeⱦH′ər/   _____

/prēzėrv′/   _____

/pəlit′əkəl/   _____

Use the four dictionary entries below to answer the next seven questions.

desert (dĕz'ərt)   *n* a dry, barren region, often covered with sand, having little or no vegetation.

inconvenient (in' kən vē n yənt)   *adj* not convenient; troublesome; causing bother, difficulty, or discomfort.

mauve (mō v)   *adj* delicate, pale purple.

pajamas (pə ja' məz *or* pə jam' əz)   *n* garments to sleep in, consisting of a coat and loose trousers.

1. Which word has only one syllable? _____

2. In which word is the accent on the second syllable? _____

3. Which word has the vowel sound heard in the word *coat*? _____

4. Which word is an adverb?   _____

5. Which word has no *schwa* sound?   _____

6. Which words are nouns?

    _____   _____

7. How many syllables are there in *inconvenient*? _____

                                                                        _____
                                                                          10

D.   Word meanings

For each sentence, select and write the number of the definition of the underlined word in the space provided.

guard (g ä r d)   *v* 1. to protect from harm.   2. to watch over to prevent escape.   3. to keep watch at
an entrance. —*n* 4. one that guards.   5. a group that performs on ceremonial occasions.   6. something that gives protection.

_____   The guard at the gate would not allow us to enter.

_____   We wanted a good dog to guard the children.

_____   It was the corporal's job to guard the main gate.

_____   Ms. Thomas is the crossing guard at the corner.

_____   Margaret says that this toothpaste is a guard against decay.

_____   Four men were assigned to guard the prisoners.

_____   An honor guard escorted the president to the platform.

lock (l o k)   *n* 1. device used to fasten something shut.   2. a section of a canal in which the water can
be raised or lowered. —*v* 3. to fasten.

_____   The large ship moved slowly through the lock.

_____   Lock the door when you go out.

                                                                        _____
                                                                          9

Dictionary Skills Assessment

A. Alphabetizing

Which groups are in alphabetical order? Circle the correct groups.

1. niece   humanity   souffle   nobody

    nightcap   humanize   soulless   noble

    nightly   humanist   soulful   nocturnal

2. ready   grouch   verbal   coffin

    reading   grouchy   verify   coffer

    readjust   ground   verse   coffee

4

B. Guide words

Which group of words would you find between the guide words below? Cross out the words that do not belong.

1. *dynamite*   *earldom*

    dynasty   eagle   earl   dying

    earl   earn   eager   easel

    early   dynamo   dynasty   each

2. *reform*   *regimen*

    refund   reflect   regent   regent

    refresh   refuse   refine   regard

    regard   regain   reel   region

2

C. Pronunciation key

Read each dictionary spelling. Then write each word the correct way.

curtain   circumference   electrician   certain   immediate   electrical

/ ə me′ dē ət /   _____

/ kėr′ tən /   _____

/ ə lek′ trə kəl /   _____

Use the four dictionary entries below to answer the next seven questions.

convey (kən vā′)   *v* to carry; to communicate; to transport.

cope (kōp)   *v* to struggle without failing; to deal with successfully.

coquette (kō ket′)   *n* a flirt.

coupon (kü pon)   *n* a printed slip of paper.

1. Which word has only one syllable? _____

2. In which word is the accent not on the second syllable? _____

3. Which word contains the vowel sound heard in the word *gate*? _____

4. Which words do not have a long vowel sound?

_____   _____

5. Which words are verbs?

_____   _____

6. Which words begin with the same two sounds?

_____   _____

7. Which words are nouns?

_____   _____

_____
10

D.   Word meanings

For each sentence, select and write the number of the definition of the underlined word in the space provided.

fly (flī)   *v* 1. to move through the air with wings.   2. to travel by airplane.   3. to run an airplane. 4. to hit a baseball high in the air. —*n* 5. flap serving as the door of a tent.   6. ball hit high in the air with a bat.

_____   The camper closed the <u>fly</u> to keep the bugs out.

_____   I didn't know that an eagle could <u>fly</u> so high.

_____   Sally is learning to <u>fly</u> a Piper Cub.

_____   Mr. Rossi is going to <u>fly</u> from Chicago to Tucson on Tuesday.

_____   Because Jack is not a good batter, he will probably <u>fly</u> out in the next inning.

_____   Do all birds <u>fly</u> south in the fall?

_____   The <u>fly</u> ball dropped safely into short left-center field.

sign (s ī n)   *n* 1. a board or poster that gives information, directions, etc.   2. a motion or gesture. —*v* 3. to put one's signature to.

_____   The car screeched to a halt at the stop <u>sign</u>.

_____   Please <u>sign</u> this birthday card for Grandmother.

7

✧   ✧   ✧

CBAs for Following Directions and Using Study Skills

In this chapter, we present examples of two CBAs developed for previously unestablished curricula. They were designed by Kim Dicker while preparing as a consulting teacher at the University of Illinois and teaching at Leal Elementary School, Urbana, Illinois. They were developed in response to problems she observed students with special needs having in the classrooms where she was consulting. As in the case of the science CBA in Chapter 5, these CBAs were designed to help teachers decide *what* to teach as well as *how* to assess problems.

The overall goal in the preparation of the CBAs was to assess and teach students to follow directions and to exhibit better study skills. Specifically, they were designed to meet the needs of a student who had serious reading comprehension problems. Initially, the author/consultant worked directly with the student to improve reading comprehension in a basal reader, using a reading CBA similar to the one presented in Chapter 1. However, even though the student's reading comprehension improved considerably as a result of repeated practice, there was poor transfer to completing reading workbook assignments in the classroom. The author/consultant and collaborating teacher began to suspect that the major stumbling blocks were in following the directions in the workbook and in general study skills. The author/consultant developed two CBAs: one for following directions and one for study skills. She then tested the student's skill areas and helped the classroom teacher develop instruc-

tional activities that focused on teaching the skill areas represented in the CBAs.

Development of the Two CBAs

The two CBAs—the directions skills CBA and the study skills CBA—pinpoint problems that individuals have on worksheets, workbook pages, dittos, and other assignments. Students today spend a good portion of each school day involved in independent seatwork filled with workbook-type activities. For some students, this work is never completed, and workbook pages pile up in the students' folders to be finished at a later date, or to be forgotten.

Students may be having difficulties with these assignments for several reasons. One possibility is that they may not know the content material. A second possibility is that they may not understand the vocabulary contained in the directions. There may be key words in the directions that they cannot pronounce or read. A third possibility is that the students may not be able to put a sentence together in a meaningful way. Even if they can read all the words, they may still not be able to do what the directions ask. A fourth possibility is that they may be having problems because of the way the workbooks and workpages have been constructed. Many workbook pages are designed like some sort of maze or puzzle. The task that is to be done might have little relevance to the content of what is to be learned. Indeed, what may seem to be interesting and exciting to the writers of such workbooks may be a nightmare to some of the students who must complete them as independent seatwork.

The solution to these problems might be (a) to write or rewrite the pages of independent seatwork assignments so that the directions are simple and relate specifically to the content area that is to be reinforced by the workpage; (b) to read the directions of the workbook pages as a group and then explain problem areas, asking the students questions about what they are to do to be sure they understand; or (c) to find out the specific difficulties the student is having with following directions and completing the work. The two CBAs presented in this chapter were designed to focus on the third solution.

The information used to develop the CBAs came from several sources: workbook pages from the Laidlaw and McMillan Series across elementary grade levels, Scott, Foresman and Company and Kottmeyer and Claus spelling books across elementary grade levels, teachers' copies of readers with suggestions for activities for workbook pages, and teacher knowledge.

Both CBAs were developed for the elementary level, but they may also be used at the junior high or high school level. The CBAs assume a reading ability of the upper primary grades (upper second, beginning third). They do not have controlled vocabularies.

The questions asked on the CBAs were chosen because of the frequency in which they occurred in the accompanying curricular materials. They are only a sample of questions that could be asked; many other kinds of questions and vocabulary words could be used. In particular, study skills cover a very broad area—much broader than that represented by the skills in our study skills CBA. Some examples of additional skill topics are identifying colors, following map directions, using table and figure references, comparing and contrasting ideas, identifying cause-and-effect relationships, and discerning facts from opinions. Teachers are encouraged to use the two CBAs presented in this chapter as guides to construct CBAs relevant to their individual needs.

Implementation of the Two CBAs

In each CBA, the series of tests may be given either to a small group or to an individual student, one on one. If a single student is given the test, the teacher might have the student read the questions orally, to ensure that the student can read all of the words.

Each series of tests is divided into three parts, one for each of three days. It is important that the first part be given on Day 1, the second on Day 2, and the third on Day 3. No set time is allotted for the tests. However, the average student should be able to finish the directions skills CBA in a 30- to 45-minute period. The study skills CBA is longer, and a student might have difficulty completing it in a single period. In this case, it may be preferable to have the student work for one period in the morning and one period in the afternoon on the first day, and then follow the same procedure for the second and third days. This arrangement would also provide some relief time for the student.

It is suggested that the teacher use the following kind of introductory words in explaining each of the tests to the students: "I'm going to give you a test to see how well you can follow directions. This is not for a grade, but how you do will give me an idea of the kinds of independent work that is best for you." The teacher should emphasize that the test is not for a grade and that the students' academic standing will not be hurt in any way by test performance. Finally, the students should be told simply to do what the directions tell them to do and to do the best they can. The teacher should not read the items to the students and should discourage cheating.

Sample Directions Skills CBA

The areas assessed on the sample directions skills CBA are understanding and independent application of the following vocabulary words: circle, check, cross, fill in the blank, add, completing, draw a line to, from, through, under, before, after, beside, underline, print, copy, write, and follow a three-part direction. Because the vocabulary of the direction itself is being assessed, the emphasis is on understanding the direction, not on deciding which word or number to choose. For example, for the direction "draw a line from *sun* to *moon*," the words *sun* and *moon* are repeated underneath the sentence, and the student is to draw the line. It is assumed that if the student is not able to draw the line, the direction is not understood and the student cannot make the appropriate choice.

Figure 7.1 is a raw data sheet for recording student performance on the directions skills CBA. The form reflects the organizational structure of the CBA. There are four items per problem type, and there are 33 problem types. Frequency and percentage-correct data for each of the three days of testing are entered on the form. The mastery criterion for each problem type across the three days is 10 of 12 responses correct, or 83 percent correct responses. In addition, 4 points are given for following the direction, 1 point is given for completing the sentence, and 1 point is given for correct sequencing.

The sample directions skills CBA is presented in the following pages. It includes a test item for each of the 33 problem types, with a new set for each of the three days.

Directions Skills Assessment Record Sheet

Student's name_____ Age _____

Tester_____ Dates_____, _____, _____

Teacher_____ Grade_____ School_____

Assessment	Problem	Day 1 **# Correct** Total	Day 2 **# Correct** Total	Day 3 **# Correct** Total	Mastery = 83% **10/12 = 83%** X̄% = Correct
Assess student's under-standing of the word *print*.	1. a, b, c, d	/4= %	/4= %	/4= %	/12= %
Assess student's under-standing of the word *write*.	2. a, b, c, d	/4= %	/4= %	/4= %	/12= %
Assess student's under-standing of the word *copy*.	3. a, b, c, d	/4= %	/4= %	/4= %	/12= %
Assess student's under-standing of the words: *Make a circle around*.	4. a, b, c, d	/4= %	/4= %	/4= %	/12= %
Assess student's under-standing of the words: *Draw a ring around*.	5. a, b, c, d	/4= %	/4= %	/4= %	/12= %
Assess student's under-standing of the words: *Draw a circle around*.	6. a, b, c, d	/4= %	/4= %	/4= %	/12= %
Assess student's under-standing of the words: *Circle the words*.	7. a, b, c, d	/4= %	/4= %	/4= %	/12= %
Assess student's under-standing of the words: *Make a cross on*.	8. a, b, c, d	/4= %	/4= %	/4= %	/12= %
Assess student's under-standing of the words: *Put a cross on*.	9. a, b, c, d	/4= %	/4= %	/4= %	/12= %
Assess student's under-standing of the words: *Put a cross beside*.	10. a, b, c, d	/4= %	/4= %	/4= %	/12= % *(continues)*

Figure 7.1. Data recording form for directions skills CBA.

Assessment	Problem	Day 1 **# Correct** Total	Day 2 **# Correct** Total	Day 3 **# Correct** Total	Mastery = 83% **10/12 = 83%** X̄% = Correct
Assess student's under- standing of the words: *Cross out.*	11. a, b, c, d	/4= %	/4= %	/4= %	/12= %
Assess student's under- standing of the words: *Put a check on.*	12. a, b, c, d	/4= %	/4= %	/4= %	/12= %
Assess student's under- standing of the words: *Check the words.*	13. a, b, c, d	/4= %	/4= %	/4= %	/12= %
Assess student's under- standing of the words: *Put a check beside.*	14. a, b, c, d	/4= %	/4= %	/4= %	/12= %
Assess student's under- standing of the words: *Fill in the blank.*	15. a, b, c, d	/4= %	/4= %	/4= %	/12= %
Assess student's under- standing of the words: *Add (a given letter) to (a given word).*	16. a, b, c, d	/4= %	/4= %	/4= %	/12= %
Assess student's under- standing of the words: *Finish a (given word) with a (given word).*	24. a, b, c, d	/4= %	/4= %	/4= %	/12= %
Assess student's under- standing of the words: *Complete the sentence with a (given word).*	29, 30, 31, 32	/4= %	/4= %	/4= %	/12= %
Assess student's under- standing of the word *underline.*	17. a, b, c, d	/4= %	/4= %	/4= %	/12= %
Assess student's under- standing of the words: *Draw a line from (given word to a given word).*	18, 19, 20, 21	/4= %	/4= %	/4= %	/12= %
Assess student's under- standing of the words: *Draw a line under.*	22. a, b, c, d	/4= %	/4= %	/4= %	/12= %
Assess student's under- standing of the words: *Draw a line through.*	23. a, b, c, d	/4= %	/4= %	/4= %	/12= %

(continues)

Figure 7.1. *Continued*

		Day 1	Day 2	Day 3	Mastery = 83%
Assessment	**Problem**	**# Correct Total**	**# Correct Total**	**# Correct Total**	**10/12 = 83% X̄% = Correct**
Assess student's understanding of the words: *Add (given) before a word.*	25. a, b, c, d	/4= %	/4= %	/4= %	/12= %
Assess student's understanding of the words: *Add (given) after the words.*	26. a, b, c, d	/4= %	/4= %	/4= %	/12= %
Assess student's understanding of the words: *Underline the word in each sentence that comes before a (given).*	27. a, b, c, d	/4= %	/4= %	/4= %	/12= %
Assess student's understanding of the words: *Underline the word in each sentence that comes after a (given).*	28. a, b, c, d	/4= %	/4= %	/4= %	/12= %
Assess student's understanding of the words in a *three-sentence direction.*	33.	/4= %	/4= %	/4= %	/12= %

Figure 7.1. *Continued*

Directions Skills   Day 1

---

1. Print the words.

   a. tree _____

   b. bed _____

   c. boy _____

   d. men _____

2. Write the words.

   a. dad _____

   b. now _____

   c. put _____

   d. pin _____

3. Copy the dates.

   a. April 18, 1983 _____

   b. May 26, 1942 _____

   c. September 4, 1957 _____

   d. June 6, 1982 _____

4. Make a circle around each word.

   a. sit   b. am   c. pat   d. dress

5. Draw a ring around each word.

   a. ball   b. new   c. cord   d. shoe

6. Draw a circle around each word.

   a. met   b. bread   c. clean   d. pep

7. Circle each word.

   a. happy   b. up   c. set   d. five

8. Make a cross on each word.

   a. go   b. flat   c. my   d. low

9. Put a cross on each word.

   a. hat   b. slow   c. good   d. now

10. Put a cross beside each word.

    a. kitten   b. coat   c. grass   d. dog

11. Cross out each word.

    a. apple   b. cow   c. mitten   d. old

12. Put a check on each word.

    a. sock   b. high   c. pup   d. girl

13. Check the words.

    a. kite   b. had   c. saw   d. pea

14. Put a check beside the words.

    a. keep   b. glove   c. sad   d. pat

15. Fill in the blanks with *er*.

    a. saf____   b. fast____

    c. happi____   d. flow____

16. Add the letter *s* to the words.

    a. coat____   b. ____hoe____

    c. la____t   d. eye____

17. Underline each word.

    a. fire   b. old   c. clean   d. nice

18. Draw a line from *yellow* to *sun*.

    yellow   sun

19. Draw a line from *old* to *man*.

    old   man

20. Draw a line from *ball* to *bat*.

    ball   bat

21. Draw a line from *pen* to *paper*.

    pen   paper

22. Draw a line under each word.

    a. see   b. cards   c. ladder   d. nickel

23. Draw a line through each number.

    a. 14   b. 28   c. 86   d. 49

24. Finish the words below with *day*.

    a. Mon____   b. to____

    c. Fri____   d. yester____

25. Add *re* before the words.

    a. ____open   b. ____do

    c. ____finish   d. ____paint

26. Add *ly* after the words.

    a. slow____   b. scarce____

    c. sad____   d. rapid____

27. Underline the word in each sentence that comes before *the*.

    a. Our cat ate the mouse.

    b. Mary had the lamb at school.

    c. Bill took the boy to school.

    d. A lamp is on the table.

28. Underline the word in each sentence that comes after *a*.

    a. Pink is a color.

    b. Soda is a sweet drink.

    c. A plant can smell good.

    d. Today is a holiday.

29. Complete the sentence with the word *happy*.

    The boy feels _____.

30. Complete the sentence with the word *soft*.

    Kittens have_____ fur.

31. Complete the sentence with the word *nice*.

    Mary has _____ shoes.

32. Complete the sentence with the word *merry*.

    Old King Cole was a _____ old soul.

33. Draw a circle. Put an X in the circle. Underline the X.

Directions Skills   Day 2

---

1. Print the words.

   a. three _____

   b. bad _____

   c. toy _____

   d. man _____

2. Write the words.

   a. old _____

   b. cop _____

   c. mat _____

   d. sit _____

3. Copy the dates.

   a. July 7, 1981 _____

   b. August 19, 1924 _____

   c. January 10, 1931_____

   d. March 24, 1954 _____

4. Make a circle around each word.

   a. sat   b. me   c. pet   d. dance

5. Draw a ring around each word.

   a. bean   b. now   c. card   d. shell

6. Draw a circle around each word.

   a. mat   b. brown   c. clown   d. pop

7. Circle each word.

   a. hope   b. on   c. sat   d. four

8. Make a cross on each word.

   a. gun   b. find   c. am   d. lot

9. Put a cross on each word.

   a. hand   b. soft   c. grass   d. not

10. Put a cross beside each word.

    a. mitten   b. boat   c. good   d. sat

11. Cross out each word.

    a. hand   b. low   c. ladder   d. one

12. Put a check on each word.

    a. coat   b. side   c. pop   d. small

13. Check the words.

    a. king   b. have   c. sun   d. pod

14. Put a check beside the words.

    a. kind   b. grove   c. sip   d. pet

15. Fill in the blanks with *es*.

    a. box____   b. candi____

    c. babi____   d. mak____

16. Add the letter *m* to the words.

    a. war____   b. ____e____ber

    c. su____ ____er   d. sea____

17. Underline each of the words.

    a. fire   b. owl   c. cloud   d. new

18. Draw a line from *blue* to *sky*.

    blue   sky

19. Draw a line from *small* to *baby*.

    small   baby

20. Draw a line from *soap* to *water*.

    soap   water

21. Draw a line from *page* to *book*.

    page   book

22. Draw a line under each word.

    a. sap b. cake c. lower d. dime

23. Draw a line through each number.

    a. 12   b. 26   c. 84   d. 45

24. Finish the words below with *time*.

    a. day _____   b. some_____

    c. any_____   d. summer__ __

25. Add *in* before the words.

    a. _____to   b. _____side

    c. _____doors   d. _____deed

26. Add *ar* after the words.

    a. sol_____   b. pol_____

    c. rad_____   d. li_____

27. Underline the word in each sentence that comes before *to*.

    a. We went to church.

    b. The children want to play.

    c. After lunch let's go to the store.

    d. Don is going to work.

28. Underline the word in each sentence that comes after *in*.

    a. There are shells in the sea.

    b. The milk is in the glass.

    c. In the pot there is dirt.

    d. Halloween is in October.

29. Complete the sentence with the word *sad*.

    John was _____ to go.

30. Complete the sentence with the word *hard*.

    This bed is _____.

31. Complete the sentence with the word *good*.

    Tom did a _____ job.

32. Complete the sentence with the word *angry*.

    He was an _____ man.

33. Draw a line. Put an X on the line. Put a circle beside the X.

Directions Skills

Day 3

1. Print the words.

   a. spree _____

   b. bud _____

   c. key _____

   d. map _____

2. Write the words.

   a. fix _____

   b. pat _____

   c. red _____

   d. bat _____

3. Copy the dates.

   a. February 19, 1980 _____

   b. October 2, 1902 _____

   c. November 5, 1943 _____

   d. December 27, 1962 _____

4. Make a circle around each word.

   a. bat   b. so   c. put   d. does

5. Draw a ring around each word.

   a. back   b. not   c. call   d. shine

6. Draw a circle around each word.

   a. mit   b. brick   c. cloud   d. pat

7. Circle each word.

   a. help   b. in   c. sit   d. fan

8. Make a cross on each word.

   a. get   b. from   c. me   d. let

9. Put a cross on each word.

   a. hop   b. soap   c. glass   d. nod

10. Put a cross beside each word.

    a. madder   b. goat   c. gold   d. mop

11. Cross out each word.

    a. stone   b. now   c. kitten   d. owl

12. Put a check on each word.

    a. hat   b. down   c. pep   d. tiny

13. Check the words.

    a. kind   b. gave   c. sum   d. put

14. Put a check beside the words.

    a. kite   b. gone   c. set   d. pop

15. Fill in the blanks with *ly*.

    a. slow____   b. rapid____

    c. sad____   d. most____

16. Add the letter *t* to the words.

    a. ha____   b. la____er

    c. ____ur____le   d. s____ar____

17. Underline each of the words.

    a. five   b. own   c. clear   d. not

18. Draw a line from *brown* to *bear*.

    brown   bear

19. Draw a line from *table* to *chair*.

    table   chair

20. Draw a line from *spoon* to *fork*.

    spoon   fork

21. Draw a line from *needle* to *thread*.

    needle   thread

22. Draw a line under each word.

    a. sip   b.   coal   c.   tower   d.   down

23. Draw a line through each number.

    a.   18   b.   22   c.   48   d.   46

24. Finish the words below with *ball*.

    a. base_____   b.   hand_____

    c. basket_____   d.   foot_____

25. Add *on* before the words.

    a. ____to   b.   ____look

    c. ____ward   d.   ____ly

26. Add *or* after the words.

    a. invent____   b.   tail____

    c. sail____   d.   monit____

27. Underline the word in each sentence that comes before *on*.

    a.   The bottles are on the table.

    b.   Mary set the flowers on the step.

    c.   I can meet you on time.

    d.   We are going on a trip.

28. Underline the word in each sentence that comes after *at*.

    a.   We will leave at noon.

    b.   The toy is at the store.

    c.   At Jim's house we play school.

    d.   She is at the doctor.

29. Complete the sentence with the word *glad*.

    I am so _____ you came.

30. Complete the sentence with the word *wet*.

    The rain made the grass _____.

31. Complete the sentence with the word *neat*.

    This room is very _____.

32. Complete the sentence with the word *hurt*.

    Tom said his leg _____.

33. Draw an X. Put a circle around the X. Underline the circle.

Sample Study Skills CBA

Study skills are defined as the ability to take the knowledge that one has acquired and apply it to a problem. This is a skill that is separate from that of acquiring the new information. Workbook pages, homework assignments, and seatwork assignments are intended to give students practice in using knowledge they have acquired. Thus, a problem arises when a student lacks the study skills needed to carry out such practice assignments.

The study skills CBA assesses the student's ability to perform following complicated directions. The emphasis in this CBA is on areas of location and on locating items on a page, in a sen-tence, and in a word. The major focus is on the sentence. The student is asked to identify who, what, where, why, how, and how many parts of the sentence. Other areas of concentration are compare and contrast; sequencing sentences for meaning; ordering numbers, months, days; and ordering the alphabet (letters). Like the direc-tions skills CBA, the study skills CBA has a recording form (Figure 7.2), again organized by problem type and scoring system across days. The scoring system is identical to that used in the directions skills CBA, with a mastery criterion of 83 percent correct for each set of problem types.

The sample study skills CBA is presented in the following pages. It includes 35 items for each of the three test days.

Directions Skills Assessment Record Sheet					
Student's name_____ Age _____					
Tester_____ Dates_____ , _____ , _____					
Classroom Teacher_____ Grade_____ School _____					
		Day 1	Day 2	Day 3	Mastery = 8
Assessment	**Problem**	**# Correct** Total	**# Correct** Total	**# Correct** Total	**10/12 = 83%** X̄% = Correct
Location: Assess student's ability to *locate a given letter in a word.*	1, 2, 3, 4	/4= %	/4= %	/4= %	/12= %
Assess student's ability to *locate a word in a list above the sentence.*	5, 6, 7, 8	/4= %	/4= %	/4= %	/12= %
Assess student's ability to *locate a word in a list below the sentence.*	9, 10, 11, 12	/4= %	/4= %	/4= %	/12= %
Sentence structure **Location of sentence parts:** Assess student's ability to *locate the WHO part of the sentence.*	13. a, b, c, d	/4= %	/4= %	/4= %	/12= %
Assess student's ability to *locate the WHERE part of the sentence.*	14. a, b, c, d	/4= %	/4= %	/4= %	/12= %
Assess student's ability to *locate the WHAT part of the sentence.*	15. a, b, c, d	/4= %	/4= %	/4= %	/12= %

(continues)

Figure 7.2. Data recording form for study skills CBA.

Assessment	Problem	Day 1 # Correct Total	Day 2 # Correct Total	Day 3 # Correct Total	Mastery = 83% 10/12 = 83% X̄% = Correct
Assess student's ability to *locate the WHEN part of the sentence.*	16. a, b, c, d	/4= %	/4= %	/4= %	/12= %
Assess student's ability to *locate the WHY part of the sentence.*	17. a, b, c, d	/4= %	/4= %	/4= %	/12= %
Assess student's ability to *locate the part of the sentence that tells HOW MANY.*	18. a, b, c, d	/4= %	/4= %	/4= %	/12= %
Assess student's ability to *locate the part of the sentence that tells HOW.*	19. a, b, c, d	/4= %	/4= %	/4= %	/12= %
Sentence structure **Choice of correct sentence parts:** Assess student's ability to *fill in the blank with the word(s) that tell WHO.*	20. a, b, c, d	/4= %	/4= %	/4= %	/12= %
Assess student's ability to *fill in the blank with the word(s) that tell WHERE.*	21. a, b, c, d	/4= %	/4= %	/4= %	/12= %
Assess student's ability to *fill in the blank with the word(s) that tell WHAT.*	22. a, b, c, d	/4= %	/4= %	/4= %	/12= %
Assess student's ability to *fill in the blank with the word(s) that tell WHEN.*	23. a, b, c, d	/4= %	/4= %	/4= %	/12= %
Assess student's ability to *fill in the blank with the word(s) that tell WHY.*	24. a, b, c, d	/4= %	/4= %	/4= %	/12= %
Assess student's ability to *fill in the blank with the word(s) that tell HOW MANY.*	25. a, b, c, d	/4= %	/4= %	/4= %	/12= %
Assess student's ability to *fill in the blank with the word(s) that tell HOW.*	26. a, b, c, d	/4= %	/4= %	/4= %	/12= %
Compare and contrast: Assess student's ability to *find words that belong with one another.*	27, 28, 29, 30	/4= %	/4= %	/4= %	/12= %

(continues)

Figure 7.2. *Continued*

Assessment	Problem	Day 1 **# Correct** Total	Day 2 **# Correct** Total	Day 3 **# Correct** Total	Mastery = 83% **10/12 = 83%** X̄% = Correct
Sequencing words and numbers: Assess student's ability to *sequence words and numbers.*	31. a, b, c, d	/4= %	/4= %	/4= %	/12= %
Sentence structure Order of sentence parts: Assess student's ability to *put words in order to make a sentence.*	32. a, b, c, d	/4= %	/4= %	/4= %	/12= %
Sentence structure Order of question parts: Assess student's ability to *put words in order to make a question.*	33. a, b, c, d	/4= %	/4= %	/4= %	/12= %
Sentence sequencing: Assess student's ability to *put sentences in a meaningful order.*	34. a, b, c, d	/4= %	/4= %	/4= %	/12= %
Assess student's ability to *eliminate the word that doesn't belong.*	35. a, b, c, d	/4= %	/4= %	/4= %	/12= %
Assess student's understanding of the words: *Draw a line under.*	36. a, b, c, d	/4= %	/4= %	/4= %	/12= %
Assess student's understanding of the words: *Draw a line through.*	37. a, b, c, d	/4= %	/4= %	/4= %	/12= %
Assess student's understanding of the words: *Add (given) before a word.*	38. a, b, c, d	/4= %	/4= %	/4= %	/12= %
Assess student's understanding of the words: *Add (given) after the words.*	39. a, b, c, d	/4= %	/4= %	/4= %	/12= %
Assess student's understanding of the words: *Underline the word in each sentence that comes before a (given).*	40. a, b, c, d	/4= %	/4= %	/4= %	/12= %

(continues)

Figure 7.2. *Continued*

Assessment	Problem	Day 1	Day 2	Day 3	Mastery = 83%
		# Correct / Total	# Correct / Total	# Correct / Total	10/12 = 83% / X̄% = Correct
Assess student's understanding of the words: *Underline the word in each sentence that comes after a (given).*	41. a, b, c, d	/4= %	/4= %	/4= %	/12= %
Assess student's understanding of the words in a *three-sentence direction.*	42.	/4= %	/4= %	/4= %	/12= %

Figure 7.2. *Continued*

Study Skills   Day 1

1. Circle the word that has the letter *o* in it.

    tree   forest   bush

2. Circle the word that has the letter *t* in it.

    side   milk   toe

3. Circle the word that has the letter *s* in it.

    swim   puppy   cat

4. Circle the word that has the letter *m* in it.

    slow   mat   pet

    pet   bat   met   bake

    rent   make   sat   let

    cat   bent   set   mat

5. Find the word *sat* in the list above and circle it.

6. Find the word *rent* in the list above and circle it.

7. Find the word *set* in the list above and circle it.

8. Find the word *bake* in the list above and circle it.

9. Find the word *sock* in the list below and underline it.

10. Find the word *nose* in the list below and underline it.

11. Find the word *much* in the list below and underline it.

12. Find the word *nice* in the list below and underline it.

    lass   sock   any   bye

    not   nose   nice   kiss

    boy   soft   tie   much

13. Circle the word(s) that tell WHO.

    a. Sam was eating dinner.

    b. Mary saw a movie.

    c. She likes milk.

    d. The boys went to the store.

14. Circle the word(s) that tell WHERE.

    a. They went swimming at the beach.

    b. There were lots of people in the store.

    c. Let's go to town.

    d. Sandy sat in the chair.

15. Circle the word(s) that tell WHAT.

    a. The table is hard.

    b. An apple is red.

    c. Candy is sweet.

    d. The music was loud.

16. Circle the word(s) that tell WHEN.

    a. I saw him yesterday.

    b. We can skate now.

    c. Scott's birthday is today.

    d. The bell will ring at three o'clock.

17. Circle the word(s) that tell WHY.

    a. Sally could not reach it because she was too short.

    b. The kittens cried because their mother left.

    c. The chair fell because its leg was broken.

    d. Ned ate the apple because it was good.

18. Circle the word(s) that tell HOW MANY.

   a. I walked many miles.

   b. Bob has six cows.

   c. Sue ate four cookies.

   d. The boy had three balloons.

19. Circle the word(s) that tell HOW.

   a. She spoke softly.

   b. Jack quickly turned off the light.

   c. The road curved sharply.

   d. The dress fit nicely.

20. Fill in the blanks with the word(s) that tell WHO.

   a. _____ was happy.
   Muffy   Soap   A lamp

   b. _____ went to a party.
   The pet   Socks   He

   c. _____ got lost.
   Shoe   A nut   We

   d. _____ is my friend.

   A mop   Book   Susan

21. Fill in the blanks with the word(s) that tell WHERE.

   a. The kids sat _____.

      on the sofa   quietly   with the dog

   b. Wood was burning _____.

      slowly   in the fireplace   with us

   c. Some bugs were hiding _____.

      in the corner   nicely   with others

   d. We were sitting_____.

      with Bob   comfortably   at the table

22. Fill in the blanks with the word(s) that tell WHAT.

   a. _____ was broken.
      Bob   The mop   Yesterday

   b. _____ brings rain.
      They   Nearby   Springtime

   c. _____ are fun to wear in the summer.
      Tom   Sandals   Pink

   d. _____ was filled to the top.

      He   The glass   Blue

23. Fill in the blanks with the word(s) that tell WHEN.

   a. I had a strange dream _____.

      last night   near the door   room

   b. The movie will finish_____.

      in the cinema   screen   in a moment

   c. He will be back _____.

      at the pool   water   in the summer

   d. We will swim _____.

      at two o'clock   to the side   the cat

24. Fill in the blanks with the word(s) that tell WHY.

   a. I can't leave now _____.

   yesterday   at the beach   because I'm not done

   b. The library is a good place to read _____.

   lots of books   because it is quiet   at the zoo

   c. That water will freeze _____.

   in the river   outside   because it is cold

   d. I will get wet_____.

   on the street   because it is raining   in the park

25. Fill in the blanks with the word(s) that tell HOW MANY.

   a. There are _____ pennies in a dollar.

      one hundred   copper   pretty

   b. A cat has _____ lives.

      clean   good   nine

   c. It rained _____ inches today.

      blue   nice   four

   d. There are _____ houses on my street.

      ten   green   great

26. Fill in the blanks with the word(s) that tell HOW.

   a. The breeze felt _____.

      six   cool   above

   b. The meeting was _____.

      good   near   ten

   c. The mother hummed _____ to her baby.

      four   sweetly   over

   d. The music _____ drifted into the room.

      there   below   gently

27. Circle the word that belongs with *fork*.

   cup   spoon   table   glass

28. Circle the word that belongs with *pear*.

   shoe   banana   dad   milk

29. Circle the word that belongs with *cap*.

   sock   hose   hat   boat

30. Circle the word that belongs with *sun*.

   train   wind   moon   paper

31. List in the proper order.

   a. Monday   Saturday   Sunday   Tuesday

      _____

      _____

      _____

      _____

   b. 12   14   15   13

      _____

      _____

      _____

      _____

   c. March   May   April   February

      _____

      _____

      _____

      _____

   d. G   J   I   H

      _____

      _____

      _____

      _____

32. Put the words in order to make a sentence.

   a. *was   Mike   hungry*

   _____ _____ _____.

   b. *on the table   was   the glass*

   _____ _____ _____.

   c. *flew   quickly   the geese*

   _____ _____ _____.

   d. *was   the race   yesterday*

   _____ _____ _____.

33. Put the words in order to make a question.

   a. *the cat   is   where*

   _____ _____ _____?

   b. *can   we do   what*

   _____ _____ _____?

   c. *when   they go   can*

   _____ _____ _____?

   d. *you know   do   how*

   _____ _____ _____?

34. Number the sentences in order.

   a. _____They took it home.

   _____It had a broken wing.

   _____The boys found a bird on the ground.

   b. _____They saw little dogs do tricks.

   _____The boys went to the circus.

   _____One little dog jumped through the hoop.

   c. _____He took his wagon with him.

   _____He brought his groceries home in the wagon.

   _____Ben's mother sent him to the grocery store.

   d. _____The rain watered it.

   _____Betty put a seed in the ground.

   _____It poked through the damp dirt.

35. Which word does not belong? Underline it.

   a. green   brown   plate   orange

   b. apple   car   banana   pear

   c. paper   nail   screw   tack

   d. grass   flower   puzzle   tree

Study Skills

Day 2

1. Circle the word that has the letter *a* in it.

   dog   cat   cow

2. Circle the word that has the letter *l* in it.

   sit   map   alike

3. Circle the word that has the letter *c* in it.

   nice   good   nap

4. Circle the word that has the letter *n* in it.

   race   almost   now

ball	red	shiny	tree
basket	club	large	mouse
kite	man	road	pin

5. Find the word *large* in the list above and circle it.

6. Find the word *club* in the list above and circle it.

7. Find the word *pin* in the list above and circle it.

8. Find the word *ball* in the list above and circle it.

9. Find the word *blue* in the list below and underline it.

10. Find the word *table* in the list below and underline it.

11. Find the word *slow* in the list below and underline it.

12. Find the word *old* in the list below and under-line it.

fur	dog	clean	ten
table	fire	dirty	blue
hungry	slow	old	cat

13. Circle the word(s) that tell WHO.

    a. Paul carried the football.

    b. Bobby walked to the store.

    c. She wrote a letter.

    d. The boy fell down.

14. Circle the word(s) that tell WHERE.

    a. They found a bird on the ground.

    b. Today we made soap in school.

    c. Put the candy in the dish.

    d. Bill went to the lake.

15. Circle the word(s) that tell WHAT.

    a. The glass is empty.

    b. A knife is sharp.

    c. Steel is strong.

    d. The candle is hot.

16. Circle the word(s) that tell WHEN.

    a. I must be at work at eight o'clock.

    b. We will eat lunch at noon.

    c. John will be here shortly.

    d. The flowers will bloom in the spring.

17. Circle the word(s) that tell WHY.

    a. Dan washed the clothes because they were dirty.

    b. The boys went to first grade because they were old enough.

    c. Meghan likes Nan because she makes her laugh.

    d. I want to go to the circus because it will be fun.

18. Circle the word(s) that tell HOW MANY.

a. Mother baked a lot of pies.

b. Bill has two baseballs.

c. Grandma has eight cats.

d. There are five cents in a nickel.

19. Circle the word(s) that tell HOW.

a. The bird sang sweetly.

b. He rapidly put his coat on.

c. John skated backwards.

d. Tom touched the stove carefully.

20. Fill in the blanks with the word(s) that tell WHO.

a. _____ was sad.

   Ben   A cup   Soap

b. _____ went to the store.

   Banana   The coat   Dad

c. _____ need new books.

   The boat   Coins   We

d. _____ can play the horn.

   She   Neck   The pot

21. Fill in the blanks with the word(s) that tell WHERE.

a. Mary went _____.

   with her lamb   to school   yesterday

b. The bird was singing _____.

   softly   in its cage   with the cat

c. Some chairs were _____.

   broken   with the table   in the closet

d. We were dancing _____.

   at the wedding   gracefully   with my uncle

22. Fill in the blanks with the word(s) that tell WHAT.

a. _____ was tall.

   Yellow   The clock   He

b. _____ are in the sky.

   Dan   Blue   Clouds

c. _____ are pretty.

   Now   Flowers   Sue

d. _____ was still.

   The air   They   Green

23. Fill in the blanks with the word(s) that tell WHEN.

a. Saturday comes _____.

   the day   after Friday   at the end

b. We will see you _____.

   in a little while   at the house   in the room

c. We will go to the coast _____.

   to the west   the new people   in the fall

d. Church begins _____.

   at the corner   at nine o'clock   the hall

24. Fill in the blanks with the word(s) that tell WHY.

a. We ate the cake _____.

   at the beach   in the kitchen   because it was good

b. It will snow soon _____.

   because the man told us   outside   in the dark

c. The flowers will bloom _____.

   at the show   because it is spring   in the garden

d. The soup will cool _____.

   on the stove   because I set ice in it   at dinner

25. Fill in the blanks with the word(s) that tell HOW MANY.

    a. There are _____ pennies in a dime.

            pretty   shiny   ten

    b. The snow was _____ inches deep.

            cold   white   three

    c. My dog is _____ years old.

            twelve   very   nice

    d. There are _____ people here.

            good   six   clean

26. Fill in the blanks with the word(s) that tell HOW.

    a. The ice cream felt _____.

            cold   chocolate   green

    b. The horse looked _____.

            brown   vanilla   mad

    c. Mary seems _____.

            near   red   nice

    d. She worked _____ on her book.

            blue   neatly   old

27. Circle the word that belongs with *garden*.

    hooks   beans   bowls   pen

28. Circle the word that belongs with *rain*.

    snow   moon   children   sun

29. Circle the word that belongs with *cup*.

    tar   ice   glass   dime

30. Circle the word that belongs with *ball*.

    bat   hose   apple   pear

31. List in the proper order.

    a. Friday   Sunday   Saturday   Monday

    _____

    _____

    _____

    _____

    b. 8   10   7   9

    _____

    _____

    _____

    _____

    c. August   June   July   May

    _____

    _____

    _____

    _____

    d. C   F   E   D

    _____

    _____

    _____

    _____

32. Put the words in order to make a sentence.

   a. *milk   like   children*

   _____ _____ _____.

   b. *to school   goes   David*

   _____ _____ _____.

   c. *is made   the ball   of rubber*

   _____ _____ _____.

   d. *to go   wanted   Bill*

   _____ _____ _____.

33. Put the words in order to make a question.

   a. *the dish   is   where*

   _____ _____ _____?

   b. *did   she say   what*

   _____ _____ _____?

   c. *when   they leave   did*

   _____ _____ _____?

   d. *can   that be   how*

   _____ _____ _____?

34. Number the sentences in order.

   a. _____ He dropped the cup.

   _____ He was washing dishes.

   _____ It broke.

   b. _____ Bill wanted to go along.

   _____ Lorna was going to the zoo.

   _____ He ran home to ask his mother.

   c. _____ It bit him.

   _____ Jack went to the zoo.

   _____ He petted a lion.

   d. _____ Two birds ate it.

   _____ Mother made a pie.

   _____ It was gone.

35. Which of the words does not belong? Underline it.

   a. yellow   blue   sun   red

   b. coat   car   hat   shoes

   c. pencil   pen   paper   cup

   d. fork   spoon   chair   knife

Study Skills   Day 3

1. Circle the word that has the letter *e* in it.

    hungry   clean   dirty

2. Circle the word that has the letter *h* in it.

    shoe   take   mop

3. Circle the word that has the letter *r* in it.

    happy   fire   nod

4. Circle the word that has the letter *w* in it.

    mouse   wagon   yard

green	cold	hat	bowls
ton	blue	car	fan
shirt	book	band	shoe

5. Find the word *ton* in the list above and circle it.

6. Find the word *cold* in the list above and circle it.

7. Find the word *band* in the list above and circle it.

8. Find the word *fan* in the list above and circle it.

9. Find the word *blow* in the list below and underline it.

10. Find the word *cable* in the list below and underline it.

11. Find the word *slide* in the list below and underline it.

12. Find the word *sold* in the list below and underline it.

fire	farm	paper	sold
slide	cable	blow	hand
fan	pen	four	pop

13. Circle the word(s) that tell WHO.

    a. Jack went to the zoo.

    b. Bill opened the door.

    c. She wore a dress.

    d. The girls had a party.

14. Circle the word(s) that tell WHERE.

    a. They were going to the show.

    b. The nickel is in his pocket.

    c. Set the bottles on the table.

    d. Sam kicked the ball in the air.

15. Circle the word(s) that tell WHAT.

    a. The banana is brown.

    b. An elephant is big.

    c. Ice is cold.

    d. The window is open.

16. Circle the word(s) that tell WHEN.

    a. I will see you at the end of the show.

    b. Our club will meet after school.

    c. We will eat lunch later.

    d. The phone will ring at two o'clock.

17. Circle the word(s) that tell WHY.

    a. Barb walked to the store because it was a nice day.

    b. She went to the market because she needed food.

    c. They drank some pop because they were thirsty.

    d. He does not like to go to the doctor because she gives shots.

18. Circle the word(s) that tell HOW MANY.

    a. The movie lasted a few hours.

    b. Jane has seven kites.

    c. Peter is four feet tall.

    d. We live one mile from school.

19. Circle the word(s) that tell HOW.

    a. Ben loved his dog dearly.

    b. She neatly wrote her paper.

    c. The car moved forward.

    d. The breeze blew gently.

20. Fill in the blanks with the word(s) that tell WHO.

    a. _____ was sorry.

       The glass   Dan   Pear

    b. _____ went to school.

       Block   The ball   She

    c. _____ are studying.

       Today   The toys   We

    d. _____ is a dancer.

       Bob   Cake   The nose

21. Fill in the blanks with the word(s) that tell WHERE.

    a. Lucy studied _____.

       at the desk   math   with Bob

    b. The cat was playing _____.

       in the yard   quietly   with a ball

    c. Those people walked _____.

       slowly   with their friends   down the street

    d. We were tanning _____.

       with the birds   on vacation   in the sun

22. Fill in the blanks with the word(s) that tell WHAT.

    a. _____ was small.

       The table   Today   Paul

    b. _____ shone at night.

       Annie   Then   The moon

    c. _____ are warm in winter.

       Afternoon   Coats   She

    d. _____ was filled with milk.

       He   Here   The glass

23. Fill in the blanks with the word(s) that tell WHEN.

    a. She left _____.

       to the right   after lunch   the dog

    b. We went home _____.

       at midnight   the book   at school

    c. They can ski _____.

       at the lodge   as soon as they dress   the house

    d. The bell rings _____.

       in the lake   at twelve o'clock   the night

24. Fill in the blanks with the word(s) that tell WHY.

    a. The window is clean _____.

       in the bucket   with Mary   because Bob washed it

    b. I read the book _____.

       with my sister   because it was exciting   in two houses

    c. She sat down _____.

       because she was tired   at my house   in a pinch

    d. Nan closed the shade _____.

       in my room   at the corner   because the sun was bright

25. Fill in the blanks with the word(s) that tell HOW MANY.

    a. There are _____ nickels in a quarter.

       five   nice   bright

    b. Plant the seeds _____ inch deep.

       lumpy   one   brown

    c. Sally ate _____ crackers.

       salty   pink   seven

    d. There are _____ people in my class.

       young   thirteen   happy

26. Fill in the blanks with the word(s) that tell HOW.

    a. The sun felt _____.

       dark   black   warm

    b. The student was _____.

       quick   nine   green

    c. The little boy walked _____.

       four   carefully   yellow

    d. The son _____ thanked his father.

       twenty   gratefully   red

27. Circle the word that belongs with *mail*.

    letter   coin   boy   silk

28. Circle the word that belongs with *adult*.

    pencil   ruler   child   chair

29. Circle the word that belongs with *milk*.

    water   grass   keys   door

30. Circle the word that belongs with *two*.

    pin   four   wall   book

31. List in the proper order.

    a. Wednesday Tuesday Friday Thursday

    _____

    _____

    _____

    _____

b. 26   24   23   25

    _____

    _____

    _____

    _____

c. December October September November

    _____

    _____

    _____

    _____

d. N   L   K   M

    _____

    _____

    _____

    _____

32. Put the words in order to make a sentence.

    a. *empty   is   the plate*

    _____ _____ _____

    b. *is   the dress   blue*

    _____ _____ _____

    c. *Sam   pop   drinks*

    _____ _____ _____

    d. *the drawer   full   is*

    _____ _____ _____

33. Put the words in order to make a question.

a. *the chair   is   where?*

_____ _____ _____

b. *are   their names   what?*

_____ _____ _____

c. *should we   come   when?*

_____ _____ _____

d. *are   you   how?*

_____ _____ _____

34. Number the sentences in order.

a. _____ Bill helped him up.

_____ Ken fell down the stairs.

_____ Ken tripped.

b. _____ Phyllis threw the ball high.

_____ The window broke.

_____ Sam and Phyllis were playing ball.

c. _____ Sally was hungry after her nap.

_____ She was not hungry any more.

_____ She ate some cake.

d. _____ There was a big crash.

_____ It woke the baby.

_____ The baby was sleeping.

35. Which of the words does not belong? Underline it.

a. purple   grey   pink   chair

b. scarf   mittens   paper   boots

c. book   meat   bread   corn

d. milk   table   coffee   tea

References

Algozzine, R., Ruhl, K., & Ramsey, R. (1991). *Behaviorally disordered? Assessment for identification and instruction: Working with behavioral disorders.* Reston, VA: Council for Exceptional Children.

Allinder, R. (1996). When some is not better than none: Effects of differential implementation of curriculum-based measurement. *Exceptional Children, 62*(6), 525–535.

Allinder, R. (1995). An examination of the relationship between teacher efficacy and curriculum-based measurement and student achievement. *Remedial and Special Education, 16*(4), 247–254.

Allinder, R., & BeckBest, M. (1995). Differential effects of two approaches to supporting teachers' use of curriculum-based measurement. *The School Psychology Review, 4*(2), 287–298.

Allinder, R., & Oats, R. (1997). Effects of acceptability on teachers' implementation of curriculum-based measurement and student achievement in mathematics computation. *Remedial and Special Education, 18*, 113–120.

Armbruster, B., Stevens, R., & Rosenshine, B. (1977). *Analyzing content coverage and emphasis: A study of three curricula and two tests* (Technical Representative N26). Urbana: University of Illinois, Center for Study of Reading.

Bagnato, S. J., Neisworth, J., & Capone, A. (1986). Curriculum-based assessment for the young exceptional child: Rationale and review. *Topics in Early Childhood Special Education, 6*(2), 97–110.

Baker, S., & Good, R. (1995). Curriculum-based measurement of English reading with bilingual Hispanic students: A validation study with second grade students. *The School Psychology Review, 24*(4), 561–578.

Baker, S., & Good, R. (1994, April). *Curriculum-based measurement reading with bilingual Hispanic students: A validation study with second-grade students.* Paper presented at the Annual Meeting of the Council for Exceptional Children/National Training Program for Gifted Education, Denver, CO.

Bernauer, J., & Cress, K. (1997). How school communities can help redefine accountability assessment. *Phi Delta Kappan, 79*, 71–75.

Blankenship, C. (1985). Using curriculum-based assessment data to make instructional decisions. *Exceptional Children, 54*, 233–238.

Blankenship, C., & Lilly, M. S. (1981). *Mainstreaming students with learning and behavior problems.* New York: Holt, Rinehart & Winston.

Bol, L., & Strage, A. (1996). The contradiction between teachers' instructional goals and their assessment practices in high school biology courses. *Science Education, 80*, 45–163.

Bondurant-Utz, J., & Luciano, L. (1994). *A practical guide to infant and preschool assessment in special education.* Needham Heights, MA: Allyn & Bacon.

Brandt, R. (1996). On authentic performance assessment. *Educational Leadership, 54*(4), 5(1).

Brolin, D. E. (1992). *Life centered career education: Competency assessment batteries.* Reston, VA: Council for Exceptional Children.

Bullard, P., & McGee, G. (1984, April). *Developing and norming a curriculum-based assessment in reading.* Paper presented at the Annual Convention of the Council for Exceptional Children, Washington, DC.

Bursuck, W. D., & Lessen, E. (1987). A classroom-based model for assessing students with learning disabilities. *Learning Disabilities Focus, 3*(1), 17–29.

Casteel, J., Roop, L., & Schiller, L. (1996). "No such thing as an expert": Learning to live with standards in the classroom. *Language Arts, 73*(1), 30–36.

Cawley, J. F., Miller, J., & Carr, S. (1990). An examination of the reading performance of students with mild educational handicaps or learning disabilities. *Journal of Learning Disabilities, 23*, 284–290.

Clark, D. (1995). Quality mathematics: How can we tell. *Mathematics Teacher, 88*, 326–328.

Cline, T., & Frederickson, N. (Eds.). (1996). *Curriculum related assessment, Cummins and bilingual children.* Monograph. Bilingual Education and Bilingualism Series No. 8. Multilingual Matters, Ltd., 1900 Frost Road, Suite 101, Bristol, PA 19007.

Coballes-Vega, C., & Salend, S. J. (1988). Guidelines for assessing migrant handicapped students. *Diagnostique, 13*(2), 64–75.

Coulter, W. A. (1985). Implementing curriculum-based assessment: Considerations for pupil appraisal professionals. *Exceptional Children, 52*, 277–281.

Cundari, L. A., & Suppa, R. J. (1988). The potential uses of curriculum-based assessment for decision making in special education. *Exceptional Children, 35*, 143–154.

Davis, L., Fuchs, L., & Fuchs, D. (1995). "Will CBM help me learn?" Students' perception of the benefits of curriculum-based measurement. *Education and Treatment of Children, 18*, 19–32.

Day, V., & Skidmore, M. (1996). Linking performance assessment and curricular goals. *TEACHING Exceptional Children, 29*(1), 59–64.

Delfino, L. (1994, November). *Curriculum-based assessment for adjudicated youth.* Paper presented at the Annual Conference of Children with Behavioral Disorders, Tempe, AZ.

Deno, S. (1985). Curriculum-based assessment: The emerging alternative. *Exceptional Children, 52*, 219–232.

Dwyer, J., & Rule, D. (1997). The effects of a kindergarten prevention program on special education referrals, classifications, and retentions. ERIC Document No ED406806.

Eckert, T., Shapiro, E., & Lutz, J. (1995). Teachers' ratings of the acceptability of curriculum-based assessment methods. *The School Psychology Review, 24*(3), 497–511.

Elliott, S., & Fuchs, L. (1997). The utility of curriculum-based measurement and performance assessment as alternatives to traditional intelligence and achievement tests. *The School Psychology Review, 26*(2), 224–233.

Epstein, M. H., Kinder, D., & Bursuck, B. (1989). The academic status of adolescents with behavioral disorders. *Behavioral Disorders, 14*, 157–165.

Epstein S. (1980). The stability of behavior: II. Implications for psychological research. *American Psychologist, 35*, 790–806.

Erpelding, D. (1990). *Integrating whole language with the basal reader to increase the use of language and comprehension of literature.* Davenport, IA: Marycrest College, MA Project. (ERIC Document Reproduction Service No. ED 350–578).

Espin, C., & Deno, S. (1995). Curriculum-based measures for secondary students: Utility and task specificity of text-based reading and vocabulary measures for predicting performance on content-area tasks. *Diagnostique, 20*(1-4), 121–142.

Espin, C., & Foegen, A. (1996). Validity of general outcome measures for predicting secondary students' performance on content-area tasks. *Exceptional Children, 62*, 497–514.

Foster, G. G., & Salvia, J. (1977). Teacher response to the label learning disabled as a function of demand characteristics. *Exceptional Children, 43*, 533–534.

Foster, G. G., Schmidt, C. R., & Sabatino, D. (1976). Teacher expectancies and the label "learning disabilities." *Journal of Learning Disabilities, 9*, 58–61.

Foster, K. (1990). *Broadening school psychological services through program evaluation and modification that emphasized curriculum-based assessment* (EdD Practicum Report). Fort Lauderdale, FL: Nova University.

Frey, B. (1995). *Portfolio assessment.* Monograph. Lewistown, PA: Adult Education and Job Training Center. (ERIC Document No. ED404503).

Fuchs, L. S. (1994). Integrating curriculum-based assessment with instructional planning for students with learning disabilities. In N. Jordan & J. Goldsmith-Phillips (Eds.), *Learning disabilities: New directions for assessment and intervention* (pp. 177–198). Needham Heights, MA: Allyn & Bacon.

Fuchs, L. S., & Deno, S. L. (1981). *A comparison of reading placements based on teacher judgment, standardized testing, and curriculum-based assessment.* Minneapolis: University of Minnesota, Institute for Research on Learning Disabilities.

Fuchs, D., & Fuchs, L. (1995). What's 'special' about special education? *Phi Delta Kappan, 76*, 522–530.

Fuchs, L. S., & Fuchs, D. (1986a). Curriculum-based assessment of progress toward long-term and short-term goals. *Journal of Special Education, 20*, 69–82.

Fuchs, L. S., & Fuchs, D. (1986b, April). *Effects of long- and short-term goal assessment on student achievement.* Paper presented at the Annual Meeting of the American Educational Research Association, San Francisco.

Fuchs, L. S., Fuchs, D., & Deno, S. L. (1982). Reliability and validity of curriculum-based informal reading inventories. *Reading Research Quarterly, 18*, 6–25.

Fuchs, L. S., Fuchs, D., & Hamlett, C. (1989). Effects of alternative goal structures within curriculum-based assessment. *Exceptional Children, 55*, 429–438.

Fuchs, L. S., Fuchs, D., & Hamlett, C. (1990). Curriculum-based measurement: A standardized long-term approach to monitoring student progress. *Academic Therapy, 25*, 615–632.

Fuchs, L. S., Fuchs, D., & Hamlett, C. (1994). Classwide curriculum-based measurement: Helping general educators meet the challenges of diversity. *Exceptional Children, 60*, 518–537.

Fuchs, L., Fuchs, D., Hamlett, C., & Ferguson, C. (1992). Effects of expert system consultation with curriculum-based measurement using a reading maze test. *Exceptional Children, 3*, 436–450.

Fuchs, L., Fuchs, D., & Karns, K. (1995). General educators' specialized adaptation for students with learning disabilities. *Exceptional Children, 61*(5), 440–459.

Fuchs, L. S., Fuchs, D., & Maxwell, L. (1988). The validation of informal reading comprehension measures. *Remedial and Special Education, 9*(2), 20–29.

Fuchs, L., Fuchs, D., & Phillips, N.H. (1995). Acquisition and transfer effects of classwide peer-assisted learning strategies in mathematics for students with varying learning histories. *The School Psychology Review, 24*(4), 604–620.

Fuchs, L. S., Fuchs, D., Tindal, G., & Deno, S. (1981). *Effects of varying item domain and sample duration on technical characteristics of daily measures in reading.* Minneapolis: University of Minnesota, Institute for Research on Learning Disabilities.

Fuchs, D., Roberts, P.H., & Barns, J. (1996). Reintegrating students with learning disabilities into the mainstream: A two year study. *Learning Disabilities Research and Practice, 11*(4), 214–229.

Gable, R., Arllen, N., & Evans, W. (1997). Strategies for evaluating collaborative mainstream insurrection: "Let the data be our guide." *Preventing School Failure, 41*, 153–158.

Gable, R. A., Enright, B., & Hendrickson, J. (1991). A practical model for curriculum-based assessment and instruction in arithmetic. *Teaching Exceptional Children, 24*(1), 6–9.

Germann, G., & Tindal, G. (1985). An application of curriculum-based assessment: The use of direct and repeated measurement. *Exceptional Children, 54*, 244–265.

Gersten, R., Vaughn, S., & Brengelman, S. (1996). Grading and academic feedback for special education students and students with learning difficulties. *Yearbook.* Alexandria, VA: Association for Supervision and Curriculum Development.

Gickling, E. E., & Havertape, J. F. (1981). Curriculum-based assessment. In J. A. Tucker (Ed.), *Non-test based assessment* (pp. 1–36). Minneapolis: University of Minnesota, National School Psychology Inservice Network.

Gickling, E., Shane, R., & Croskery, K. (1989). Developing mathematics skills in low-achieving high school students through curriculum-based assessment. *School Psychology Review, 18,* 344–355.

Gickling, E. E., & Thompson, V. (1985). A personal view of curriculum-based assessment. *Exceptional Children, 52,* 205–218.

Gilbert, J. C., & Burger, P. (1990). *Performance-based assessment resource guide.* Denver: Colorado State Department of Education.

Gillung, T. B., & Rucker, C. N. (1977). Labels and teacher expectations. *Exceptional Children, 43,* 464–465.

Ginn & Co. (1982). *The Ginn reading program.* Lexington, MA: Author.

Gong, B., & Reidy, E. (1996). Assessment and accountability in Kentucky's school reform. *Yearbook of the National Society for the Study of Education, 95*(1), 215–233.

Gordon, E. (1995). Toward an equitable system of educational assessment. *The Journal of Negro Education, 64,* 360–372.

Graue, M., & Smith, S. (1996). Parents and mathematics education reform: Voicing the authority of assessment. *Urban Education, 30,* 395–421.

Guernsey, M. A. (1990). Curriculum-based assessment and the regular classroom teacher. *Illinois Schools Journal, 69*(2), 15–19.

Haring, N. G., Lovitt, T. C., Eaton, M. D., & Hansen, C. L. (1978). *The fourth R: Research in the classroom.* Columbus, OH: Merrill.

Hintze, J., Shapiro, E., & Lutz, G. (1994). The effects of curriculum on the sensitivity of curriculum-based measurement in reading. *Journal of Special Education, 28,* 188–202.

Howell, K., & Evans, D. (1995). A comment on "Must instructionally useful performance assessment be based in the curriculum?" *Exceptional Children, 61,* 394–396.

Idol, L. (1993). *Special educator's consultation handbook* (2nd ed.). Austin, TX: PRO–ED.

Idol, L. (1997). Reading success: A specialized literacy program for leraners with challenging needs. Austin, TX: PRO-ED.

Idol, L., Nevin, A., & Paolucci-Whitcomb, P. (in press) *Collaborative consultation* (3rd ed.). Austin, TX: PRO–ED.

Idol, L., & West, J. F. (1993). *Effective instruction of difficult-to-teach students: An inservice and preservice professional development program for classroom, remedial, and special education teachers.* Austin, TX: PRO–ED.

Idol-Maestas, L. (1981). A teacher training model: The resource/consulting teacher. *Behavioral Disorders, 6,* 108–121.

Idol-Maestas, L. (1983). *Special educator's consultation handbook.* Austin, TX: PRO–ED.

Idol-Maestas, L., Paolucci–Whitcomb, P., & Nevin, A. (1986). *Collaborative consultation.* Austin, TX: PRO–ED.

Jenkins, J. R., & Pany, D. (1976a). Curriculum biases in reading achievement tests. *Journal of Reading Behavior, 10,* 345–357.

Jenkins, J. R., & Pany, D. (1976b). Standardized achievement tests: How useful for special education? *Exceptional Children, 44,* 448–453.

Johnston, P. H. (1981). *Prior knowledge and reading comprehension test bias.* Unpublished doctoral dissertation, University of Illinois, Urbana.

Jonietz, P. L. (1990, October). *Developing collaboratively an international school special needs plan for multicultural, multilingual, and multinational secondary students.* Paper presented at the Council for Exceptional Children Symposium on Culturally Diverse Exceptional Children, Albuquerque, NM.

Joyce, B. G., & Wolking, W. D. (1988). Curriculum-based assessment: An alternative approach for screening young gifted children in rural areas. *Rural Special Education Quarterly, 8*(4), 9–14.

Karns, K., Fuchs, L., & Fuchs, D. (1995). Curriculum-based measurement: Facilitating individualized instruction and accommodating student diversity. *LD Forum, 20*(2), 16–19.

King-Sears, M. (1997). Best academic practices for inclusive classrooms. *Focus on Exceptional Children, 29*(7), 1–22.

Lewis, A. (1997). Changing assessment, changing curriculum. *Education Digest, 62*(7), 13–15.

Lilly, M. S. (1979). *Children with exceptional needs: A survey of special education.* New York: Holt, Rinehart & Winston.

Marston, D., & Magnusson, D. (1985). Implementing curriculum-based assessment: Considerations for pupil appraisal professionals. *Exceptional Children, 52,* 266–276.

Mathes, P., Fuchs, D., & Fuchs, L. (1995). Accommodating diversity through Peabody classwide peer tutoring. *Intervention in School and Clinic, 31,* 46–50.

Mehrens, W. A., & Clarizio, H. F. (1993). Curriculum-based measurement: Conceptual and psychometric considerations. *Psychology in the Schools, 30,* 241–254.

Morison, P., White, S., & Feuer, M. (Eds.). (1996). *The use of IQ tests in special education decision making and planning.* National Academy of Sciences Board bulletin. Washington, DC: Board on Testing and Assessment, National Research Council, 2101 Constitution Avenue, NW., Washington, DC 20418. (ERIC Document No. ED393261)

Nelson, N. W. (1989). Curriculum-based language assessment and intervention. *Language, Speech, and Hearing Services in Schools, 20*(2), 170–184.

Nitko, A. (1995). Is the curriculum a reasonable basis for assessment reform? *Educational Measurement, 14,* 5–10.

Norris, P., Fuchs, L., & Fuchs, D. (1994). Effects of classwide curriculum-based measurement and peer tutoring: A collaborative researcher-practitioner interview study. *Journal of Learning Disabilities, 27,* 420–434.

Notari, A. R., & Drinkwater, S. S. (1991). Best practices for writing child outcomes: An evaluation of two methods. *Topics in Early Childhood Special Education, 11*(3), 92–106.

Ortiz, A. A., & Wilkinson, C. Y. (1991). Assessment and intervention model for the bilingual exceptional student (AIM for the BESt). *Teacher Education and Special Education, 14,* 35–42.

Pallrand, G. (1996). The relationship of assessment to knowledge development in science education. *Phi Delta Kappan, 78*(4), 315.

Parke, C., & Lane, S. (1996). Learning from performance assessments in math. *Educational Leadership, 54*(4), 26(4).

Parker, D., & Picard, A. (1997). Portraits of Susie: Matching curriculum instruction, and assessment. *Teaching Children Mathematics, 3*(7), 376–377.

Paulsen, K. (1997). Curriculum-based measurement: Translating research in to school-based practice. *Intervention in School and Clinic, 32*, 162–167.

Pearson, P. D. (1982). *Asking questions about stories*. Boston: Ginn.

Peterson, J., Heistad, D., Peterson, D., & Reynolds, M. (1985). Montevideo individualized prescriptive instructional management system. *Exceptional Children, 52*, 239–243.

Resnick, L. B., Wang, M. C., & Kaplan, J. (1973). Task analysis in curriculum design: A hierarchically sequenced introductory mathematics curriculum. *Journal of Applied Behavior Analysis, 6*, 679–710.

Roberts, A., & Rust, J. (1994). Role and function of school psychologists, 1992–93: A comparative study. *Psychology in the Schools, 31*, 113–119.

Roberts, M., & Shapiro, E. (1996). Effects of instructional ratios on students' reading performance in a regular education program. *Journal of School Psychology, 34*, 73–91.

Rogan, J., LaJeunesse, C., & Miller, C. (1995). Facilitating inclusion: The role of learning strategies to support secondary students with special needs. *Preventing School Failure, 39*(3), 35–39.

Rosenfield, S., & Shinn, M. R. (Eds.). (1989). Mini-series on curriculum based assessment. *School Psychology Review, 18*, 287–370.

Russell, D. (1995). Collaborative portfolio assessment in the English secondary school system. *The Clearing House, 68*, 244–247.

Rydell, L. (1990). *The least biased assessment: Implications for special education* (Crosscultural Special Education Series, Vol. 4). Sacramento: Resources in Special Education.

Scott, Foresman & Co. (1978). *Spelling: Words and skills*. Glenview, IL: Author.

Seidenberg, P. L. (1986). *Curriculum-based assessment procedures for secondary learning disabled students: Student centered and programmatic implications* (Long Island University Transition Project Learning How to Learn: A High School/College Linkage Model to Expand Higher Educational Opportunities for Learning Disabled Students, Position Paper Series: Document No. 4). Brooklyn: Long Island University.

Seidenberg, P. L. (1987). *The unrealized potential: College preparation for secondary learning disabled students. A guide for secondary school administrators, faculty, and parents* (Long Island University Transition Project Learning How to Learn: A High School/College Linkage Model to Expand Higher Educational Opportunities for Learning Disabled Students, Position Paper Series: Document No. 10). Brooklyn: Long Island University.

Shanks, R. D., Jr. (Ed.). (1986). *Instructional and curriculum guidelines for the resource room program* (ED 278203). Grand Island, NE: Grand Island School District.

Shapiro, E. S., & Eckert, T. L. (1993). Curriculum-based assessment among school psychologists: Knowledge, use, and attitudes. *Journal of School Psychology, 31*, 375–384.

Shapiro, E. S., & Eckert, T. L. (1994). Acceptability of curriculum based assessment by school psychologists. *Journal of School Psychology, 32*, 167–183.

Shinn, M. R., Powell-Smith, K., & Good, R. (1997). The effects of reintegration into general education reading insurrection for students with mild disabilities. *Exceptional Children, 64*, 59–79.

Skakun, V. (1988). Integration—how can we make it work? In D. Baine, D. Sobsey, L. Wilgosh, & G. Kysela (Eds.), *Alternative futures for education of students with severe disabilities*. Edmonton, Alberta, Canada: University of Alberta, Department of Educational Psychology.

Smith, M., & Levin, J. (1996). Coherence, assessment, and challenging content. *Yearbook for the National Society for the Study of Education, 95*(1), 104–124.

Smith, T. E., & Dowdy, C. (1992). Future-based assessment and intervention for students with mental retardation. *Education and Training in Mental Retardation, 27*, 255–260.

Stodden, R. A., & Ianacone, R. N. (1986). *Curriculum-based vocational assessment handbook: A guide to the implementation of curriculum-based vocational assessment activities* (rev.). Washington, DC: Dependents Schools (DOD), European Area.

Stoner, G., Carey, S., & Ikeda, M. (1994). The utility of curriculum-based measurement for evaluating the effects of methylphenidate on academic performance. *Journal of Applied Behavior Analysis, 27*, 101–113.

Swisher, J., & Clark, G. M. (1991). Curriculum-based vocational assessment of students with special needs at the middle school/junior high school levels: The practical arts evaluation system (PAES). *Journal for Vocational Special Needs Education, 13*(3), 9–14.

Thomas, A., & Grimes, J. (Eds.). (1990). *Best practices in school psychology—II*. Silver Spring, MD: National Association of School Psychologists.

Thompson, D., Beckmann, C., & Senk, S. (1997). Improving classroom tests as a means of improving assessment. *Mathematics Teacher, 90*(1), 58(7).

Thousand, J. W., & Villa, R. A. (1990). Strategies for educating learners with severe disabilities within their local home schools and communities. *Focus on Exceptional Children, 23*(3), 1–24.

Tindal, G. (1992). Evaluating instructional programs using curriculum-based measurement. *Preventing School Failure, 36*(2), 39–42.

Tindal, G., & Nolet, V. (1995). Curriculum-based measurement in middle and high schools: Critical thinking skills in content areas. *Focus on Exceptional Children, 27*, 1–22.

Tindal, G., & Parker, R. (1989). Development of written retell as a curriculum-based measure in secondary programs. *School Psychology Review, 18*, 328–343.

Tucker, J. (1985). Curriculum-based assessment: A special issue. *Exceptional Children, 52*, 199–204.

Tuinman, J. J. (1974). Determining the passage-dependency of comprehension questions on five major tests. *Reading Research Quarterly, 2*, 207–223.

Umbreit, J. (1995). Functional assessment and intervention in a regular classroom setting for the disruptive behavior of a student with attention deficit hyperactivity disorder. *Behavioral Disorders, 20*(4), 267–278.

Umbreit, J. (1996). Functional analysis of disruptive behavior in an *inclusive* classroom. *Journal of Early Intervention, 20*(1), 18–29.

Van Zant, S., & Brown, S. (1997). Evaluating student success. *Thrust for Educational Leadership, 26*, 18–20.

Webb, N. (1994). Special education: With new court decisions backing them, advocates see inclusion as a question of value. *The Harvard Education Letter, 10*(4), 1–3.

Wiederholt, J. L. (1974). Planning resource for the mildly handicapped. *Focus on Exceptional Children, 8*(5), 1–11.

Wiggins, G. (1995). Curricular coherence and assessment: Making sure that the effect matches the intent. *Yearbook for the Association for Supervision and Curriculum Development, 95*(1), 101–119.

Wiggins, G. (1996). Practicing what we preach in designing authentic assessments. *Educational Leadership, 54*(4), 19(8).

Wilcox, S., & Zielinski, R. (1997). Using the assessment of students' learning to reshape teaching. *Mathematics Teacher, 90*(3), 223–227.

Wisconsin Department of Education. (1985). *Educational assessment: A guide for teachers of the learning disabled* (Bulletin No. 5232). Madison: Author, Division for Handicapped Children and Pupil Services.

Wixson, K., Peters, C., & Potter, S. (1996). The case for integrated standards in English Language Arts. *Language Arts, 73*(1), 20(10).

Appendix: The Mechanics of Composition

Capitalization

445[a] Every sentence except a very short parenthetical sentence within another should begin with a capital letter:

> *The* day was beautiful.

> *Mary* left yesterday (she had been here a week) for New York City.

446 Every line of poetry should begin with a capital:

> "*Poems* are made by fools like me,
> *But* only God can make a tree."

447 The first word of a direct quotation should begin with a capital letter:

> The girl said, "*Wait* for me."

448 The first word of a formal statement or resolution should be capitalized:

> Resolved, *That* the world is growing better.

449 Every proper noun (52)[a] and every adjective derived from a proper noun (279) should be capitalized: *Boston, John Smith, Grand Army of the Republic, French, American.*

450 The names of the days of the week, special holidays, and the names of the months should be capitalized: *Sunday, June.*

451 Names of the seasons are not capitalized ordinarily:

> I like *summer* better than *winter.*

452 Names of particular associations and proper names resulting from membership in these associations should be capitalized: *Republican Party, Democrat, Methodist, Garden Club.*

Note: Classes, schools, and colleges are capitalized when they refer to the particular:

> John is a senior in *Brown College;* he attended *Oak High School.*

> The *Junior Class* invited Miss Smith to speak.

The use of capitals seems to be optional in some instances in which class names are used to refer to particular classes:

> The *Juniors* (or *juniors*) have come.

453 Some abbreviations, such as the following, are usually written with capitals: MS, MSS, *A.D., B.C., No., C.O.D.*

454 Important historical events and numbered school courses should be capitalized: *Battle of Hastings, World War II, Declaration of Independence, Science 11.*

School subjects, unless derived from proper names, are not capitalized except in numbered courses:

> We study *history* and *English.*

455 The words *east, west, north* and *south* are capitalized when they mean particular sections of the country, but they are not capitalized when they mean directions:

> He came from the *South.* (a section of the country)

Note. From *Plain English Handbook* by J. M. Walsh and A. K. Walsh, 1951, Wichita, KS: McCormick-Mathers. Copyright 1951 by McCormick-Mathers.
[a]Numbers in boldface and in parentheses refer to sections of *Plain English Handbook*.

He went *south* from town. (a direction)

The compounds of these words follow the same rule:

He lives in the great *Northwest.*

Is Hutchinson *northwest* of Wichita?

456 Nouns and personal pronouns (127) referring to God or to Christ are capitalized; but some authorities do not capitalize the personal pronoun when its antecedent (124) is expressed:

I know He is the *Lord.*

Jesus loves his friends.

457 The words *Bible, Scriptures,* and names of books of the Bible should begin with capital letters.

458 The titles of books, literary articles, pictures, musical compositions, chapters of books, poems, plays, stories, newspapers, and magazines should be capitalized. Prepositions, articles, auxiliary verbs, and conjunctions are not capitalized unless they begin the title. If an article begins the title of a magazine or newspaper, it is not capitalized unless it begins a sentence:

"Ode on a Grecian Urn"

He reads the *Saturday Evening Post.*

460 The initials of a person's name should be capitals.

461 Titles used with proper names should be capitalized:

We think that *Captain Smith* would make a good school *principal,* but he prefers to be a *captain.*

He saw *Principal* John Moore at the meeting of *principals* and *superintendents.*

462 When a title is used as a proper noun referring to a particular person, it is correct to capitalize it:

The *President* of the United States spoke today.

Ann went with *Mother* and me to see her *mother.*

Note: There is much disagreement among authorities as to the application of this rule. It seems the preference to capitalize the word *president* when it refers to the President of the United States whether it refers to a particular man or not, especially when it is preceded by *the.* Capitalization of such a term as *mother, father, uncle, sister,* or *cousin,* when it refers to a particular person, is considered optional by most writers; but some consider the use of the capital obligatory when the title is used in direct address. If, however, a possessive immediately precedes such a term, no capital is used. The following are correct:

I went with *Mother* to Chicago.

I went with my *mother* to Chicago.

Will you help me, *Father,* with this work?

I went with my *father* to New Orleans.

463 Common nouns are capitalized when they are strongly personified.

Come, lovely *Autumn,* and make us glad.

464 A common noun, such as *river, mountain, park, lake, gulf, ocean, street, avenue, hotel, church, school, club, society,* or *company,* is properly capitalized when it becomes a part of a particular name:

Is Lowell *School* near Belmont Park?

Does Clifton *Avenue* cross Maple *Street?*

Note: There is lack of agreement as to the application of this rule. Some good authorities capitalize only the first word in names of which these words are part. Many newspapers use the form given below; the schools seem to prefer the form already illustrated:

Is Lowell *school* near Belmont *park?*

Does Clifton *avenue* cross Maple *street?*

If the common noun precedes the particular name, it is capitalized in the newspapers:

He lives near *Lake* Erie.

Punctuation

Period

465 A period should be placed at the end of every declarative (25) and every imperative (26) sentence unless it is used as an exclamatory (28) sentence or is a very short sentence used parenthetically within another sentence (445). An elliptical expression (5, 482) used as a substitute for a sentence is followed by a period or other end punctuation:

Jean went to Europe last summer. (declarative)

Let me see your new book. (imperative)

Fred Jones (he is president of our class) will arrange the program. (parenthetical sentence with no capital, 445, and no period)

Yes. (elliptical)

Note: The polite request disguised as a question, so frequent in letters, is followed by a period, not a question mark (506).

Will you please send your latest catalogue.

466 Use periods after initials and most abbreviations: *A.D., B.C., C.O.D., No., Geo. F. Smith, LL.D.*

There are exceptions, such as *MS, MSS,* and *per cent.* Consult the dictionary as a guide to the handling of abbreviations. Do not use a period after a contraction or after a part of a name used as a whole:

Ben Brown *isn't* here.

Note: Only one period is necessary at the end of a sentence even if it ends with an abbreviation, but a question mark (506) may follow a period used after an abbreviation at the end of a sentence:

A great battle was fought in the year 490 B.C.

What battle was fought in the year 490 B.C.?

467 Three periods are used to show the omission of material:

He did his best . . . yet he never quite succeeded.

Note: The period is used between the integral and decimal parts of a mixed fraction; and it may be used between figures indicating hours and minutes, though the colon (473) is generally preferred:

The lake is 62.35 miles long.

He arrived at 10.45 p.m.

Semicolon

468 Use a semicolon between two clauses of a compound sentence (401) when they are not joined by a conjunction (355-359) unless they are very short and are used informally (475):

The rain came in torrents; we did not know what to do. (This may be punctuated as two sentences.)

He came; he saw; he went away.

469 The semicolon is used between two clauses of a compound sentence which are joined by connectives such as *therefore, hence, ever, nevertheless, accordingly, thus, then:*

> The day was very cold; therefore we did not go for a ride.

470 The semicolon is used between clauses which are joined by conjunctions if the clauses are long, or if the clauses have commas within themselves:

> John arrived last night, I am told; and on his arrival at the hospital, he found his father still alive.

Note: The semicolon may be used for clearness:

> We invited Don Webb, the captain of the team; Sue Mills, the president of our class; and Joe Wynn, the chairman of our group.

471 The semicolon usually precedes *as, namely,* or *thus* when used to introduce examples:

> Four boys were mentioned; *namely,* Henry, Clarence, Merle, and Clyde.

Colon

472 The colon is used to introduce formally a word, a list, a statement or question, a series of statements, or a long quotation. An expression such as *as follows* or *the following* usually precedes the list:

> He brought *the following* fruit: apples, peaches, pears.

473 A colon is used after the salutation of a business letter and is used between the parts of a number denoting time:

> Dear Sir:

> He came at 6:15 this morning.

Comma

474 Many authorities insist upon using a comma between the clauses of a compound sentence (401) if they are joined by such a conjunction as *but, for, or, yet,* or *and.* Other authorities contend that the use of the comma here is merely optional. If, however, the clauses are long and have commas within them, a semicolon should be used to separate them (see 470):

> Robert entered the race, but he did not win.

> Robert entered the race but he did not win. (also accepted)

475 Very short clauses making up a series and not joined by conjunctions may be separated by commas (468, 483):

> She came, she looked, she went away.

476 An adverbial clause (398) which precedes a main clause (386), unless it is very short, is set off by a comma:

> When my cousin came to spend the day with me, she found me work.

> If you expect to succeed, you must prepare yourself.

The comma is usually omitted when the adverbial clause follows the main clause:

> My cousin found me at work when she came to spend the day with me.

477 A comma should be used to set off *yes, no,* or *well* when used at the beginning of a sentence:

> Yes, you may go.

Other introductory words, such as mild exclamations, are usually set off by commas:

> Ah, who can tell what may happen?

478 Nonrestrictive phrases and clauses should be set off from the rest of the sentence by a comma or commas. A nonrestrictive phrase or clause is a nonessential phrase or clause; that is, it is a phrase or a clause which could be omitted without changing the meaning of the main clause:

> Edgar Allan Poe, who wrote "The Raven," is a great American poet. (The clause *who wrote "The Raven"* is not necessary to the meaning of the main clause.)

> Boys who study will learn. (The clause *who study* is necessary to the meaning.)

> The girl who sells the tickets is a member of the class. (*Who sells the tickets* is necessary.)

> Jane Gray, who sells the concert tickets, is a member of our class. (The clause is not necessary; it merely explains that the girl sells tickets.)

> The boy, seeing the cloud, hurried home. (The phrase is not necessary.)

> The girl holding the flag is Margaret. (The phrase is necessary to the meaning.)

> Wishing to see the parade, we went to town early. (A participial phrase, 380-3, which stands at the beginning of a sentence is followed by a comma.)

> The task being done, we went home. (absolute, 95)

479 Items of a parenthetical nature are set off by commas. Two commas are necessary when the expression is within the sentence and no other mark is used. These items include persons addressed, appositives, items in addresses and dates, as well as independent phrases and clauses:

> Will you help me, Harry, with this work?

> Nan Gray, my favorite cousin, is here.

> Tom came from Dallas, Texas, yesterday.

> Jane was born on June 12, 1932, in Wichita.

> That boy is, I believe, a dependable chap.

Note: When an appositive (97) is a part of the proper name, or is closely connected with the word it explains, no comma is used.

> Edward the Confessor was there.

> My cousin Nell lives in Arizona.

480 A direct informal quotation equivalent to a sentence should be separated from explanatory matter by a comma or commas. But a short sentence quoted within another sentence may be so restricted in meaning that no comma is needed:

> The girl said, "Wait for me."

> "Wait for me," the girl said.

> "Wait," the girl said, "until I come."

> Her cheerful greeting was always "How do you do today?"

Warning: Use no comma before an indirect quotation or quotation marks unless there is a need:

> Fred said that he went to Chicago.

> Longfellow wrote "The Psalm of Life."

481 Items in a date are set off by commas:

> They were married on Tuesday, May 6, 1946.

Note: In a date consisting of month and year only, the use of commas is optional:

In August, 1950, (or August 1950) we were on vacation.

482 Use commas for explanatory matter in connection with a direct quotation, unless stronger punctuation is necessary (495):

> "It is time," she said, "for me to go home."

> "It is time to go," she said; "it is very late."

483 Use commas to separate the items of a series of words, phrases, or clauses:

> The farmer sold corn, hay, oats, potatoes, and wheat.

> They came from east, from west, from north, and from south.

> He arose, he smiled, he began to speak.

484 A series of adjectives of the same rank modifying the same noun are separated by commas unless they are joined by conjunctions. No comma is used after the last adjective:

> We saw tall, slender, graceful trees.

> A steep and narrow path led on.

Note: When the adjective next to the noun seems to be a part of the noun, no comma is used before it:

> He is a courteous young man. (Courteous modifies *young man*.)

485 A comma may be used for clearness:

> Ever since, Frank has been a better boy.

> The boy, not the girl, was to blame.

> Whatever you do, do well.

Quotation Marks

486 Quotation marks are used to enclose a direct quotation. They are not used with indirect quotations:

> "You are to blame," she said.

> He said that he would go home.

487 Quotation marks or italics are used to distinguish a word or letter, the name of which is being discussed:

> You may parse the word "they" in that sentence.

Note: Never use quotation marks where they are not required by the rules of mechanics. It is improper to use quotation marks for mere emphasis or adornment in sign painting or on cafe menus.

488 Quotation marks are used with the titles of articles, chapters of books, and titles of short poems and stories (italics are used for titles of books and periodicals and the names of ships, 514B):

> He read Whittier's "Maud Muller."

> I read Hawthorne's *The Scarlet Letter*.

Note: Most authorities still accept quotation marks with the title of books. (One line drawn under a title indicates that it should be italicized in print.)

489 A quotation of several paragraphs or stanzas should have quotation marks at the beginning of each paragraph and at the end of the last paragraph or stanza.

490 In reporting narration (524C) or conversation, each speech, no matter how short, should be in quotation marks. An uninterrupted quotation in one paragraph, though long, should have but one set of quotation marks:

> "Do you know me?" he asked.

> "I am not sure," she replied.

> "I am your old schoolmate, Edgar Jones," he explained.

491 Place nicknames and words or phrases used ironically in quotations:

> My friend "Shorty" was there.

His "limousine" was a Model T.

Note: Many people also use quotation marks to distinguish technical terms and slang. Often it is better to avoid the use of slang and faulty diction than to apologize for it with quotation marks. If the slang phrase is too expressive to admit substitution, assume responsibility for using it instead of quoting it.

492 A quotation within a quotation should be enclosed in single quotation marks, and a quotation within that should be in double marks:

"I was embarrassed," Mary admitted, "when I said, 'I agree with Shakespeare, "All the world's a stage."'"

493 A question mark or an exclamation mark is placed inside the quotation marks if it is a part of the quotation; outside, if it applies to the main clause. The period or the comma is always placed inside the quotation marks; the semicolon is placed outside:

"Are you ill?" she asked.

Did Father say, "Wait until tomorrow"?

He gave a quotation from "The Raven."

"The music was beautiful," she remarked.

Note: If both the main clause of the sentence and the quotation are interrogative, only one question mark (506) is used:

Did Fred ask, "Where have you been?"

494 When a quotation is interrupted, an extra set of marks must be used:

"Come," he said, "expecting to have a good time."

495 There is an impression among students that all interruptions of quotations are marked by commas. Use the marks which should be used, regardless of the quotation:

"You have delayed too long already," he said. "Success does not come to him who tarries."

"I have been wrong," she admitted; "there is no denying that."

Apostrophe

496 Use the apostrophe to indicate the omission of letters from words. It should be placed immediately above the point of omission:

The man *isn't* here.

497 The apostrophe may be used with *s* to denote plurals of letters, figures, signs, symbols, and words considered merely as words (85):

She used two *a*'s, three *b*'s, two 8's (or 8s), two *and*'s (or *and*s).

498 The apostrophe is used in forming the possessive of nouns and pronouns. To form the possessive singular, add the apostrophe and *s* (115):

The *bird's* song is beautiful.

To form the possessive of a singular or plural noun that does not end in *s*, add the apostrophe and *s* (115, 117):

The *salesman's* samples included *men's* hats.

To form the possessive plural of a noun whose plural ends in *s*, add an apostrophe only (116):

Boys' suits are on sale.

Note: Some words have two forms (115): Burns' or Burns's, James' or James's. (The second form seems preferred.)

Warning: The possessives *its*, *his*, *hers*, *ours*, *yours*, and *theirs* (141) do not use the apostrophe, but such words as *either*, *one*, and *other* do use the apostrophe:

> The cat wants *its* (not it's) dinner. (*Its* is possessive.)
>
> *It's* time to go home. (*It's* is a contraction, 141, 496.)
>
> One must do *one's* duty.

The apostrophe is often omitted from proper times: *Pikes Peak*.

Dash

499 A dash is used to mark a sudden change or break in a sentence:

> The boy went—where did he go?
>
> "There is no—" The speaker could not go on. (No period is needed after a dash which breaks off a sentence.)

500 The dash may be used instead of the marks of parentheses:

> Smith told me—but don't mention this—that he was bankrupt.

501 The dash may be used before a summarizing statement:

> He planned, he worked, he sacrificed—all these he did that he might succeed.

502 The dash may be used for emphasis:

> For a thousand dollars—a mere thousand dollars—he betrayed his friend.

Note: A dash may be used to indicate the omission of words or letters:

> Shakespeare lived 1564–1616.
>
> Have you seen Captain H—lately?

Parentheses

503 Parentheses may be used to enclose matter apart from the main thought:

> If you come to see me (and I hope you do come), be sure to bring your camera.

Matter enclosed in parentheses within a sentence, even though it forms a complete declarative or imperative sentence, need not begin with a capital and need not end with a period, if the sentence is short. But if it is interrogative, it ends with a question mark (506). See the examples under 445 and 465; also, the sentence in parentheses in the example just given.

504 A punctuation mark belonging to matter given before that set off by parentheses should be placed after the second parenthesis mark (see the sentence given in 503):

> When you receive your appointment (and I hope you receive it soon), you must tell me of your plans.

Brackets

505 Brackets are used to enclose explanatory matter which one adds in editing the work of another writer:

> It was this poem ["The Raven"] that made Poe famous.

Question Mark

506 Place a question mark after every direct question. Although the very short declarative sentence (25) within parentheses (465) does not require a period, the short interrogative sentence (27) thus used must close with a question mark:

> Have you seen my new hat?

When you come to see me (why not come soon?), I will tell you about my trip to Denver.

Note: If the main clause of a sentence and the dependent clause are both interrogative (27), only one question mark (493) is used. No question mark is used after an indirect question. After a polite request a period may be used instead of a question mark:

Did the coach inquire, "When did you return?"

He asked what the trouble was.

Will you please send the check at once.

507 A question mark within parentheses expresses uncertainty:

He came here on May 5 (?), 1928.

Exclamation Mark

508 The exclamation mark is used after words, expressions, or sentences to show strong feeling:

Fire! Fire!

Hyphen

509 A hyphen should be used to join words combined into a single adjective modifier:

well-to-do, self-supporting, far-flung.

Adverbs ending in *ly* are not usually changed into compound modifiers:

a *beautifully illustrated* story.

510 The hyphen is omitted when certain compound modifiers follow the word modified, but other compounds retain the hyphen in this position:

His mother is *self-supporting.*

His mother is *well liked.*

Use your dictionary as a guide to correct handling of compounds.

511 Hyphens should be used in compound numbers from twenty-one to ninety-nine.

512 The words *half* and *quarter* when used as prefixes are generally followed by the hyphen.

513 New compounds are hyphenated; but after a time the hyphen may be omitted and the compound written as a solid. Words which have but recently lost the hyphen except in very formal writing are *tonight, tomorrow, today.* A good dictionary is the only safe guide to the correct use of hyphens.

514 When it is necessary to divide a word at the end of a line, the division should be made between syllables and a hyphen placed at the end of the line. Never place a hyphen at the beginning of a new line.

Abbreviations and Contractions

514A The following rules should be observed in using abbreviations and contractions:

1. The use of many abbreviations in formal writing indicates carelessness on the part of the writer. However, there are a few abbreviations which may be used even in the most formal writing: *A.D., B.C., a.m., p.m.,* and others.

2. It is considered impolite to abbreviate titles such as the following when used before the last name only: *captain, general, colonel, professor, president.* Abbreviations of the following titles,

however, are proper in any writing: *Mr., Mrs., Ms., Messrs., Dr.*

3. The rule is to place a period after each abbreviation, but there are exceptions to the rule (see 466).

Contractions and Roman numerals used in sentences do not require periods after them:

He *doesn't* live here.

James II was king of England.

Note: See *Webster's New International Dictionary*, Second Edition, pages 2989–3000, for a list of standard abbreviations.

Italics

514B The following rules should be observed in using italics:

1. In writing longhand and in typing, place one line under a word to indicate that it should be printed in italics.

2. Italicize foreign terms which have not become naturalized. The dictionary is the only safe guide in determining these.

3. Italicize a word, phrase, or letter used as a subject of discussion:

The word *receive* is often misspelled.

4. Use italics to indicate the titles of books, magazines, newspapers, paintings, and the names of ships:

We have just read *Vanity Fair* by Thackeray.

5. Most authorities agree that an article (276) or the name of a city used in the title of a magazine or newspaper need not be italicized:

We read the Kansas City *Star*.

6. It is permissible to italicize a word for emphasis, but some authorities discourage this.

Numerals

514C The following rules should be observed in using numerals:

1. Dates, street numbers, and page numbers should be written in figures:

Columbus discovered America on *October 12, 1492.*

He lives at *16* (not *sixteen*) Spruce Street.

2. The sign $ is not used for a sum less than one dollar:

The knife cost sixty-five cents.

3. The general rule for writing numbers is to spell out the number if it may be done in one or two words:

He gave me a *thousand* dollars.

If the number requires the spelling of several words, it should be written in figures:

He gave me *1397* copies of the paper.

4. When several numbers are mentioned in a short space, use figures for all.

5. A number which represents a person's age or one denoting the hour of the day is usually spelled out:

At *three o'clock* there is to be a meeting of the boys who are between *sixteen* and *eighteen* years of age.

6. Do not begin a sentence with figures:

Twenty-five (not *25*) boys played in the game.

7. It is not necessary, except in special instances, to place numerals in parentheses after writing numbers; but when they are used, each should follow the number it repeats:

I am sending you *fifteen* (*15*) bushels of wheat.

Author Index

Subject Index